Crossing borders and queering citizenship

Manchester University Press

Contemporary American and Canadian Writers

Series Editors
Nahem Yousaf and Sharon Monteith

Also available
The quiet contemporary American novel   Rachel Sykes
Sara Paretsky: Detective fiction as trauma literature
    Cynthia S. Hamilton
**Making home: Orphanhood, kinship, and cultural memory
    in contemporary American novels**   Maria Holmgren Troy,
    Elizabeth Kella, Helena Wahlstrom
Thomas Pynchon   Simon Malpas and Andrew Taylor
Jonathan Lethem   James Peacock
Mark Z Danielewski   Edited by Joe Bray and Alison Gibbons
Louise Erdrich   David Stirrup
**Passing into the present: contemporary American fiction of
    racial and gender passing**   Sinéad Moynihan
Paul Auster   Mark Brown
Douglas Coupland   Andrew Tate
Philip Roth   David Brauner

Crossing borders and queering citizenship

Civic reading practice in contemporary American and Canadian writing

Zalfa Feghali

Manchester University Press

Copyright © Zalfa Feghali 2019

The right of Zalfa Feghali to be identified as the author of this work has been asserted by her in accordance with the Copyright, Designs and Patents Act 1988.

Published by Manchester University Press
Oxford Road, Manchester M13 9PL
www.manchesteruniversitypress.co.uk

British Library Cataloguing-in-Publication Data is available

ISBN 978 1 7849 9309 2 hardback
ISBN 978 1 5261 6393 6 paperback

First published by Manchester University Press in hardback 2019

This edition published 2022

The publisher has no responsibility for the persistence or accuracy of URLs for any external or third-party internet websites referred to in this book, and does not guarantee that any content on such websites is, or will remain, accurate or appropriate.

Typeset by Newgen Publishing UK

For my grandparents,
Anna, who never learned to read, and Adamos,
who always read to her

Contents

Series editors' foreword		viii
Acknowledgements		x
Introduction: why queer(y) citizenship?		1
1	Reading: an act of queering citizenship	17
2	Autobiographical acts of reading and the work of Gloria Anzaldúa and Dorothy Allison	35
3	Métis and two-spirit vernaculars in the writing of Gregory Scofield	57
4	Performing the border and queer *rasquachismo* in Guillermo Gómez-Peña's performance art	93
5	The antianaesthetic and 'a community of readers' in Erín Moure's *O Cidadán*	125
6	Reading for hemispheric citizenship in Junot Díaz's *The Brief Wondrous Life of Oscar Wao*	153
Conclusion: Yann Martel's lonely book club		173
Bibliography		182
Index		201

Series editors' foreword

This innovative series reflects the breadth and diversity of writing over the last thirty years, and provides critical evaluations of established, emerging and critically neglected writers – mixing the canonical with the unexpected. It explores notions of the contemporary and analyses current and developing modes of representation with a focus on individual writers and their work. The series seeks to reflect both the growing body of academic research in the field, and the increasing prevalence of contemporary American and Canadian fiction on programmes of study in institutions of higher education around the world. Central to the series is a concern that each book should argue a stimulating thesis, rather than provide an introductory survey, and that each contemporary writer will be examined across the trajectory of their literary production. A variety of critical tools and literary and interdisciplinary approaches are encouraged to illuminate the ways in which a particular writer contributes to, and helps readers rethink, the North American literary and cultural landscape in a global context.

Central to debates about the field of contemporary fiction is its role in interrogating ideas of national exceptionalism and transnationalism. This series matches the multivocality of contemporary writing with wide-ranging and detailed analysis. Contributors examine the drama of the nation from the perspectives of writers who are members of established and new immigrant groups, writers who consider themselves on the nation's margins as well as those who chronicle middle America. National labels are the subject of vociferous debate and including American and Canadian writers in the same series is not to flatten the differences between them but to acknowledge that literary traditions and tensions are cross-cultural and that North American writers often explore and expose precisely these tensions. The series recognises that situating a writer in a cultural context involves a multiplicity of influences, social and geo-political, artistic and theoretical, and that contemporary fiction defies easy categorisation. For example, it examines writers who invigorate the genres in which they have made their mark alongside writers whose aesthetic goal is to subvert the idea of genre altogether. The challenge of defining the roles of writers and assessing their reception by reading communities is central to the aims of the series.

Overall, *Contemporary American and Canadian Writers* aims to begin to represent something of the diversity of contemporary writing and seeks to engage students and scholars in stimulating debates about the contemporary and about fiction.

Nahem Yousaf
Sharon Monteith

Acknowledgements

Overall, this book took a long time to write. I am grateful for the patience, guidance, good faith, and support of series editors Sharon Monteith and Nahem Yousaf, and the fantastic team at Manchester University Press, Paul Clarke and Laura Swift, as well as the anonymous readers.

I have been fortunate to be a citizen of a wonderful community of scholars, mentors, colleagues, and friends who have patiently and generously put up with my deep anxiety and *many* mistakes as this book went through its many stages of: my thanks to all.

My family, Maria, Nazih, Joseph, Michael, Susana, and Tomas, made this project possible. Gavan Lennon made it happen, though all mistakes are mine.

I thank Gregory Scofield, Erin Moure, Nightwood Editions, and House of Anansi Press for their generosity in granting permissions to reprint the following:

Selected excerpts from 'O Cidadán' copyright © 2002 by Erin Moure. Reproduced with permission from House of Anansi Press Inc., Toronto. www.houseofanansi.com

'Mixed Breed Act' from *kipocihkân* by Gregory Scofield, Nightwood Editions, 2009, www.nightwoodeditions.com

'The Poet Leaves a Parting Thought' from *kipocihkân* by Gregory Scofield, Nightwood Editions, 2009, www.nightwoodeditions.com

'kipocihkân' from *kipocihkân* by Gregory Scofield, Nightwood Editions, 2009, www.nightwoodeditions.com

'Epitaph' from *Louis: The Heretic Poems* by Gregory Scofield, Nightwood Editions, 2011, www.nightwoodeditions.com

'When It Comes To Your Turn', 'Survival Poetry', 'Answer For My

Brother (Who Are The Metis?)', and 'Making New History', all from *The Gathering: Stones for the Medicine Wheel* by Gregory Scofield, Polestar, 1993.
'Policy of the Dispossessed' from *Native Canadiana: Songs from the Urban Rez* by Gregory Scofield, Polestar, 1996.

Introduction: why queer(y) citizenship?

In Thomas King's 1993 short story, 'Borders', readers follow an Indigenous woman and her son as they set off from their home on the reserve and attempt to cross the Canada–US border that cuts across the 49th parallel. The US border guard does not allow them to cross into the United States because the mother declares their citizenship as Blackfoot and not 'Canadian' or 'American'. The pair attempt to return and are not allowed to cross into Canada for the same reason.[1] Despite attempts by border guards on both sides to elicit an 'acceptable' answer from them, the mother steadfastly refuses to offer the declaration that they come from any 'side' of the border other than the 'Blackfoot side' ('Borders' p. 135). As a result of what has been variously read as either the border guards' ignorance or the mother's stubbornness, the mother and the story's narrator spend three nights between the two border checkpoints in no man's land – the literal borderlands – sleeping in their car until a media frenzy forces the US border guards to let the pair through on the basis of their Blackfoot citizenship.

King's short story highlights the relationship between citizenship, the state, and national borders, and, in particular, emphasises the erosion of Indigenous rights and sovereignty as they play out at North American borders, as suggested by one reporter who earnestly (but ignorantly) asks the young narrator 'how it [feels] to be an Indian without a country' (p. 142). The mother's refusal to acknowledge any 'side' of the border undermines and ultimately rejects the idea that her citizenship can be bounded by either a figurative or literal modern nation state whose borders were drawn at the expense of Indigenous people in North America. The Canada–US border, in fact, as it runs across the 49th parallel and is touted as 'the world's longest undefended border', originated from the negotiations that were to become the 1794 Jay Treaty. The Treaty, which is still legally binding today (as well as in the fictive universe of King's short story), included stipulations that protected Indigenous peoples whose lands straddled this new political boundary. Indigenous people crossing the border were not required to adhere to US and (then Great Britain) Canadian border control and customs regulations.[2] It is ironic, then, that the other questions asked of the mother in 'Borders' include whether she is carrying 'any firearms or tobacco' ('Borders' p. 135).

As it meditates on the need for recognition, rights, and representation as they are made manifest by the artifice and limits of nationhood, 'Borders' effectively emphasises the idea that, as Karl Hele puts it, 'borders are lived experiences' (xv), and 'mere lines drawn upon the water often disrupted or even erased altogether by the lived experiences of First People'.[3] In this way, the story negates a view of citizenship and national identity as contingent on conceptions of the 'fraternity' that emerges from the policing of national borders, or, the 'deep, horizontal comradeship' critiqued by political scientist Benedict Anderson in his iconic work on imagined communities.[4] This kind of fraternity, Anderson would have it, is rooted in an understanding of nationhood and community that ignores and takes part in the ongoing erasures and elisions of peoples and histories, what Anderson calls 'the actual inequality and exploitation' that takes place in the activity of nation building.[5] It is important, then, to read work by Indigenous writers like King, whose writing serves to 'undermine established beliefs and to introduce other, typically marginalised viewpoints', especially in relation to the activity of citizenship.[6]

Crossing borders and queering citizenship recognises the limited imaginings of political and national communities, and reimagines the contours of contemporary citizenship. As it connects queer and citizenship theories to the idea of an engaged reading subject, this book offers a new approach to studying the act of reading, arguably a basic function of literature, as well as theorising reading as an integral element of the basic unit of the state: the citizen. This book explores how the act of reading across borders can be understood as a civic act that queers citizenship, and it does so through discussing seven US and Canadian writers in whose work borders proliferate and citizenship is unravelled: US–Mexico borderlands lesbian writer Gloria Anzaldúa, lesbian US southern white trash author Dorothy Allison, Canadian Métis poet Gregory Scofield, Mexican-American performance artist Guillermo Gómez-Peña, queer Canadian language poet Erín Moure, Dominican-American novelist Junot Díaz, and Canadian author Yann Martel. Each of these writers offers a literary engagement with citizenship that advocates for an alternative model of belonging through civic readerly engagement, with no recourse to the reification of political borders yet without an outright rejection of state citizenship. In my interpretation of their work, then, I use the term 'queer' to denote the ways in which the concept and structure(s) of citizenship are critiqued, troubled, and unsettled, not only by their writing, but by their status, to varying 'degrees', as 'peripheral peoples', excluded from having full membership in their respective polities on the basis of one or more of their identifications, what sociologist Carlos A. Forment calls 'those groups who are excluded from or marginalised within the polity despite having rights to inclusion'.[7] In this book, then, 'queer' is, as queer theorist David Halperin puts it, that which is 'at odds with the normal, the legitimate, the dominant'.[8] The writing by 'peripheral peoples' examined in this book not only engages with citizenship but also positions the reader to queer it.

One impulse to and justification for rethinking citizenship is that it has been almost universally recognised as exclusionary. As social scientists Engin F. Isin and Patricia Wood note, 'citizenship, despite modern, universalist rhetoric, has always been a group concept – but it has never been expanded to all members of any polity'.[9] Semiotician Walter Mignolo sees the very ideas of citizenship and the citizen as racist, and 'tied to a racial hierarchy of human beings that depends on universal categories of thought created and enacted from the identitarian perspectives of European Christianity and by white males'.[10] Rethinking citizenship is valuable, according to legal scholar Carl Stychin, because 'part of the value of citizenship discourse is the way in which it can be deployed to re-imagine the nation as a space for the performance of a range of different projects, in which there is no single authentic way of relating to the nation'.[11] In participatory democracies, the work of citizens is 'in the public sphere, carrying rights and entitlements but also responsibilities to fellow citizens and to the community which defines citizenship'.[12] However, each of the writers under examination here advocates what sociologist Yasemin Soysal has called 'a new mode of membership, anchored in the universalistic rights of personhood, [which ultimately] transgresses the *national* order of things' (emphasis added).[13] This works on the assumption that there is a need to 'shift ... the major organizing principle of membership in contemporary polities: [one in which] the logic of personhood supersedes the logic of citizenship' but not one that allows the exclusionary thrust of contemporary state citizenship to continue unimpeded.[14] To queer citizenship, what I argue each of the writers under examination here engages in, is to also explore the reader as a queer, sexual(ised) citizen, which, as queer theorist Jeffrey Weeks has described, is a 'hybrid being, breaching the public/private divide which Western culture has long held to be essential'.[15] The recognition that readers are hybrid beings who can read for the empowerment hybridity can engender is explored in more detail in the next chapter. In this book, the role of hybridity is sometimes understated but more often explicit, recognising the ways in which all citizens are hybrid beings but remain anchored, for as long as it exists conceptually, to the state. Likewise, queering underpins my analysis throughout as an intersectional, feminist praxis that can be used productively as a strategy in the decolonisation of citizenship and the establishment of alternative community building practices that resist and change the exclusions of citizenship rather than accept and adapt to them. This understanding is premised on the idea that feminist and queer critical frames can be used as tools to unravel the exclusionary practices deployed by the concept and practice of state-sanctioned citizenship.

The interest of queer theorists in and preoccupation with the unsettling and troubling of dominant and mainstream frameworks of 'Western' thought is useful in the unravelling of citizenship in that it provides an overarching and inclusive vocabulary with which to describe the exclusionary and marginalising processes of citizenship. Of course, queer theory is fraught. But not all the writers discussed in this book identify as queer, and not all readers are queer, either. However, the critical practice of queering as it takes place in the act of reading can translate to civic action, understood in this book as the opening up of new discursive areas from which to safely articulate improved citizenship practices that foreground and value *recognition*, *rights*, and *representation* for all members of a polity. These spaces offer not only discursive areas to rehearse these ideas, but also the community support and language needed to transform acts of reading into actualised political changes to state-sanctioned citizenship. The first chapter theorises these spaces further and sets my theory of queering citizenship as a critical lens used in my analysis of Anzaldúa, Allison, Scofield, Gómez-Peña, Moure, Díaz, and Martel.

Introduction

As it enquires after and constructs a model for queering citizenship through reading, this book can be situated alongside existing theories of reading and particularly emergent theories of the citizen-reader, which cast the reading experience as one in which readers can find 'another sense of' citizenship.[16] This form of citizenship lies beyond state-sanctioned notions of nationality and belonging and constitutes what literary critic Lauren Berlant might call a gentler, 'intimate public sphere' that 'renders citizenship a condition of social membership produced by personal acts and values'.[17] Berlant's view of citizenship here is convincing, but focalised on the individual. As they theorise the other ways of belonging advanced by their figure of a citizen-reader, critics Danielle Fuller and DeNel Rehberg Sedo rightly criticise scholarship of paying too 'little attention to the reader-reader interaction and [giving] no sense of the ways that non-academic readers might employ various reading practices as part of their everyday lives as social beings'.[18] In these scenarios, citizen readers 'express a version of citizenship outside the public domain of politics'.[19] Where Berlant, Fuller, Rehberg Sedo, and others find this alternative sphere a space for new (or renewed) articulations of belonging and citizenship that offer 'the promise of belonging', these models may inadvertently diminish the importance of resisting the exclusionary powers of state citizenship.[20] This book aims to do the opposite.

My arguments here are premised on the importance of citizens' relationship to the state as one that is in dire need of interrogation, because, as Gillian Roberts reminds us, 'rights are not upheld in the same way for all individuals, as evidenced by the distinction between legal and cultural belonging'.[21] When critics and theorists formulate sites at which alternative citizenship networks can be generated, citizenship as it relates to the state is allowed to escape scrutiny of its exclusionary civic practices. Further, these spaces of alternative citizenship, while theorised as locally democratising, progressive spaces of resistance, can easily be mobilised to regressive, conservative ends that uphold the values of patriarchal, heteronormative, white supremacy and seek to further curtail state-sanctioned civic rights on the basis that alternative models for belonging exist. This book, therefore, advances a model for reading that has as its agenda the queering or unsettling of state citizenship *as it stands* and as it impacts the lived experiences of real, civically disenfranchised and disempowered groups in the United States and Canada as they are represented in the literary texts under discussion. This is not at odds with the creation of alternative spaces of citizenship and belonging, but rather a project that stands alongside these existing theoretical frameworks, working towards more impactful and inclusive conclusions and policies.

As well as its engagement with studies of reading, this book works to hemispherically connect contemporary border studies, Indigenous studies and the politics of recognition, critical race studies, queer theory, postcolonial studies, and reception and audience theories.[22] Bringing these separate but related fields together to examine work by authors whose writing contests and resists claims by a particular national context (in this case, the United States or Canada) works to reframe our understanding of what is generally called 'American studies', centring the reader as a powerful agent of literary validation as well as civic action. In this way, while this book positions itself as working within American studies, it also, as Caroline F. Levander and Robert S. Levine put it, seeks to 'chart new literary and cultural geographies' in the Americas through its exploration of queering citizenship.[23] It also alleviates the concerns expressed by Gillian Roberts and David Stirrup that the last decade's 'newly reconfigured American Studies' has sought only to 'expand [the field's] object, rather than its method, of study'.[24] In its engagement with hemispheric American studies, this book looks first to the borders of North America as it theorises a reader capable of queering citizenship.

Crossing borders and queering citizenship begins, then, from a rereading of Gloria Anzaldúa's *Borderlands/La Frontera: The New Mestiza* (1987), which is generally considered to be a 'foundational' text in studying North American border identities. The borderlands Anzaldúa alludes to in the title of her work are specific: she is referring to the US–Mexico borderlands where she grew up. Rife with controversy, the US–Mexico borderland region took the shape that it retains to this day in 1848 with the Treaty of Guadalupe Hidalgo, the treaty that ended the US–Mexico War that had begun in 1846. The stipulations of the Treaty stated that Mexico cede the equivalent of 55 per cent of its pre-war territory to the United States in exchange for $15 million. The stipulations also assured the safety of pre-existing property rights of Mexican citizens in the transferred territories. However, the US Senate modified the Treaty and subsequently seized much of the privately owned land.

In *Borderlands/La Frontera*, Anzaldúa demonstrates the dramatic consequences of the Treaty for ordinary Mexican citizens: overnight,

Introduction

they were Mexicans living in 'America' – the naturalisation process took much longer than had been negotiated – and second-class citizens. Many towns, villages, and families had been split in two, one half on the Mexican side and the other on the American side. Those left living on the American side were no longer recognised as Mexican; nor were they recognised as American. Instead, they occupied uncertain territory, their citizenship status ambiguous. They viewed Mexico as their home and the United States as an occupying force. These groups' lives were changed by the creation, imposition, and enforcement of a border in their midst. Anzaldúa's formulation of the new *mestiza* focuses on the 'hybrid' character of the borderland experience in general, and the hybrid nature of those who inhabit the borderlands in particular. She presents a framework of hybridity and arguably, citizenship, that extends beyond the borderlands referred to in the title of her well-known text: 'the Borderlands are physically present wherever two or more cultures edge each other, where people of different races occupy the same territory, where under, lower, middle and upper classes touch, where the space between two individuals shrinks with intimacy'.[25] This book discusses Anzaldúa as not only the foundational figure of border studies, but also reframes her active involvement in feminist movements as part of the broader narrative of US feminism in the 1970s and 1980s.

North American borders have served as important signifiers of national security and identity since the original settlement of the continent, but their narratives have become especially polarised in the last 30 years, and especially since the 2016 election of Donald Trump to the US presidency.[26] The reality of and discourse around borders since 9/11 has become increasingly politically charged, and at the time of writing, Donald Trump's 27 January 2017 Executive Order, known more popularly as the Muslim Ban, figures North American borders as sites where citizenship and national identity can be contested by the state and is an attempt to strip away civic rights from citizenship status. Precursors to this Executive Order are numerous, with a rise since 2001 of figures in the United States and Canada such as Brigitte Gabriel, for example, who urges Americans and Canadians to monitor their borders because '[t]he terrorists are using our borders to infiltrate our country' and legislation such as the Secure Fence Act of 2006 which doubled the funding of border patrol agents on both the United States' northern and southern borders.[27]

Of course, discursive appeals that describe American borders as weak and understand citizens as being in need of protection predates Donald Trump; for example, after September 2001, one of the more controversial changes in border security in the United States was the Real ID Act of 2005. This Act, which stipulated that '[n]ot withstanding any other provision of law, the Secretary of Homeland Security shall have the authority to waive all legal requirements [that] such Secretary, in such Secretary's sole discretion, determines necessary to ensure expeditious construction of the barriers and roads',[28] allowed Secretary of Homeland Security Michael Chertoff to 'waive in their entirety' seven pieces of legislation relating to the environment to extend triple fencing through the Tijuana River National Estuarine Research Reserve near San Diego.[29] Crucially, the Act also established new categories of acceptable identification documentation for those crossing into the United States from its borders with both Mexico and Canada, in addition to broadening and further defining 'terrorist' activity in the wake of 9/11. The legislative establishment and implementation of new definitions of identification papers stands as a violation of treaty obligations with cross-border Indigenous peoples, and, within the United States, impacts voting rights for other minority and historically disenfranchised populations, including African Americans, Mexican Americans, and others. In the context of this book, the Real ID Act of 2005 is an excellent example of the intersection of the status of citizenship and the discourse around North American borders, even though it became law over a decade ago. The continued return in legal and scholarly treatments of North American borders to the site of the US–Mexico border as a metonym for questions of citizenship renders this particular border significant, even while it has also become the 'originary' site of burgeoning alternative articulations of civic identity that this book explores.

Indeed, according to Claudia Sadowski-Smith, 'by the turn of the twenty-first century ... the U.S.-Mexico frontier has evolved into one of the most prominent sites for analyses of border transgressions that emphasize contemporary diasporic practices of hybrid place-making and non-absolutist citizenship'.[30] To the north, an imbalance between scholarship on the US–Mexico and Canada–US borders can be easily traced; the latter had long been the 'longest undefended border in the world' until 9/11.[31] However, as Victor Konrad and Heather N. Nicol observe, 'the time-word rhetoric about the "longest undefended border in the world" has disappeared both in Canada and the United

States. In its place a new, "post-9/11" border culture has emerged in the Canada-U.S. borderlands'.[32] As it engages with border studies, this book contributes to a noticeably undertheorised area of North American studies: the Canada–US border.[33]

While no Canadian legislation as controversial as the Real ID Act exists (though perhaps the Canadian Anti-Terrorism Act and the related Canadian Senate Bill S-7, the 2013 Combatting Terrorism Act qualify), questions of citizenship have always played a significant role on the Canada–US border, particularly in the context of Indigenous peoples' cross-border territorial rights.[34] One need only consider an incident from July 2010, when the United Kingdom declined to issue visas to the Iroquois Nation's lacrosse team that had been due to compete in the World Lacrosse Championship. The UK claimed that their Iroquois passports are not currently recognise as *state-issued* travel documents and later clarified that it would waive the visa requirement and accept the Iroquois document if it was 'accompanied by a United States passport'. This was despite then-Secretary of State Hillary Clinton's 'one-time' letter of assurance to the UK government that the team would be allowed back into the United States on their tribal passports. Secretary Clinton's (unintentionally) ironic guarantee that the lacrosse team would be allowed back into the United States sparked a controversy that eventually led the US State Department to 'confirm' in a statement that it had no treaty obligation with the Iroquois Nation to recognise their passports, despite the Iroquois existing legally as a confederacy of six nations. This is one example in a range of others that has seen legal Indigenous citizenship described as 'a fantasy document' or, as in Thomas King's 'Borders', dismissed as irrelevant because it is 'not on the forms'.[35]

Just as Anderson's understandings of imagined communities, Anzaldúa's new *mestiza*, and conceptions of borders in narratives of hemispheric American studies represent nodes in this book, so does the work of political historian T. H. Marshall, whose formulation of modern citizenship is a typical starting point in studies of the field. In 1950 Marshall delivered a series of lectures at the University of Cambridge that has since become a benchmark and reference point for most theoretical work on citizenship in the post-Second World War era. In 'Citizenship and Social Class', Marshall sees citizenship as 'a direct sense of community membership based on loyalty to a civilization which is a common possession'.[36] Here, Marshall presents a causal relationship between membership in a community, civilization, and citizenship. This concept of citizenship is also contingent on a certain understanding of the modern nation state, which 'encompasses the notions of the people as a nation, the sovereignty of these people as a nation, and the state as the sum total of its individualised citizens'.[37] In these views, the citizen is a political entity and the smallest unit that makes up the state. As such, the citizen does not only enjoy the rights that come with membership in the political community, but also assumes the duties that come with citizenship. In this framework, citizenship defines identity.[38] Yasemin Soysal notes: 'Citizenship defines bounded populations, with a specific set of rights and duties, excluding "others" on the grounds of nationality.'[39] Marshall's specific definition, with operative words such as 'rights', 'duties', and 'common possession', is often seen as the bedrock of citizenship and leads clearly to the development of citizen 'rights'. His reading of citizenship is examined further in the next chapter.

Despite Marshall's significance within citizenship theory, the writing explored in this book assumes an engagement with participatory theories of citizenship rather than the representative democracies of the United States and Canada, themselves standing as 'representative' of certain manifestations of exclusion. In such a framework of participatory democracy, 'citizen action and self-government [are put] at the centre of political life'.[40] Far from the stark and severe delineation between civil, political, and social citizenship that Marshall advocates, or the crude corollary understanding of citizens which sees them as having an amorphous balance between rights and obligations, citizenship in a participatory democracy works by 'transforming strangers into citizen-neighbours through common conversations and projects'.[41] This focus on individuals and their roles in a community while still maintaining the accountability of the state is key to understanding the basic terrain upon which the writers examined in this book position readers to rethink and queer citizenship.

It is, of course, far easier to theorise a queered citizen or citizenship rather than to put it into practice, principally because there are no simple answers to the questions of how and where this process is to take place. Critical theorist Nancy Fraser's articulation of subaltern counterpublics is helpful here. As she puts it, subaltern counterpublics are 'parallel discursive areas where members of subordinated social groups invent and circulate counterdiscourses to formulate oppositional interpretations of their identities, interests, and needs'.[42] These counterpublics provide a model for the shift away from the public/private binary that characterises dominant discourses of citizenship. If we are to view citizenship as not simply a delicate relationship between rights and duties, but as a complex nexus where the discourse and performance of citizenship intersect and intervene, or as Isin and Wood suggest, as a combination of political 'status and practice' (or performance), then the distinction between public and private spheres and, by extension, public and private citizenship, is also inevitably blurred.[43] When read alongside Fraser's notion of subaltern counterpublics, these constitute a site at which the queering of citizenship can take place, and in each of the chapters to come, this theoretical site is made manifest by the civic work of the active reader.

This book, therefore, offers not only a 'model' for 'queering citizenship' but also a theory for understanding the various ways in which peripheral or minority writers, like Anzaldúa, Allison, Scofield, Gómez-Peña, Moure, Díaz, and Martel work to interrogate, critique, and queer the concept of citizenship. I read their work in service of a relationship with a state that does not require nations and their borders to be 'reified through assertions of border controls and appeals to nationhood', as we see in the actions of the border guards in Thomas King's 'Borders', but instead through queer readings that hold states accountable and engender civic belonging, as we see in the actions of the story's Blackfoot mother, who tells her son Blackfoot creation stories as they sleep in their car, parked between two border checkpoints.[44] The task of this book is to 'identify the terrain' of queering citizenship and the potential it can hold for readers.[45]

As it theorises reading as a civic act in the queering and querying of citizenship, *Crossing borders and queering citizenship* crosses and re-crosses North American borders, moving back and forth to the US–Mexico border and across the 49th parallel, and exploring the work of American and Canadian writers whose work is concerned with questions of recognition, rights, and representation in their critiques of the state and citizenship. This book's contribution to their projects is in its theorisation of the reader of these literary texts as an active agent in this critique, so that readers are imbued with power beyond 'empathetic' reading (though empathy is certainly welcomed).[46] This discursive move allows for the possibility of co-situating the critique and connecting authors from the 'periphery' of the polity to 'mainstream' readers in a meaningful way.

If this introduction has been concerned with the 'why' of querying and queering citizenship, the first chapter works to explain the 'how'. Fusing theories of citizenship, postcoloniality, active reading, and queering, the chapter offers a starting point in exploring how reading is a powerful tool that can be mobilised in service of civic struggles for recognition, rights, and representation. Each of the subsequent chapters focuses on a writer whose work, whether autobiographical or fictional, poetry or prose, performance or epistolary, is preoccupied with how the recognition and dismantling of borders – physical or figurative, political or socially constructed, geographical or psychic – gestures towards a citizenship that is founded on principles vastly different than those we might recognise today. Anzaldúa, Allison, Scofield, Gómez-Peña, Moure, Díaz, and Martel may represent only a few 'ways' of being 'peripheral', but their readerly solutions to the problem of civic exclusion are applicable beyond one particular minority group, and are elegant, creative, and transformative.

Notes

1 Thomas King, 'Borders', in *One Good Story, That One: Stories* (Minneapolis: Minnesota University Press, 2013 [1993]), pp. 131–47. All subsequent references to the short story will appear parenthetically in the text.
2 The Jay Treaty. Treaty of Amity, Commerce, and Navigation, signed at London November 19, 1794, with additional article Original in English. Submitted to the Senate June 8, Resolution of advice and consent, on condition, June 24, 1795. Ratified by the United States August 14, 1795. Ratified by Great Britain October 28, 1795. Ratifications exchanged at London October 28, 1795. Proclaimed February 29, 1796. http://avalon.law.yale.edu/18th_century/jay.asp (accessed 15 June 2013).
3 Karl S. Hele, ed., *Lines Drawn upon the Water: First Nations and the Great Lakes Borders and Borderlands* (Waterloo, ON: Wilfrid Laurier Press, 2008), pp. xv and xi.
4 Benedict Anderson, *Imagined Communities: Reflections on the Origin and Spread of Nationalism* (London and New York: Verso, 1991), p. 7.
5 Ibid., p. 7.
6 Arnold E. Davidson, Priscilla L. Walton, and Jennifer Andrews, *Border Crossings: Thomas King's Comic Inversions* (Toronto: University of Toronto Press, 2003), p. 29.

Introduction

7 Carlos A. Forment, 'Peripheral Peoples and Narrative Identities: Arendtian Reflections on Late Modernity', in *Contesting the Boundaries of the Political*, ed. Seyla Benhabib (Princeton: Princeton University Press, 1996), pp. 314–30, at p. 314.
8 David Halperin, *Saint Foucault: Towards a Gay Hagiography* (New York: New York University Press, 1995), p. 62.
9 Engin F. Isin and Patricia Wood, *Citizenship and Identity* (London: Sage, 1999), p. 20.
10 Ibid., p. 313.
11 Carl Stychin, *A Nation by Rights: National Cultures, Sexual Identity Politics, and the Discourse of Rights* (Philadelphia: Temple University Press, 1998), p. 200.
12 David Bell and John Binnie, *The Sexual Citizen: Queer Politics and Beyond* (Cambridge: Polity Press, 2000), p. 36.
13 Yasemin Nohŏglu Soysal, *Limits of Citizenship: Migrants and Postnational Membership in Europe* (Chicago: Chicago University Press, 1994), p. 159.
14 Ibid., p. 164.
15 Jeffrey Weeks, quoted in Bell and Binnie, *The Sexual Citizen*, p. 36.
16 Danielle Fuller and DeNel Rehberg Sedo, *Reading Beyond the Book: The Social Practices of Contemporary Literary Culture* (London: Routledge, 2013); Lynne E. F. McKechnie, Knut Oterholm, Paulette M. Rothbauer, and Kjell Ivar Skjerdingstad, eds, *Plotting the Reading Experience: Theory/Practice/Politics* (Waterloo, ON: Wilfrid Laurier University Press, 2016); DeNel Rehberg Sedo, *Reading Communities: From Salon to Cyberspace* (Basingstoke: Palgrave Macmillan, 2011); Anouk Lang, ed., *From Codex to Hypertext: Reading at the Turn of the Twenty-First Century* (Amherst: University of Massachusetts Press, 2012); Elizabeth Long, *Book Clubs: Women and the Uses of Reading in Everyday Life* (Chicago: University Press of Chicago, 2003); Karen Littau, *Theories of Reading: Books, Bodies, and Bibliomania* (Cambridge: Polity, 2006); Janice Radway, *A Feeling for Books: The Book-of-the-Month Club, Literary Taste, and Middle Class Desire* (Chapel Hill: University of North Carolina Press, 1999).
17 Lauren G. Berlant, *The Queen of America Goes to Washington City: Essays on Sex and Citizenship* (Raleigh: Duke University Press, 1997), p. 5.
18 Fuller and Rehberg Sedo, *Reading Beyond the Book*, p. 39.
19 Danielle Fuller, 'Citizen Reader: Canadian Literature, Mass Reading Events and the Promise of Belonging', The Fifth Eccles Centre for American Studies Plenary Lecture pamphlet series (London: Eccles Centre & The British Library, 2011), p. 4.
20 Lauren Berlant, *The Female Complaint: The Unfinished Business of Sentimentality in American Culture* (Durham, NC: Duke University Press, 2008), p. ix.

21 Gillian Roberts, *Prizing Literature: The Celebration and Circulation of National Culture* (Toronto: University of Toronto Press, 2011), p. 11.
22 See for example, Gloria Anzaldúa, *Borderlands/La Frontera: The New Mestiza* (San Francisco: Aunt Lute Books, 1997 [1987]); Renato Rosaldo, *Culture and Truth: The Remaking of Social Analysis* (London: Routledge, 1993); Emily Hicks, *Border Writing: The Multidimensional Text* (Minneapolis: University of Minnesota Press, 1991); Héctor Calderón and José David Saldívar, *Criticism in the Borderlands: Studies in Chicano Literature, Culture, and Ideology* (Durham, NC: Duke University Press,1991), José David Saldívar, *Border Matters: Remapping American Cultural Studies* (Oakland: University of California Press, 1997); Claudia Sadowski-Smith, *Border Fictions: Globalization, Empire, and Writing at the Boundaries of the United States* (Charlottesville and London: University of Virgina Press, 2008); Claudia Sadowski-Smith, *Globalization on the Line: Culture, Capital, and Citizenship at U.S. Borders* (New York: Palgrave, 2002); Amritjit Singh and Peter Schmidt, *Postcolonial Theory and the United States: Race, Ethnicity, and Literature* (Jackson: University Press of Mississippi, 2000); Caroline F. Levander and Robert S. Levine, eds, *Hemispheric American Studies* (New Brunswick and London: Rutgers University Press, 2008); Rachel Adams, *Continental Divides: Remapping the Cultures of North America* (Chicago: University of Chicago Press, 2009); John Carlos Rowe, *Post-Nationalist American Studies* (Oakland: University of California Press, 2000); David Staines, ed., *The Canadian Imagination: Dimensions of a Literary Culture* (Cambridge, MA: Harvard University Press, 1977); Ian Angus, *A Border Within: National Identity, Cultural Plurality, and Wilderness* (Montreal and Kingston: McGill-Queen's University Press, 1997): W. H. New, *Borderlands: How We Think about Canada* (Vancouver: University of British Columbia Press,1998); Davidson *et al.*, *Border Crossings*; Winfried Siemerling, *The New North American Studies Reader: Culture, Writing, and the Politics of Re/Cognition* (New York: Routledge, 2005); Ila Nicole Sheren, *Portable Borders: Performance Art and Politics on the U.S. Frontera since 1984* (Austin: University of Texas Press, 2015); Rachel St John, *Line in the Sand: A History of the Western U.S.-Mexico Border* (Princeton: Princeton University Press, 2011).
23 Levander and Levine, *Hemispheric American Studies*, p. 3.
24 Gillian Roberts and David Stirrup, *Parallel Encounters: Culture at the Canada-US Border* (Waterloo, ON: Wilfrid Laurier University Press, 2013), pp. 2–3.
25 Anzaldúa, *Borderlands/La Frontera*, p. 19.
26 See, for example, the USA PATRIOT Act of 2001 and the Real ID Act of 2005 (discussed further below).

27 Jennifer Leclaire, 'Because They (Islam) Hate', *The Voice*. www.thevoicemagazine.com/culture/society/brigitte-gabriel-because-they-hate.html (accessed 12 October 2010). In addition to other spurious claims, Gabriel suggested that Hezbollah intend to invade the United States through its shared border with Mexico.

28 It should be noted here that the Real ID Act was passed as a rider on an appropriations bill funding the wars in Iraq and Afghanistan. The Act has seen resistance from environmental groups in addition to civil liberties advocates. For more, see 'An Act making Emergency Supplemental Appropriations for Defense, the Global War on Terror, and Tsunami Relief, for the fiscal year ending September 30, 2005, and for other purposes' (11 May 2005). www.gpo.gov/fdsys/pkg/PLAW-109publ13/content-detail.html (accessed 17 October 2010).

29 The following Acts were waived by Secretary Chertoff: The Endangered Species Act of 1973, The Migratory Bird Treaty Act of 1918, the National Environmental Policy Act of 1969, the Coastal Zone Management Act of 1972, the Clean Water Act of 1972, the Clean Air Act of 1963, and the National Historic Preservation Act of 1966. Chertoff's waiver of these Acts in favour of legislation that is undeniably a reaction to 9/11, further emphasises my point that the events of 9/11 represented a break in the way the United States dealt with its borders. The Real ID Act further stipulates that his decisions are not subject to judicial review, and in December 2005 a federal judge dismissed legal challenges by the Sierra Club, the Audubon Society, and others to Chertoff's decision.

30 Sadowski-Smith, 'Introduction', p. 2.

31 At a conference I attended at the University of North Dakota's Borderlands Institute in 2010, a United States government representative clearly stated that the border was no longer considered 'undefended'; rather, within government circles, it is termed the 'longest *unsecured* border'.

32 Victor Konrad and Heather N. Nicol, *Beyond Walls: Re-inventing the Canada-United States Borderlands* (Aldershot and Burlington: Ashgate, 2008), p. 2.

33 Examinations of the Canada–US border have tended to focus on cultural production and circulation. See for example Waldemar Zacharasiewicz and Christoph Irmscher, eds, *Cultural Circulation: Dialogues between Canada and the American South* (Vienna: Verlag der Österreichischen Akademie der Wissenschaften, 2013); Roberts and Stirrup, *Parallel Encounters*; Gillian Roberts, *Discrepant Parallels: Cultural Implications of the Canada-US Border* (Montreal: McGill-Queens University Press, 2015).

34 For more on this, see 'UK Refuses to Grant Visas to Iroquois Lacrosse Team' (15 August 2010). www.bbc.co.uk/news/world-us+canada-10634044 (accessed 16 August 2010).

35 Gale Courey Toensing, 'Canadian Border Agent Confiscated Haudenosaunee Passport, Called It "Fantasy Document"', *Indian Country Media Network* (17 August 2011). https://indiancountrymedianetwork.com/travel/canadian-border-agent-confiscated-haudenosaunee-passport-called-it-fantasy-document/ (accessed 20 September 2011).
36 T. H. Marshall, *Class, Citizenship, and Social Development* (Chicago: University of Chicago Press, 1964), p. 91.
37 Maria-Barbara Watson-Franke, 'To Teach "the Correct Procedure for Love": Matrilineal Cultures and the Nation State', in *The Political Interests of Gender Revisited: Redoing Theory and Research with a Feminist Face*, ed. Anna G. Jónasdóttir and Kathleen B. Jones (Manchester: Manchester University Press, 2009), pp. 104–21, at p. 104.
38 Suad Joseph, 'Women between Nation and the State in Lebanon', in *Between Woman and Nation: Nationalism, Transnational Feminism, and the State*, ed. Cora Kaplan, Norma Alarcon, and Minoo Moallem (Durham, NC: Duke University Press, 1999), pp. 162–81, at p. 163.
39 Soysal, *Limits of Citizenship*, p. 2.
40 Holloway Sparks, 'Dissident Citizenship: Democratic Theory, Political Courage, and Activist Women', *Hypatia* 12:4 (1997): pp. 74–110, at p. 78.
41 Ibid., p. 78.
42 Nancy Fraser, 'Rethinking the Public Sphere: A Contribution to the Critique of Actually Existing Democracy', in *Habermas and the Public Sphere*, ed. Craig Calhoun (Cambridge, MA and London: MIT Press, 1992), pp. 109–42, at p. 123.
43 Isin and Wood, *Citizenship and Identity*, p. 10.
44 Soysal, *Limits of Citizenship*, p. 2.
45 Bell and Binnie, *The Sexual Citizen*, p. 49.
46 See, for example, David Kidd and Emanuele Castano, 'Reading Literary Fiction Improves Theory of Mind', *Science* 342:6156 (2013): pp. 377–80, and even Loris Vezzali, Sofia Stathi, Dino Giovannini, Dora Capozza, and Elena Trifiletti, 'The Greatest Magic of Harry Potter: Reducing Prejudice', *Journal of Applied Social Psychology* 45 (2015): pp. 105–21.

1

Reading: an act of queering citizenship

The very idea of queering citizenship can be confounding. In an essay entitled 'Queer Citizenship/Queer Representation: Politics Out of Bounds?' Kathleen B. Jones and Sue Dunlap investigate the idea of what they call queer citizenship, based on 'the building of a different kind of democratic community' as one they are unable to define or pin down.[1] In exploring US and Canadian literary texts that reflect on the limitations of contemporary understandings of citizenship, this book posits a queering of citizenship using parameters that move beyond simplistic understandings of citizens as the basic units of the state. In this way, queer citizenship works by 'transforming strangers into citizen-neighbours through common conversations and projects',[2] a transformation that all the authors under examination in this book present in their writing. Here, I theorise how readers can be positioned to enact such a process.

This chapter sketches the conceptual terrain of a queered citizenship by first critically engaging with queer theory, citizenship studies and the concept of an 'act' of citizenship, as well as theories of active reading. Taken together, these ideas underpin the notion that the act of reading can be a transgressive civic act that constitutes reading subjects as empowered citizens. Accordingly, the chapter proceeds along several strands of argument. First, I provide a brief history of citizenship theory, before moving on to consider how queer theory and citizenship studies can intersect to consolidate the idea of an 'act of citizenship'. My focus then moves to the importance of postcolonial theory, active reading practices, and reader-response theory in constituting a civic subject discursively capable of engaging in radical acts of citizenship: the citizen. The concluding section brings these strands together to affirm that reading can be an act of queering citizenship, and shows how each of the authors explored in this book appropriates and resignifies the idea of an 'act' of citizenship in different but complementary ways to advocate their own political and artistic positions in a framework where 'queer' and 'citizenship' are not paradoxical.

The context of queer citizenship

As I note in the introduction, T. H. Marshall posits citizenship as 'a direct sense of community membership based on loyalty to a civilization which is a common possession'.[3] My exploration of the writers in this book suggests that theories of citizenship based on this premise are no longer useful given what Jones and Dunlap describe as 'the concerns raised by new social movements'.[4] However, despite criticism he has received that his theory of citizenship is narrow and has only limited applicability outside England, Marshall remains a significant figure and his work has led to important developments in contemporary citizenship theory.[5] The main branches of contemporary citizenship theory can be broadly understood in three ways: those that emerge from the liberal democratic paradigm; communitarian theories of democracy; and the participatory theories of democracy in which this book intervenes. These theories of democracy inevitably make implicit assumptions about citizen behaviour (and in some cases, 'human nature'), and have significant implications for how citizenship operates and is practised within a political system that defines itself as a democracy.

Marshall's work can be clearly linked to the liberal democratic paradigm, famously posited by political theorists such as Thomas Hobbes, John Rawls, Ronald Dworkin, and Robert Nozik. They see citizens as inherently (but legitimately) self-interested individuals who have socially and politically contracted to respect each other. Previous to the social contract these individuals would have lived in a 'state of nature', in which life, as Hobbes famously described, would have been 'nasty, brutish, and short'.[6] The social contract would have secured individuals' natural rights to life, liberty, health, and property. The liberal democratic paradigm is perhaps the most dominant (and certainly the most recognisable) in contemporary political systems.[7]

On the other hand, communitarian theory operates with a far less suspicious view of citizens, and is based on ideals of positive rights rather than 'natural' rights. Robert Putnam, one of the more well-known exponents of communitarian theory, understands this kind of system as one that is contingent on social capital, which he sees as key to building and maintaining democracy. Communitarian theory suggests that values and beliefs are formed in the public sphere, in which debate takes place, but this debate is almost always focused on the community rather than the individual. In its most basic form, communitarian theory stands in direct opposition to the liberal democratic paradigm because of its views on the basic 'character' of citizens.[8]

However, this book (and the authors under study in it) contends that citizenship is limited and curtailed by intersecting national, sexual, racial, gendered, and class identifications and is, as a result, exclusionary. Instead, a queered citizenship is able to represent 'multiply excluded alien partnerships between strangers and friends'.[9] In the United States and Canada, notions of multicultural citizenship and 'group-differentiated rights', posited by political theorists such as Will Kymlicka, and questions around the politics of recognition, theorised by political scientist and Indigenous scholar Glen Sean Coulthard, can be usefully repurposed to envision and fashion a political system that is participatory without losing the state-sanctioned 'integrity' required for it to be 'convincing'.[10] In this framework, 'queer' offers a way of understanding the process of interrogation that must take place in order to push the boundaries of how citizenship is theorised. As Jones and Dunlap put it: 'if citizenship is "queered" through the incorporation of identities, actions, and locales represented by the previously marginalised, then, by definition, its process of normalization has been disrupted.'[11]

But it is still necessary to approach queer citizenship cautiously, for as Jones and Dunlap note, it is an oxymoron, and 'invites the construction of a paradox'.[12] If we are to understand 'queer' as marginal and outside the bounds of 'mainstream' representation, how can it be represented within citizenship, which is itself a process of normalisation and state containment? In fact, merely opening up the concepts of representation and citizenship disrupts their processes of normalisation, making them, as Judith Butler suggests, 'signify in ways that none of us can predict in advance'.[13] Indeed, the issues of normalisation and disruptions figure significantly in the work of Anzaldúa, Allison, Scofield, Gómez-Peña, Moure, Díaz, and Martel. While each critiques 'mainstream' citizenship while also opening it up to different articulations of what this book calls a queered citizenship, each also risks the kind of normalisation or containment that has marginalised or excluded them in the first place. In this sense, queer citizenship is oxymoronic as it insists on the erasure of the public/private binary, replacing it with a simultaneity of the private and the public that can be at once promising and perplexing.

To 'queer' citizenship is neither to merely think in opposition to dominant discourses of citizenship, nor is it to theorise a community that is not defined by its 'common possession' of a civilisation. Rather, it is to consider a community based on a new understanding of the important role difference can play. As a result it is committed to, as Jones and Dunlap suggest, 'building a different kind of democratic'[14] locale and one that, as philosopher and political scientist Seyla Benhabib might put it, recognises peripheral communities as 'polyvocal, multilayered, decentered and fractured systems of action and signification'.[15] An effective entry point into this logic is to consider the intersections between queer theory and citizenship studies in order to craft the necessary framework for queering citizenship.

Queer theory and citizenship studies

While queer theory emerged, at least in part, from the perceived limitations of identity politics, it has certainly evolved over the last three decades. It is certainly also true that queer theory and studies have developed and renewed themselves since their initial scholarly emergence. As it is used in this book, queer studies self-consciously positions itself in a post-9/11 critical frame, since the events of 9/11 represent a significant break or rupture in approaches to understanding citizenship and, in some senses, civic responsibility, particularly in North America. As David Eng, Judith Halberstam, and José Esteban Muñoz note, the renewal of queer studies – the built-in self-critique that leads to recalibration and renewal which itself is part of the promise of queer studies – 'insists on a broadened consideration of the ... global crises that have configured historical relations among political economies, the geopolitics of war and terror, and national manifestations of sexual, racial, and gendered hierarchies'.[16] While the authors here are perhaps focusing primarily on the United States in their conception of the 'national', the same logic is certainly applicable in the Canadian context.[17] Indeed, Eng et al. rightly understand queer studies as an international, and as I contend in this book, *cross-border* critical endeavour, urging it to become and remain relevant in a contemporary political context. They ask: 'What does queer studies have to say about empire, globalization, neoliberalism, sovereignty, and terrorism? What does queer studies tell us about immigration, citizenship, prisons, welfare, mourning, and human rights?'[18] If we are to take Judith Butler's 1993 assertion that it is necessary to 'affirm the contingency of the term [queer], to let it be vanquished by those who are excluded by the term but who justifiably expect representation by it, to let it take on meanings that cannot now be anticipated by a younger generation whose political vocabulary may well carry a very different set of investments', then it is clear that this understanding of queer is precisely what is at stake when intersecting queer studies with questions of citizenship.[19] As a result it must remain 'open to a continuing critique of its [own] exclusionary operations'.[20] This understanding allows queer studies to remain relevant at any political or social juncture; indeed, it is the 'capacity of queer studies to mobilize a broad social critique of race, gender, class, nationality, and religion, as well as sexuality' that affords it the efficacy it (sometimes controversially) enjoys.[21]

Similarly, theories of citizenship, stemming broadly from theories of democracy, have also sought to remain relevant in changing political and historical contexts. The participatory theories of democracy this book engages with can in part be considered as reactions to the ostensible limitations, and in some cases, failures, of contemporary dominant political systems. However, even participatory theories of democracy are limited in their ability to translate to action *on the ground*. The articulation of queer citizenship I put forward over the course of this chapter attempts to reimagine the terrain upon which action can be taken. While citizenship is perhaps first and foremost a political category of identification by the state, reconsidering the concept as both discourse and performance in both concrete and theoretical terms is beneficial in that it allows for a renewed understanding of how to achieve this kind of political and civic change called for by the authors in this study.

Most crucial to my analysis is the now almost universally accepted notion that citizenship can be divided into two constituent parts: its practice, performance, or habitus, and its legal status or discourse.[22] According to citizenship theorist Engin F. Isin, 'critical studies of citizenship over the last two decades have taught us that what is important is not only that citizenship is a legal status but that it also involves practices of making citizens – social, political, cultural, and symbolic'.[23] *Acts* of citizenship, Isin argues, are distinct from civic *actions*, in that acts of citizenship produce actors, while actors *actualise* both these acts and themselves through the action.[24] Isin notes that to 'investigate acts of citizenship in a way that is irreducible to either status or habitus, while still valuing this distinction, requires a focus on those moments when, regardless of status and substance, subjects constitute themselves as citizens – or, better still, as those to whom the right to have rights is due'.[25] Such actions are able to disrupt the established order of citizenship. As Isin notes, 'Acts rupture or break the given orders, practices, and habitus'.[26] As I discuss the work of the seven writers explored in this book, I argue that in disrupting the normalising flow of the habitus of citizenship, the status of citizenship is then compromised and must adjust itself. Accordingly, it is certainly accurate to describe 'the enactment of citizenship [as] paradoxical because it is dialogical'.[27]

This shift from investigating citizenship as a balance between the practice and status of citizenship is useful in that it places primacy on the performance of a 'deed', which Isin and Nielsen understand as holding great potential. As they note: 'Acts of citizenship create a sense of the possible and of a citizenship that is "yet to come".'[28] This view connects well to that of Jones and Dunlap, whose ideas suggest that the potential of queer citizenship is its futurity. Significantly, Isin and Nielsen's notion of acts of citizenship 'leads to a rather sharp break with current citizenship studies in that it stretches the field well beyond the dominant liberal trajectory that dwells on a linear, formal and legal language of status, rights, obligations, and order'.[29] As a result the nature of this strand of citizenship studies can be likened to the nature of queer studies, in that its future outlook is as important as its current configuration.

Despite a focus on what is 'yet to come', Isin and Nielson believe that 'acts' of citizenship are effective 'in so far as they help organize public presentations or appearances of often-contradictory statements from actors who claim rights or impose social responsibilities'.[30] Introducing the notion of the public here resonates well with Jurgen Habermas' work on the public sphere, as he theorises the development and role of the public sphere as 'a body of "private persons" assembled to discuss matters of "public concern" or "common interest"'.[31] Nancy Fraser elaborates further on this, noting that 'the idea of "the public sphere" in Habermas' sense is a conceptual resource'.³² This conceptual resource provides us with the vocabulary necessary to such a task and allows us to analyse what Habermas describes as:

> a theatre in modern societies in which political participation is enacted through the medium of talk. It is the space in which citizens deliberate about their common affairs, and hence an institutionalized arena of discursive interaction. This arena is conceptually distinct from the state; it is a site for the production and circulation of discourses that can in principle be critical of the state.³³

Where Habermas theorises the space where political participation can offer a critique of the state, he stops short of suggesting how this theatre, while 'conceptually distinct from the state' can engage with the state. In the same way, feminist theorists M. Jacqui Alexander and Chandra Talpade Mohanty provide both theoretical and practical strategies for the *decolonisation* of citizenship. According to them, 'Decolonization involves thinking oneself out of the spaces of domination, but always *within* the context of a collective or communal process'.³⁴ It is only through 'action and reflection, through praxis' that this decolonisation can occur, and most significantly, only through a feminist – or more fittingly, *queer* – framework of theory and praxis at both the local and global levels.³⁵ They suggest that 'to talk about feminist praxis in global contexts would involve shifting the unit of analysis from local, regional, and national culture to relations and processes across cultures. Grounding analysis in particular, local feminist praxis is necessary, but we also need to understand the local in relation to larger, cross-national processes'.³⁶ What Alexander and Mohanty gesture towards, therefore, is a cross-border issue balancing the global and the local and the public and private with the basic principle that 'nation and citizenship [are] largely premised within normative parameters of masculinity and heterosexuality'.³⁷ In so doing they identify the very notions that can be resisted through a queering of citizenship.

This conceptual site where the practice of queering citizenship takes place is also evocative of what Holloway Sparks calls dissident citizenship. In her understanding, dissident citizenship is defined 'as the practices of marginalized citizens who publicly contest prevailing arrangements of power by means of oppositional democratic practices that augment or replace institutionalized channels of democratic opposition when those channels are inadequate or unavailable'.[38] Again, the idea of public contestation surfaces here, supplementing Fraser's articulation. Crucially, for Fraser, subaltern counterpublics work dialectically:

> On the one hand, they function as spaces of withdrawal and regroupment; on the other hand, they also function as bases and training grounds for agitational activities directed toward wider publics. It is precisely in the dialectic between these two functions that their emancipatory potential resides. This dialectic enables subaltern counterpublics partially to offset, although not wholly to eradicate, the unjust participatory privileges enjoyed by members of dominant social groups in stratified societies.[39]

This comment identifies the various strata of society that enjoy the privileges of citizenship more than others – recalling Carlos A. Forment's understanding of peripheral peoples noted earlier. According to Ann Travers, '[subaltern] counterpublics play an important role in the stratified societies of the West in that they allow for the consolidation of identity and regroupment while supporting more effective efforts for inclusion in the larger society'.[40] In this model, dissident citizenship 'encompasses the often creative oppositional practices of citizens who, either by choice or (much more commonly) by forced exclusion from the institutionalized means of opposition, contest current arrangements of power from the margins of the polity'.[41] *Crossing borders and queering citizenship* shows how reading can be one of these creative oppositional practices.

Reading and the civic subject

To map how the very act of reading can transform reading subjects into citizens, I rely on reader-response theory and theories of identification and disidentification to provide critical vocabulary, as well as drawing on postcolonial theories of *métissage* and hybridity to theorise the relationship between the author, the reader, and the text in the context of queer citizenship.

Reader-response criticism, the strand of literary theory that is interested in examining the reader's role in the reading process, originally emerged from the debate surrounding a particular group of texts: Louise Rosenblatt's *Literature as Exploration* (1968) and *The Reader, the Text, the Poem* (1978), David Bleich's *Readings and Feelings* (1975) and *Subjective Criticism* (1978), Wolfgang Iser's *The Implied Reader* (1972) and *The Act of Reading* (1978), Stanley Fish's *Is There a Text in this Class?* (1980). and Norman Holland's *Poems in Persons* and *Five Persons Reading* (1975).[42] Partly in response to what they saw as New Criticism's single-minded focus on close textual analysis, these critics foregrounded the role of the reader in creating meaning, in a process of collaboration with the author. Louise Rosenblatt summarises the process as one 'in which the reader selects out ideas, sensations, feelings, and images drawn from his past linguistic, literary, and life experience, and synthesizes them into a new experience'.[43] While the popularity of reader-response criticism has waned since its initial emergence in the 1970s and 1980s, it would be inaccurate and short-sighted to assume that it no longer represents a useful and effective way of understanding reading practices, even in the twenty-first century. Particularly appropriate is J. P. Surber's reminder that we 'must not lose sight of the facts that readers not only produce interpretations of texts but are produced as subjects by the texts they read',[44] evocative, of course, of Louis Althusser's theory of interpellation which describes how we are ideologically formed and identify as subjects.[45] Indeed, questions of identity are crucial to understanding the role of the reader. In this vein, Patricinio Schweikart asks: '[If] the meaning of the work is the experience of the reader, what difference does it make if the reader is a woman, [for example]?'[46] For example, Schweikart identifies the different processes at work when female readers read female-authored texts and when female readers read male-authored texts. More relevant to this book is an examination of the processes that take place when readers encounter texts authored by those in peripheral positions. Surber's and Schweikart's respective comments relate directly to how readers identify before reading and how reading can then transform their identifications.

Diana Fuss understands the process of identification as relational, requiring the presence of a distinct 'other' to use as a point of reference. Her theorisation of identification is rooted in a rereading of Freud's understanding of the same process, which he sees as the central process by which an individual's subjectivity is constituted. Fuss traces Freud's reworking of the notion of identification to incorporate his work on hysteria, the Oedipus complex, narcissism, and the id-ego-superego structure, while also focusing on identification in terms of theories of gender and sexuality.[47] In this book, the process of identification is mobilised to advance a queer political framework.

Equally important to this framework of identification in the context of community building is the process of disidentification. Not to be understood as the mere 'opposite' of the process of identification, disidentification works by distancing oneself from a certain identifying trait or characteristic. In *Disidentifications: Queers of Color and the Performance of Politics* (1999), José Esteban Muñoz suggests disidentification has the potential to be a strategy of resistance against dominant paradigms of identity, particularly in relation to how performance art allows for a space in which queer Latina/o subcultures can resist the racism and homophobia implicit in hegemonic norms. As he puts it, 'Disidentification is a strategy that resists a conception of power as being a fixed discourse. Disidentification negotiates strategies of resistance within the flux of discourse and power'.[48] As a strategy of resistance, disidentification does not function as a counter-stance; that is, it is not a reaction, but rather positive action in and of itself.

The processes of identification and disidentification are thus key to a community that is based on the queering of citizenship. Significantly, neither function in an exclusionary fashion; that is, it is perfectly possible to hold one identification while simultaneously holding its apparent opposite identification (for example, the identification as both male and female, or both masculine and feminine, or various permutations of all). Indeed, towards the end of *Bodies that Matter* (1993), Judith Butler describes disidentification as 'the uneasy sense of standing under a sign to which one does and does not belong'.[49] Both Butler and Muñoz connect disidentification to performance, which is useful to my understanding of the site of queer citizenship as negotiating the discursive and performative aspects of citizenship. Disidentification functions by resisting the binary relationship between ostensibly 'oppositional' identifications, negotiating the space between the two terms and enacting a shift in their potency. In this sense, the processes of identification and disidentification operate in tandem, and are significant tools in the queering of citizenship. Indeed, Muñoz gestures towards this queering, noting that 'the minoritarian subject employs disidentification as a crucial practice of contesting social subordination through the project of worldmaking'.[50] According to Muñoz, 'The promises made by disidentification's performance are deep. Our charge as spectators and actors is to continue disidentifying with this world until we achieve new ones'.[51] Significantly, Muñoz asks for actors and spectators – and those who occupy peripheral positions – to *continuously* disidentify with the hegemonic paradigms that they intend to critique in a discursive move that signals the need for both continuous re-evaluation of mainstream norms and simultaneous self-critique.

Muñoz loads his use of the terms 'spectators' and 'actors' so that it functions as a reminder of the performance art context from which he writes. He is also canny in his identification of citizens in general, and peripheral people specifically, as being spectators *before* being actors or agents within the civic context. More relevant to the context of this study would be to replace 'spectators' and 'actors' with 'readers', as I show below. This somewhat pessimistic view of civic agency does not preclude Muñoz from understanding disidentification to be positive action that instigates change. Indeed, according to Jonathan Dean, some iterations of 'disidentificatory relations open up scope for solidarity within and across social categories, and potentially militate against the tendency to think of membership of social groups in divisive and exclusive terms'.[52] Dean also notes that 'Muñoz repeatedly emphasises how disidentification is an unambiguously positive social force integral to both the deconstruction of identity barriers and minoritarian cultural production and political mobilisation'.[53] Whether or not disidentification is unambiguously positive, it is certainly a useful strategy of resistance against the normalising thrust of citizenship and is a key tool in conceptualising a site where citizenship is queered.

Employing an analysis inflected by reader-response theory comes with its own risk: that of sidelining the role of the author. This is consistent with the unsettling drive of queer studies. Unbalancing and re-evaluating the relationship between author and reader is one of the broader dynamics behind the queering process and it is the middle term – the text – that is integral to this process. The site of the subaltern counterpublic, which is a potential site at which the subversive process of queering occurs, thus shifts continuously between the author and the reader via the text, unbalancing the conventional relationship between each term. As one of the very sites of the queering of citizenship, the reader also partakes in Sparks' dissident citizenship. As such this figure can also be seen as a dissident citizen. Reading therefore becomes an act of dissent as well as an act of assent, suggestive of the processes of identification and disidentification described above. Further, the text operates as the *mediator* that provides the citizen-reader with agency. For example, in *The Psychic Life of Power*, Butler 'emphasizes the subversive potential of unstable identities and misrecognition'.[54] Similarly, Sarah Salih notes that 'if the subject is hailed by a name that is constitutive of a social identity-in-inferiority, the symbolic term is exceeded by the psychic or imaginary'.[55] Reader-response criticism works alongside the processes of identification and disidentification so that the reader is transformed into an active agent who both reads and co-creates the text. Specifically, this reader *identifies* with the text authored by a peripheral person and thus identifies with both the subject matter of the text *and* the author. That is not to say that the reader feels herself as occupying the same position as the author (such a conclusion would suggest a crude, simplistic understanding of the process of identification, completely undermining any sense of intersectional identity), but rather the reader disidentifies with the exclusionary processes that marginalise the author.

The processes I describe above are elucidated in further detail by Françoise Lionnet, whose understanding of the concept and processes of *métissage* – hybridity – is relevant to the hybrid nature of identity and, by extension, routes to civic inclusion. Specifically, she focuses on understanding the potential of hybridity as a process and practice, and how it can then resist hegemonic forces. This book argues for *métissage* as a strategy to negotiate conflicting cultural influences in texts with a focus on themes of dislocation, displacement, and exile – appropriate in the context of peripheral peoples under study. In terms of the processes of identification and disidentification, Lionnet and Shu-Mei Shi highlight the need to study the strategies through which minority formations interact with one another.[56] Lionnet and Shi suggest that instead of only engaging with and against majority groupings in a vertical relationship, minority groups can usefully interact laterally and intersectionally with both majority and minority groupings. Writing on francophone, African, and African American literatures, Lionnet suggests that one important strategy in thinking past hegemony is the concept and practice of *métissage*. Lionnet's definition of *métissage*, which she sees as the 'braiding of cultural forms though the simultaneous revalorization of oral traditions and reevaluation of Western concepts [that] has led to the recovery of occulted histories' builds on work by Edouard Glissant, the Martinician writer, poet, and literary critic.[57] According to Lionnet,

'*Métissage* is a form of *bricolage*' which has the potential of 'bring[ing] together biology and history, anthropology and philosophy, linguistics and literature'.[58] It is also a reading practice that is crucial in understanding and articulating what she calls 'a politics of solidarity'. In order to understand and practise *métissage*, she believes that

> [w]e have to articulate new visions of ourselves, new concepts that allow us to think *otherwise*, to bypass the ancient symmetries and dichotomies that have governed the ground ... *Métissage* is such a concept and a practice: it is the site of undecidability and indeterminacy, where solidarity becomes the fundamental language of political action against hegemonic languages.[59]

The role of language is important here, as Lionnet distinguishes between the different roles it can play: language as solidarity and resistance, on the one hand, and language as domination, on the other. This new language of resistance, however, can only be enunciated by those individuals who have engaged in a re-visioning of thought and moved beyond those 'ancient symmetries and dichotomies' which characterise hegemonic languages and ideologies. Lionnet provides an excellent example of this, maintaining that *métissage*, and its Spanish counterpart *mestizaje*, as terms and concepts, denote processes that cannot be represented in English – which in this case is the language of the mainstream (and, often, the coloniser). There is no English equivalent for either '*mestizaje*' or '*métissage*', save for miscegenation, which only denotes part of the meaning of the former terms. These concepts refer to the processes of the genetic, cultural, and linguistic intermingling that regularly take place at sites where differences are exposed to each other. They are also used to describe an individual possessing *mestizaje* or *métissage* as a trait or characteristic, as in one's *métis*-ness or *mestiza*-ness. In fact, in English, only the products of such mixing or intermingling are named: 'half-breed', 'mixed-blood', 'mixed-race', and so on. Each description contains a value judgement based on notions of purity, as if 'breed', 'blood', and 'race' are unitary categories that do not lend themselves well to contamination, mixture, or dilution. As Lionnet puts it: 'these expressions always carry a negative connotation, precisely because they imply biological abnormality and reduce human reproduction to the level of animal breeding'.[60] The easy comparison to draw here is that of the mule: part horse, part donkey, the mule is widely considered stubborn, stupid, and fickle – yet studies have shown that in addition to its physical superiority, the mule exhibits higher cognitive ability than its 'pure' parent animals.[61] Most significantly, the mule is sterile; its inability to procreate is considered by many as proof that such crossbreeding is unnatural, wrong, and biologically untenable in terms of evolutionary survival.

Lionnet's call to move beyond and bypass traditional Western dualistic modes of thought – those modes which are incapable of truly representing *métissage* and *mestizaje* – is a political call to action and resistance against systems of exclusion and domination. These calls to action can be enacted through the process of reading that takes place at a site, where, as Françoise Lionnet suggests, 'multiplicity and diversity are affirmed. This space is not a territory staked out by exclusionary practices'.[62] This site of *métissage* could otherwise be described as the site at which queer citizenship exists, located in the interstices of the binary relationships and dichotomies that characterise traditional modes of thought, and seeking to build bridges between all minority communities in order to achieve social and political change. Lionnet explains what kind of work must be done:

> a radical and subversive *appropriation* of the cultural codes by a subject who constructs herself through her discourse. Underlining the ruptures of the historical perspective, this subject projects herself in the fictitious and the fabulous, thereby authorizing herself to assume her own destiny through utterances that allow her to construct her own symbolic context.[63]

Lionnet's formulation provides the necessary clarity to allow an understanding of the process of queering. The focus here is also on agency, for this subject 'assumes [her] own destiny' and is able to 'construct her own symbolic context'.[64] This is also valid for the reading subject whose reading is an act that, as Isin and Nielsen understand it, enables 'the production of subjects, whether citizens, strangers, aliens, or outcasts'.[65] Indeed, for them, the emancipatory potential of such an act is clear: 'The essence of an act, as distinct from conduct, practice, behaviour, and habit, is that an act is a rupture in the given.'[66] This rupture – a queering – works well alongside Lionnet's understanding of *métissage* as a site of inclusion rather than exclusion and serves to promote and enhance the possibility of lateral alliances of which a queered citizenship is capable.

If we are to understand *métissage* 'as a concept of solidarity which demystifies all essentialist glorifications of unitary origins, be they racial, sexual, geographic, or cultural', then this book shows that one strategy to achieve this is through reading.[67] In connecting queer theory, citizenship studies, and reader-response theory to craft a methodological approach in which the act of reading constitutes civic subjects who queer citizenship, this book's exploration of Gloria Anzaldúa, Dorothy Allison, Gregory Scofield, Guillermo Gómez-Peña, Erín Moure, Junot Díaz, and Yann Martel is but a small gesture of solidarity.

Notes

1. Kathleen B. Jones and Sue Dunlap, 'Queer Citizenship/Queer Representation: Politics Out of Bounds?' in *The Political Interests of Gender Revisited: Redoing Theory and Research with a Feminist Face*, ed. Anna G. Jónasdóttir and Kathleen B. Jones (Manchester: Manchester University Press, 2009), pp. 189–207, at p. 203.
2. Holloway Sparks, 'Dissident Citizenship: Democratic Theory, Political Courage, and Activist Women', *Hypatia* 12:4 (1997): pp. 74–110, at p. 76.
3. Jones and Dunlap, 'Queer Citizenship/Queer Representation', p. 203.
4. Ibid., p. 203.
5. For more on this, see Nancy Fraser and Linda Gordon, 'Contract versus Charity: Why is there no Social Citizenship in the United States?' *Socialist Review* 23:3 (1992): pp. 45–65.
6. Thomas Hobbes, *Leviathan* (Cambridge: Cambridge University Press, 1991 [1651]), p. 78.
7. For more on the liberal democratic paradigm, see: Ronald Dworkin, *Is Democracy Possible Here? Principles for a New Political Debate* (Princeton: Princeton University Press, 2006); William Kymlicka, *Liberalism, Community and Culture* (Oxford: Clarendon Press, 1991); Robert Nozick, *Anarchy, State, and Utopia* (Oxford: Blackwell, 1974); John Rawls, *A Theory of Justice* (Delhi: Universal Law Publishing Co., 2008 [1971]); Michael J. Perry, *The Political Morality of Liberal Democracy* (Cambridge: Cambridge University Press, 2010).
8. For more on communitarian theory, see: Gad Barzilai, *Communities and Law: Politics and Cultures of Legal Identities* (Ann Arbor: University of Michigan Press, 2003); Daniel Bell, *Communitarianism and Its Critics* (Oxford: Clarendon Press, 1993); Henry Tam, *Communitarianism: A New Agenda for Politics and Citizenship* (Basingstoke: Macmillan, 1998); David Rasmussen, ed., *Universalism vs. Communitarianism* (Cambridge, MA: MIT Press, 1990).

9   Jones and Dunlap, 'Queer Citizenship/Queer Representation', p. 203.
10 Will Kymlicka, *Multicultural Citizenship: A Liberal Theory of Minority Rights* (Oxford: Oxford University Press, 1995); Glen Sean Coulthard, 'Subjects of Empire: Indigenous Peoples and the "Politics of Recognition" in Canada', *Contemporary Political Theory* 6:4 (2007): pp. 437–60.
11 Jones and Dunlap, 'Queer Citizenship/Queer Representation', p. 203.
12 Ibid., p. 191.
13 Judith Butler, *Bodies that Matter: On the Discursive Limits of Sex* (London: Routledge, 1993), p. 29.
14 Jones and Dunlap, 'Queer Citizenship/Queer Representation', p. 203.
15 Seyla Benhabib, *The Claims of Culture: Equality and Diversity in the Global Era* (Princeton: Princeton University Press, 2002), pp. 25–6.
16 David L. Eng, Judith Halberstam, and José Esteban Muñoz, 'What's Queer about Queer Studies Now?' *Social Text* 23:3–4 (2005): pp. 1–17, at p. 1.
17 Gary Kinsman's work is particularly relevant in this context, although I will not rehearse his arguments here to avoid repetition. See, for example, Gary Kinsman and Patrizia Gentile, *The Canadian War on Queers: National Security as Sexual Regulation* (Vancouver: University of British Columbia Press, 2010) and Gary Kinsman, *The Regulation of Desire* (Montreal: Black Rose Books, 1996).
18 Eng *et al.*, 'What's Queer about Queer Studies Now?' p. 2.
19 Judith Butler, 'Critically Queer', *GLQ* 1 (1993): pp. 17–32, at p. 21.
20 Eng *et al.*, 'What's Queer about Queer Studies Now?' p. 3.
21 Ibid., p. 4.
22 Engin F. Isin confirms that 'citizenship studies often proceeds with a focus on the three ontic aspects of citizenship: extent (rules and norms of exclusion and inclusion), content (rights and responsibilities), and depth (thickness or thinness of belonging)'. We can suggest that these aspects of citizenship 'arrive at the scene too late' and do not provide substantive methods for understanding and interpreting the acts and actors of citizenship (see Engin F. Isin, 'Theorizing Acts of Citizenship', in *Acts of Citizenship*, ed. Engin F. Isin and Greg M. Neilsen (London and New York: Zed Books, 2008), pp. 15–43, at p. 37).
23 Ibid., p. 17.
24 Ibid., p. 37.
25 Ibid., p. 18.
26 Ibid., p. 36.
27 Ibid., p. 18.
28 Engin F. Isin and Greg M. Nielsen, eds, 'Introduction', in *Acts of Citizenship* (London and New York: Zed Books, 2008), pp. 1–12, at p. 4.
29 Ibid., p. 11.
30 Ibid., p. 10.

31 Jurgen Habermas, *The Structural Transformation of the Public Sphere: An Inquiry into a Category of Bourgeois Society*, trans. Thomas Burger with Frederick Lawrence (Cambridge, MA: MIT Press, 1989).
32 Nancy Fraser, 'Rethinking the Public Sphere: A Contribution to the Critique of Actually Existing Democracy', in *Habermas and the Public Sphere*, ed. Craig Calhoun (Cambridge, MA and London: MIT Press, 1992), pp. 109–42, at p. 112.
33 Jurgen Habermas, quoted in ibid., p. 110.
34 M. Jacqui Alexander and Chandra Talpade Mohanty, eds, 'Introduction: Genealogies, Legacies, Movements', in *Feminist Genealogies, Colonial Legacies, Democratic Futures* (New York and London: Routledge, 1997), pp. xiii–xlii, at p. xxviii.
35 Ibid.
36 Ibid., p. xix.
37 Ibid., p. xiv.
38 Sparks, 'Dissident Citizenship', p. 75.
39 Nancy Fraser quoted in ibid., p. 85.
40 Ann Travers, 'Parallel Subaltern Feminist Counterpublics in Cyberspace', *Sociological Perspectives* 46:2 (2003): pp. 223–37, at p. 230.
41 Sparks, 'Dissident Citizenship', p. 75.
42 Louise Rosenblatt, *Literature as Exploration* (London: Heinemann, 1968 [1938]) and *The Reader, The Text, The Poem: The Transactional Theory of the Literary Work* (Carbondale: Southern Illinois University Press, 1978); David Bleich, *Readings and Feelings: An Introduction to Subjective Criticism* (Urbana: NCTE, 1975) and *Subjective Criticism* (London: Johns Hopkins University Press, 1978); Wolfgang Iser, *The Implied Reader: Patterns of Communication in Prose Fiction from Bunyan to Beckett* (Munich: Wilhelm Fink, 1972) and *The Act of Reading: A Theory of Aesthetic Response* (London: Johns Hopkins University Press, 1978); Stanley Fish, *Is There a Text in the Class? The Authority of Interpretive Communities* (London: Harvard University Press, 1980); Norman Holland, *Poems in Persons: A Psychology of the Literary Process* (New York: Norton, 1973) and *Five Readers Reading* (London: Yale University Press, 1975).
43 Louise Rosenblatt, 'The Transactional Theory of the Literary Work: Implications for Research', in *Researching Response to Literature and the Teaching of Literature: Points of Departure*, ed. C. R. Cooper (Norwood: Ablex, 1985), pp. 33–53, at p. 40.
44 J. P. Surber, *Culture and Critique: An Introduction to the Critical Discourses of Cultural Studies* (Boulder: Westview Press, 1998), p. 245.
45 Louis Althusser, 'Ideology and Ideological State Apparatuses', in *Lenin and Philosophy and other Essays*, trans. Ben Brewster (New York and London: Monthly Review Press, 1971), pp. 121–76.

46 Patricinio Schweikart, 'Toward a Feminist Theory of Reading', in *Gender and Reading: Essays on Readers, Texts, and Contexts*, ed. Elizabeth A. Flynn and Patricinio Schweikart (Baltimore: Johns Hopkins University Press, 1996), pp. 31–62.
47 For more on this, see Sigmund Freud, *Group Psychology and the Analysis of the Ego*, trans. James Strachey (London: Hogarth Press, 1922).
48 José Esteban Muñoz, *Disidentifications: Queers of Color and the Performance of Politics* (Minneapolis and London: University of Minnesota Press, 1999), p. 12.
49 Butler, *Bodies that Matter*, p. 219.
50 Muñoz, *Disidentifications*, p. 200.
51 Ibid.
52 Jonathan Dean, 'The Lady Doth Protest Too Much: Theorising Disidentification in Contemporary Gender Politics'. Working Paper in Ideology in Discourse Analysis 24 (2008). www.essex.ac.uk/idaworld/paper240708.pdf (accessed 15 November 2008), n.p.
53 Ibid.
54 Sarah Salih, *Judith Butler* (London and New York: Routledge, 2002), p. 129.
55 Ibid.
56 Françoise Lionnet and Shu-Mei Shi, eds, *Minor Transnationalism* (Durham, NC and London: Duke University Press, 2005).
57 Françoise Lionnet, *Autobiographical Voices* (Ithaca and London: Cornell University Press, 1989), p. 4.
58 Ibid., p. 8.
59 Ibid., p. 6.
60 Ibid., p. 13.
61 For example, see Leanne Proops, Faith Burden, and Britta Osthaus, 'Mule Cognition: A Case of Hybrid Vigour?' *Animal Cognition* 12:75 (2009): pp. 75–84.
62 Lionnet, *Autobiographical Voices*, p. 5.
63 Françoise Lionnet, *Postcolonial Representations: Women, Literature, Identity* (Ithaca and London: Cornell University Press, 1995), p. 175.
64 Ibid., p. 175.
65 Isin and Nielsen, 'Introduction', p. 6.
66 Isin, 'Theorizing Acts of Citizenship', p. 25.
67 Lionnet, *Autobiographical Voices*, p. xi.

2

Autobiographical acts of reading and the work of Gloria Anzaldúa and Dorothy Allison

In a 2007 interview for the Voices of Feminism Oral History Project, Dorothy Allison shares her experiences of being a feminist activist and organiser in the 1960s and 1970s while at college in Florida. She reveals how, attending one women's meeting, she realised why she did not belong there:

> When I went to the women's meeting ... these people can afford to talk about this stuff, but I could lose my scholarship and be on the street. So I walked out, then didn't go back. And that's the whole thing of, this is what the middle class women are going to do, and that's all very well and good, but people like me, no, for three reasons: one, incest; two, violence; and three, being queer.[1]

Allison's experiences as a young student at a time when the feminist movement was mobilising and working towards the Equal Rights Amendment expose the now well-documented concerns raised by minority women about feminist movements in the twentieth century ignoring issues of intersectionality and echo the anxiety of lesbian Chicana writer Gloria Anzaldúa who, in 1991, warned that lesbian writers sometimes struggle to avoid 'getting sucked into the vortex of homogenization'.[2] Indeed, a few years later, in a telephone interview in 1995, Anzaldúa expresses pleasant surprise at her work being read in the same tradition as W. E. B. Du Bois, John Dos Passos, Jack Kerouac, Virginia Woolf, Paula Gunn Allen, and Audre Lorde because this suggested that her writing had become part of an American literary canon, something she would not have expected given the difficulties she had faced as a graduate student trying to write about Chicano literature.[3]

Gloria Anzaldúa and Dorothy Allison's writing in many ways anticipates the work of Scofield, Gómez-Peña, Moure, Díaz, and Martel, and serves, among other functions, as a reminder of the longstanding importance of treating reading as a civic act of queering citizenship. As I note in the Introduction, Anzaldúa's work in *Borderlands/La Frontera: The New Mestiza* (1987) galvanised the field of border studies, and she is read most often for Chicana nationalist and queer feminist engagement with the US–Mexico border. Anzaldúa is famous for her formulation of the new *mestiza*, a figure of resistance against totalising understandings of identity and belonging in the space of the US–Mexico borderlands. Queer southern writer Dorothy Allison's work, ranging from her essays, poetry, short stories, and longer writing, including her first novel, the National Book Award finalist *Bastard Out of Carolina* (1993), is concerned with the intersection of race, class, and sexuality as these realities connect to the representation and experience of growing up as 'white trash'.

This chapter constructs a relationship between Anzaldúa and Allison's writing. Although there is only one public record of the two having potentially met, when they appeared independently as presenters at the 1993 Kentucky Women's Writers Conference,[4] and there is no archive of correspondence except for Anzaldúa having kept one of Allison's essays in her personal collection, both writers regularly appear alongside each other in course syllabi on queer writing and are part of a recognised strand of feminist activism, particularly in the 1980s and 1990s.[5] Here, they are read together for their autobiographical writings, which offer personal accounts of the histories of their communities. Anzaldúa and Allison's autobiographical strategies engage in the *métissage* and *bricolage* described by Francoise Lionnet, and work to heal Anzaldúa and Allison of the personal trauma wrought by their personal and community circumstances. Ultimately, what I call their autobiographical acts allow each to theorise and practise alternative queer feminist communities of belonging, or, in the language of citizenship studies, multiple alternative civic *habita*. Their use of the autobiographical mode works to 'deploy discourses of identity to organize acts of remembering that are addressed to multiple addressees or readers' and their use of direct address offer readers concrete models for civic action.[6]

Reading these two authors together allows us to begin the recovery of an as-yet-unwritten history of radical queer feminism in the twentieth century, mapping linked networks of influence that suggest a burgeoning strand of intersectional feminism that has not yet been examined in existing literary histories of the movement. More broadly, by exposing tangible connections between the experiences of civic marginalisation faced by Chicana and 'white trash' communities, this chapter reads Anzaldúa and Allison as having separately but equally theorised feminist spaces for a queered citizenship.

Both Anzaldúa and Allison use writing and storytelling as a way of healing from personal trauma, but also as a way of relating the historical narratives of their broader (and bordered) communities. Anzaldúa, for example, begins *Borderlands/La Frontera* with her history of the peopling of the Americas, before moving through time to contextualise her writing within the Chicano Civil Rights Movement and as emerging from the US–Mexico border, which she famously describes as '*una herida abierta* [an open wound] where the Third World grates against the first and bleeds' (*Borderlands* p. 25). Anzaldúa is concerned with being able to relate the silenced histories of not only the Chicanos, who 'did not know [they] were a people until 1965' (*Borderlands* p. 85) but also women who have 'been silenced, gagged, caged, bound into servitude with marriage, bludgeoned for 300 years, sterilized and castrated in the twentieth century' (p. 44). Anzaldúa's search for belonging and representation finds an echo in Dorothy Allison's writing which is explicit in its focus on representing 'the central fact' of her life, that she was 'born in 1949 in Greenville, South Carolina, the bastard daughter of a white woman from a desperately poor family'.[7] This central fact, according to Allison, 'has had dominion over [her] to such an extent that [she has] spent her life trying to overcome or deny it' (*Trash* p. vii), and Anzaldúa's writing also emphasises this 'barbwire' existence (*Borderlands* pp. 24–5). In telling personal histories of their seemingly separate communities, both Anzaldúa and Allison work towards healing and empowerment and theorise queer feminist sites at which the civic belonging they are denied as peripheral peoples can be realised.

Personal community histories

Born in 1942 on the US side of the US–Mexico border, Anzaldúa and her family were migrant workers, constantly changing locations to find employment. When she was eight years old, Anzaldúa's family 'settled' in Hargill, Texas, where she attended school. Although she was a US citizen, parts of Anzaldúa's life that should have been seen as entitlements were presented to her as privileges. Anzaldúa's First Amendment right to freedom of expression did not extend to speaking Spanish at recess, or correcting people if they mispronounced her name: 'If you want to be American, speak "American." If you don't like it, go back to Mexico where you belong' (*Borderlands* p. 75), one school teacher threatened. On attending university, Anzaldúa began to write and engage with feminist groups, and her focus on the intersection of feminism and Chicano/a culture led her to publish *This Bridge Called My Back* (1981) with Cherríe Moraga. The collection of feminist theory by self-described radical women of colour has been described by one reviewer as 'a vermilion ink bloom on the crisp white wedding dress of the U.S. feminist movement' and sparked debate among white feminists about their own practices.[8]

This Bridge Called My Back even influenced Allison, who cites the collection as having helped change her understanding of 'what feminism meant'.[9] As she puts it: 'It was a matter, then, not only of looking at the personal racism that blights all our lives, but of examining the institutional racism that shapes our convictions of who is or can be *right*, and what it is that we really know as feminists' (*Skin* p. 115). Allison's own experiences at the first feminist meeting she attended had been validated, then, and the act of reading *This Bridge Called My Back* imbued her with a sense of responsibility to '[insist] on a shared vision of feminism' (p. 115) that she had not encountered before.

Allison's childhood experiences of sexual violence and extreme poverty allow her insight into the complex and problematic label of 'white trash', which in her writing, she has taken on to confront as it 'had been applied to [Allison and her] family in crude and hateful ways' (*Trash* p. xv). Allison was physically and sexually abused from the age of five by her stepfather for almost a decade, a fact of her life that seemed to fulfil the 'expectations' that came with the label of 'white trash'. When, as a young teenager, Allison moves with her family to Florida, she is able to see 'other futures' for herself, different from the expectations of being 'trash': 'In that new country, we were unknown. The myth of the poor settled over us and glamorized us' (*Skin* p. 21).

Both Anzaldúa and Allison's personal experiences are key to their later understandings of intersectional feminism. For example, Anzaldúa notes that women like her, but especially the undocumented

Mexican woman, suffer a double oppression, first as women of colour in a whitewashed United States, and second as women: 'Not only does she have to contend with sexual violence, but like all women, she is prey to a sense of physical helplessness' (*Borderlands* pp. 34–5). Her awareness of this leads her to reflect on how this process of double oppression and alienation is enacted and perpetuated: 'Culture forms our beliefs. We perceive the version of reality that it communicates. Dominant paradigms, predefined concepts that exist as unquestionable, unchallengeable, are transmitted to us through the culture. Culture is made by those in power – men. Males make the rules and the laws; women transmit them' (p. 38). While Anzaldúa places blame on women on continuing to perpetuate an unfair system, she also recognises the broader systemic issues at work. Likewise, Allison is aware that there is a more pervasive, intangible system that has the power to stamp these labels on people: 'Everything in our culture ... is presented as if it is being seen by one pair of eyes, shaped by one set of hands, heard by one pair of ears. Even if you know you are not part of that imaginary creature ... you are still shaped by that hegemony, or your resistance to it' (*Skin* p. 16).

Anzaldúa's resistance to systemic, institutionalised racism and misogyny comes in the form of her challenge to the Chicano movement. Indeed, *Borderlands/La Frontera* was written in the mid-1980s and published in 1987 as a reaction to the Chicano movement. The Chicano Civil Rights Movement, which began in the 1960s, lasted until well into the 1980s. The aim of the Chicano Civil Rights Movement was to gain equal rights as a minority group in the United States. The Chicano movement, or *El Movimiento Chicano*, is considered to have officially begun in 1965, when César Chávez helped found the National Farm Workers Association. However, as it progressed, the Chicano movement also 'ignited a political debate between Chicanas and Chicanos based on the internal gender contradictions prevalent within *El Movimiento*'.[10] This pattern was also reflected in the literature of the movement. Early Chicano movement literature, while playing an important role in the Chicano national psyche and championing Chicano rights, tended to reproduce other social inequalities such as misogyny and homophobia.

The literature of the Chicano movement, sometimes known as the Chicano literary renaissance, was characterised by an affirmation of what Alurista describes as 'a nationalist fervor founded on the most ancient and pre-colonial cultural origins available to the modern Xicano writer'.[11] This nationalism focused on reminding Chicanos that they were not immigrants, but that the United States had occupied Mexican territory. As Luiz Valdez put it: 'America was not a country, the United States was a country. America was a continent, a continent where mixed-blooded, Spanish-speaking people constituted the majority.'[12] The literature of the Chicano movement was inherently political, basing itself on the historical dialectic Valdez utilised above, and intended to 'combat the onslaught of Anglo-American acculturation'.[13] Alma M. García suggests that the Chicano movement 'manifested a paradoxical agenda of civil rights and equal opportunity demands, on the one hand, and a more separatist ethnic nationalist rebellion, on the other'.[14] The Chicana feminist movement emerged as a result of the realisation that *Chicanismo*, or Chicano cultural nationalism, did not account for the experiences of *Chicanas*. As a result, the Chicana feminist movement 'represented a struggle that was both nationalist and feminist' and worked against what García calls 'the culturally accepted role of woman, as defined by a cultural nationalist ideology, [which] relegated women to subordinate positions within the Chicano movement'.[15] Crucially, the Chicana feminist movement strove to avoid the same homogenising thrust of the Chicano movement. For example, in their introduction to *Chicana Feminisms: A Critical Reader*, Arredondo *et al.* carefully 'use the term Chicana to convey the politicized nature of [their] project' based on the tacit recognition that in terms of Chicana womanhood, 'regardless of whether one uses Chicana, Mexicana, Tejana, or another term, heterogeneity is critical to understanding the overall Chicana experience'.[16]

Allison's resistance is, at least partially, routed through the protagonist and narrator of her first novel, *Bastard Out of Carolina* (1993), a partially autobiographical coming of age work that follows Ruth Anne Boatwright, called Bone by her family, as she grows up in a 'white trash' family and endures abuse from her stepfather, Daddy Glen. In the opening pages of the novel, Allison tells the story of Bone's birth and describes how she was named:

> I am Ruth for my aunt Ruth, and Anne for my mama ... Other than the name, [Aunt Ruth and Granny] got just about everything else wrong. Neither Aunt Ruth or Granny could write very clearly and they hadn't bothered to discuss how Anne would be spelled, so it wound up spelled three different ways on the form. As for the name of the father ... They

> tried to get away with just scribbling something down, but if the hospital didn't mind how a baby's middle name was spelled, they were definite about having a father's last name. So Granny gave one and Ruth gave another, the clerk got mad, and there I was – certified a bastard by the state of South Carolina.[17]

From the moment of her birth, then, Bone is marked as outside the acceptable boundaries of subjecthood. On her birth certificate, the word 'Illegitimate' is stamped, and cannot be erased. This serves to solidify and strengthen the view that her mother has of herself, a view that Bone will later struggle with – that the myth of the 'noble poor' of the South does not apply to her, that she is in fact, 'white trash'.

Bone's mother repeatedly attempts to change her daughter's birth certificate so that it does not read 'illegitimate'. But when she visits the courthouse to request a new document, the clerk tells her that a different one cannot be issued, because 'This is how it's got to be. The facts have been established' (*Bastard* p. 4). To the clerk, and the system he represents, the facts are, of course, that Bone's mother had sex out of wedlock and most likely does not know who the father is. She therefore *deserves* nothing more than what she already has – and that sentence extends to her daughter, too.

In *Two or Three Things I Know for Sure* (1995), originally a performance piece but revised for publication shortly after the release of *Bastard Out of Carolina*, Allison attempts to further contextualise the 'facts' above. Directly addressing the reader, she writes:

> Let me tell you about what I have never been allowed to be. Beautiful and female. Sexed and sexual. I was born trash in a land where the people all believe themselves natural aristocrats. Ask any white Southerner. They'll take you back two generations, say, 'Yeah we had a plantation.' The hell we did. I have no memories that can be bent so easily, I know where I come from, and it is not that part of the world. My family has a history of death and murder, grief and denial, rage and ugliness – the women of my family most of all.[18]

Allison draws a distinction between two different perceptions of poverty – those of the noble, honorable poor and the ungrateful poor. The latter group, to which her family has belonged for generations, is characterised as 'no good, lazy, shiftless' (*Two or Three* p. 3) and branded as such. As John Hartigan puts it, 'if "hillbilly" burns, "white trash" "brands"'.[19] Despite their racial standing as 'white', they possess no upward mobility because their lives are seemingly predetermined nor, it could be argued, is there even the possibility of change. In fact, those who are branded 'white trash' stand as a reference point for those white who are *not* trash, as Matt Wray notes when he asserts: 'The term white trash helps solidify for the middle and upper classes a sense of cultural and intellectual superiority.'[20]

Whites' deployment of the modifier 'trash' to part of their own 'racial' group is designed to differentiate themselves from whiteness' lower-class constituents: 'white poverty necessitates a differentiation within whiteness itself, the signs of which are visible characteristics … Bodies become coded as trashy when associated with unregulated reproduction, unrestrained or perverse sexuality, and lax work ethic.'[21] Allison echoes this in a description of the women in her family: 'Solid, stolid, wide-hipped baby machines. We were all wide-hipped and predestined' (*Two or Three* p. 33). Accordingly, the term 'trash', put in conversation with 'white', is problematic:

> White trash names a kind of disturbing liminality: a monstrous, transgressive identity of mutually violating boundary terms, a dangerous threshold state of being neither one nor the other. It brings together into a single ontological category that which must be kept apart in order to establish a meaningful and stable symbolic order. Symbolic orders are those shared representations of reality and collective systems of classification that are key elements in bringing about social solidarity. White trash names a people whose very existence seems to threaten the symbolic and social order. As such, the term can evoke strong emotions of contempt, anger, and disgust. This is no ordinary slur.[22]

Here, white trash is cast as both an issue of class and race, despite the fact that within its very naming, its racial standing is intended to be clear. That once whiteness descends below a certain level of class or social standing it becomes racialised speaks to the interconnectedness of class and race in the perception of whites, or Anglos, as Anzaldúa calls them.

In the South, 'white trash' 'has served as a container for regional legacies of violence, incest, racial brutality, illiteracy, and indolence'[23] that have been maintained since William Byrd's observations of whites on the other side of the Virginia–North Carolina border he was surveying in 1728 as 'indolent wretches'[24] and W. J. Cash's description of southern white 'crackers'.[25] In tracing the literary descent of Dorothy Allison, David Reynolds suggests that Allison forces her reader to 'confront white trash as realistic human characters, possessing both positive and negative attributes'.[26] Unlike her literary ancestors, including James Agee and Erskine Caldwell and even extending to Hunter S. Thompson and Nelson Algren, whose stereotypical and often romanticised depictions of white trash communities continue to shape contemporary understanding of the term, Allison humanises her characters so that her readers recognise 'persons of [that] social class not as subhuman trash but as human, flawed, and extraordinary', as Moira P. Baker puts it.[27] Allison's Bone, then, is crafted as a character who, as Sharon Monteith puts it, does 'battle against the circumstances that reduce [her] to "trash"',[28] even while Allison writes: 'My people were not remarkable. We were ordinary, but even so we were mythical. We were the *they* everyone talks about – the ungrateful poor' (*Skin* p. 13).

In writing Bone as an avid reader, Allison gives Bone access to a range of literary texts, almost always after the depiction of a violent encounter with Daddy Glen: 'The librarian gave me *Black Beauty, Robinson Crusoe,* and *Tom Sawyer.* On my own I found copies of *Not as a Stranger, The Naked and the Dead, This Gun for Hire,* and *Marjorie Morningstar*' (*Bastard* p. 119). Reading these books offers Bone a literal excuse to be out of the house: 'I found a hiding place in the woods near Aunt Alma's where I could camp for hours with a bag of Hershey Kisses and a book ... and only went home after dark' (p. 119) as well as a more figurative escape into the lives of castaways, assassins, aspiring actresses, and doctors – all futures that seem out of reach for Bone and for Allison, until Allison recognises the power of storytelling, which she describes elsewhere: 'Sometimes I became people I had seen on television or read about in books, went places I'd barely heard of, did things that no one I knew had ever done, particularly things that girls were not supposed to do. In the world as I remade it, nothing was forbidden; everything was possible' (*Two or Three Things* p. 2).

Along these lines, Anzaldúa and Allison credit reading with exposing them to the possibility for other futures for themselves. But it is the autobiographical act that offers a space for each to heal from their personal and community circumstances. For Anzaldúa, reading and writing is a process by which identities can be negotiated and realised, and in an essay in Betsy Warland's *Inversions: Writings by*

Dykes, Queers, and Lesbians (1991) she is explicit: 'Reading is one way of constructing identity.'[29] She is also helpfully clear about the relationship she wants to build with readers: 'Making meaning is a collaborative affair. Similar class, ethnic, and sexual identity is a strong component of the bond between writer and reader. This intimate interactive relationship I have with readers has to do with a colored queer feminist mestiza identity.'[30]

In Allison's case, reading allowed her to learn about writing, and in particular to write in refutation of 'stories in which poor southern characters were framed as if they were brain-damaged, or morally insufficient, or just damn stupid' (*Trash* p. ix). Explaining her writing process, Allison notes that 'It is quite literally the case that I wrote out loud, reading the stories out loud over and over until they were closer to what I wanted' (p. ix). Allison's self-consciously readerly writing process strove to both express her own feelings – 'Sometimes I was so angry, I wrote to stop my own rage' – and to correct misconceptions, stereotypes, and myths surrounding white trash communities: 'We are not stupid. We do pretty well with what we have' (p. ix). The autobiographical occasion also became a way for Allison to 'say things that otherwise [she] had no other way to talk about'.[31] It also informed her writing process and narrative strategies; in the case of *Bastard Out of Carolina*, Allison's aims were to 'get the reader inside Bone – inside this whole community of people who are viciously hated – so the reader can get a different view of it'.[32]

Concerned as they are with resisting the stereotypes and marginalisation that have dominated the depiction and representation of their communities' identities, Anzaldúa and Allison engage in self-representation and healing through their autobiographical acts. This self-representation is then extended to their broader communities through their narrative strategies and choice of genre. As Albert E. Stone puts it, 'autobiography is a rich cultural medium for exploring the necessary interplay between the particular and the general', and for Allison, an opportunity 'to claim my family, my true history, and to tell the truth not only about who I was but about the temptation to lie' (*Skin* p. 34).[33] Further, Allison acknowledges that 'writing *Bastard Out of Carolina* became, ultimately, the way to claim my family's pride and tragedy' (*Skin* p. 34).

If, as Stone puts it, 'An autobiographical act, therefore, makes a writer at once the creator and the recreator of his or her personal identity',[34] then both Anzaldúa and Allison are able to craft personal narrative identities designed not only for their individual self-representation and empowerment but also to engage readers, who, according to Anzaldúa, 'want to interact, to repeat back or reflect or mirror – to add to the dialogue' whereas 'in the past, the reader was a minor character in the triangle of author-text-reader'.[35] Sidonie Smith and Julia Watson confirm that in autobiographical writing, the narrator and the reader are 'engaged in a communicative action that is fundamental to autobiographical acts and the kinds of intersubjective truth they construct'[36] and Smith, writing on women and autobiographical acts, suggests that

> particularly in the dramatic passages of her texts, where she speaks directly to the reader about the process of constructing her life story, she reveals the degree of her self-consciousness about the process of constructing her position as a woman writing in an androcentric genre. Always, then, she is absorbed in a dialogue with her reader, that 'other' through whom she is working to identify herself and to justify her decision to write about herself in a genre that is men's.[37]

If both Anzaldúa and Allison are writing not only for self-realisation, but also directly to readers, their work can and should be usefully read as offering to readers a model for a different kind of belonging, what this book calls a queering of citizenship. As peripheral peoples, both authors find themselves, as Lourdes Torres suggests, 'marginalized by multiple discourses, and existing in a borderland' which 'compels them to reject prescriptive positions and instead leads them to create radical personal and collective identities'.[38] These radical identities enact a queering of citizenship through the act of reading.

Queer communities

Anzaldúa and Allison's autobiographical acts position them to formulate new grounds upon which to build new communities based on radical senses of civic belonging. As Lourdes Torres suggests, minority women writers 'create a new discourse which seeks to incorporate the often contradictory aspects of their gender, ethnicity, class, sexuality, and feminist politics'.[39] For Anzaldúa and Allison, this new discourse also takes the form of a community founded on a radical intersectional politics that resists the coercive elements of traditional citizenship.

Anzaldúa's theorisation and practice of a new community that springs from a collective new consciousness is perhaps the major reason her work remains influential today. Coupled with her very personal treatment of the experience of living on the physical US–Mexico border, but also on the invisible borders of gender, sexuality, and race, the multi-generic nature of *Borderlands/La Frontera* engages with the way borders police people's lives. Indeed, her work is seen to retain much of its original influence and political potential, its cross-disciplinarity providing new and varied methodologies to analyse borders in a multiplicity of contexts. Anzaldúa and her work have also played an important role in refocusing American studies as a transnational discipline. In her presidential address to the American Studies Association in 2004, Shelley Fisher Fishkin identified Anzaldúa's *Borderlands/La Frontera* as epitomising the transnational nature of American studies, and credited her work for opening up a space for 'American studies scholars [to] increasingly recognize that understanding requires looking beyond the nation's borders, and understanding how the nation is seen from vantage points beyond its borders'.[40] Anzaldúa's work, much like Anzaldúa herself, is able to blur the boundaries of a range of different theoretical approaches and contexts, including postcolonial, feminist, border, and queer theories, in addition to other disciplines including sociology and anthropology. It is virtually impossible to find a collection or anthology on Chicana/o literature, feminist theory, or border studies without a section inspired by Anzaldúa's work and Gita Rajan and Radhika Mohanram have noted how, because of Anzaldúa's work, 'critical focus ... shifted from exile and diaspora to borders, and the crossing and re-crossing of physical, imaginative, linguistic, and cultural borders'. They see Anzaldúa's work as 'largely responsible for this new direction in post-colonial studies'.[41]

Courtney George identifies the 'patriarchal southern social structures' at work in *Bastard Out of Carolina* and suggests that the novel 'interrupts' what she calls 'the larger imagined South' by depicting 'a resisting community of queer "white trash" women'.[42] Allison resists myths of the South as well as its patriarchal structure through the act of writing, confirming what Scott Romine in *The Narrative Forms of Southern Community* calls the 'coercive' and 'cohesive' character of the South.[43] In so doing, Allison theorises a cohesive queer southern community of women that resists the South's coercive patriarchal frame. This community can be usefully read as intersectional. Indeed, as she names herself 'queer white trash', Allison is, as Kimberlé Crenshaw puts it, 'subverting the naming process in empowering ways'.[44]

Within race studies, Anzaldúa's treatment of *mestizaje* (in a culturally specific sense rather than a broader framework) has been used in parallel with other processes of racial mixture, such as *métissage* in the case of Canada or other former French colonies, and *creolite* in the Caribbean. On a broader level, the *mestiza* as a figure of resistance is also used in conjunction with the *métis(se)* and the *mulatta*. Critics such as Rafael Pérez-Torres, José David Saldívar, and Suzanne Bost insist on the potential of the *mestiza*, as both a literal figure and as a conceptual tool, to instigate change. As Bost notes: 'Despite its ambivalent history, *mestizaje* is an enabling concept because it suggests ways in which race dynamics in the United States could be re-examined with greater attention to such contradictions.'[45] The ambivalent history of *mestizaje* – the fact that the process has a history rooted in colonial enterprises characterised by violence, rape, and war and motivated by essentialised and totalised understandings of identity – makes it all the more powerful. In fact, as Suzanne Bost has noted, it is precisely because mixed identities such as the *mestiza*, *mulatta*, or *métis(se)* challenge these universalised notions of identity that they have so much potential.

Mestizaje need not be restricted to thinking only of racial mixture, but also to consider the ways, as I have above, in which whiteness can be unravelled to render it visible. In the case of 'white trash', whiteness is reclassified as a trait that marks out poverty as well as, owing to the US Eugenics Records Office's 'Eugenic Family Studies', 'poor breeding' and 'genetic defectives'. According to Carsten Schinko, Allison 'uses the slur not so much for its transgressive promises but in "self-defense," in an attempt to write off the ghosts that haunt her',[46] but in a way that allows her 'to elude objectification … freeing her to explore the fluidity of self and memory'.[47]

In terms of critical engagement within Chicana feminist writing, Arredondo *et al.* foreground the work of Anzaldúa and engage especially with her notion of Chicanas' bodies as *bocacalles*. This term quite literally translates to 'an intersection'. However, as Arredondo *et al.* put it, 'a more provocative translation of *bocacalle* as mouth/street evokes images of women shouting in the street or the assertion of Chicana feminisms as public discourse demanding to be heard'.[48] Certainly Anzaldúa demanded to be heard; representing an important break from the mainly male-dominated pool of 'traditional' Chicano writers, Anzaldúa's *Borderlands/La Frontera* was written from the position(s) of queer Chicana womanhood, featured code-switching between English, dialects of Spanish, and Nahuatl, and mixed poetry and prose, inspiring a generation of Chicanas to write about their experiences as border-crossers with hybrid identities.[49] Until then, the Chicano movement had been represented in literature by a small circle of male writers who generally wrote in English, and often for a mainstream, English-speaking audience. Anzaldúa's work stood out as her multi-generic writing articulated a deliberately feminist Chicanismo. She also wrote in multiple languages, leaving most of the Spanish dialects and Nahuatl untranslated. Her decision to do this is decidedly political, since as she puts it, 'we Chicanos no longer feel that we need to beg entrance, that we need always to make the first overture – to translate to Anglos, Mexicans and Latinos, apology blurting out of our mouths with every step. Today we ask to be met halfway' (*Borderlands* p. 20).

Likewise, Allison's feminist work is concerned with excavating 'the categories by which we categorize and dismiss each other' in order to 'resist destruction, self-hatred, or lifelong hopelessness' and to 'see ourselves as human, flawed, and extraordinary' (*Skin* p. 36). For both authors, intersectionality plays a significant role, with Vincent King describing Allison's feminism as 'postmodern' insofar that it is 'politically charged, highly ethical, socially aware, and ultimately, affirmative'[50] and Anzaldúa's 'reinterpret[ation] of history', her creation of 'a new culture – *una cultura mestiza* – with [her] own lumber, own bricks and mortar, and own feminist architecture' constitutes the shaping of new myths with new symbols (*Borderlands* p. 44). As an 'invitation from the new *mestizas*' to anyone interested in joining this new community characterised by mutual dialogue, Anzaldúa's writing aims to be transformative (p. 20) in the same way that Allison's works to 're-vision' the white trash label, 'reordering the narrative of access and representational power to reclaim for poor white female "trash" a legitimate place in southern, and national, identities'.[51]

If, as Lionnet notes, 'the very notion of *métissage* is something culturally specific', then Anzaldúa and Allison's foregrounding of intersectional politics into their queer communities of resistance constitutes an undeniable kind of cultural *métissage*.[52] While Anzaldúa's borderlands are quite specific – those of the US–Mexico border – she is quick to clarify that her analysis is not exclusive to the physical borderlands of her ancestry. As she now famously puts it: 'the Borderlands are physically present wherever two or more cultures edge each other, where people of different races occupy the same territory, where under, lower, middle and upper classes touch, where the space between two individuals shrinks with intimacy'.[53] In this vein, it may be useful to consider Renato Rosaldo's characterisation of borders as 'sites where identities and cultures intersect' which are 'always in motion'.[54] This is significant as Rosaldo does not specify or limit his conception of borders to physical locations – so they could be, for example, internal to one individual, something that Anzaldúa's formulation would certainly advocate. In this way, Anzaldúa and Allison's new communities allow their citizens to claim membership to multiple identifications without relinquishing their sense of belonging. Accordingly, the idea of borders as intersecting and connecting, rather than merely separating, identities, communities and cultures is crucial to how these communities work. Anzaldúa's presentation of an alternative subject, the new *mestiza*, empowered by her *mestizaje*, is here a strategy to open up a site at which *mestizaje*, *métissage*, and the multifaceted identifications of peripheral peoples can become acceptable 'currency' in debates surrounding identity and citizenship. Thus, employing the new *mestiza*'s identification with borderlands (in the broad understanding of the term) makes it possible to resist marginalisation through the act of reading.

For Anzaldúa, the *mestiza* consciousness is attainable by any individual from any group of people. Having originated from Anzaldúa's conception of *mestizaje*, the new *mestiza* consciousness is not restricted to those who identify as *mestiza/o*. In fact, according to Anzaldúa, the new *mestiza* consciousness is a result of the *mestiza*'s need to 'work out a synthesis' of her constituent parts (*Borderlands* p. 102). According to Anzaldúa, 'its energy comes from continual creative motion that keeps breaking down the unitary aspect of each new paradigm' (p. 102).[55] The new *mestiza* also overcomes the trauma and subsequent silencing and denial of colonial conquest, violence, and rape. Anzaldúa sees this new *mestiza* consciousness as 'greater than the sum of its severed parts' (p. 102). As such, her new *mestiza* is capable of crossing all borders and questioning all social constructions of identity, history, language, race, sexuality, and gender. Not only is this figure one of hope, but it is also one of distinct political potential; the *mestiza* is both genetically and politically capable of identifying with other *mestiza* figures (other hybrid or marginalised identities) and of working to resist the systems which oppress them. Most importantly to Anzaldúa, the new *mestiza* has an interest in forming solid alliances and unlikely partnerships on the basis of shared experiences, whether marginalisation or belonging.

This interest in forming alliances is also at the core of Allison's theorisation of an alternative community of belonging. In an essay entitled 'Neighbors', Allison writes: 'I have always wanted to be a good neighbor, the kind of person who talks across the fence and shows up at the block party with a plate full of barbecue. Nor do I see any reason why this kind of ambition shouldn't reside in a woman who is also a trashy lesbian, a political activist, and an honest writer' (*Skin* p. 73). For Allison, then, community belonging can take the form of neighbourliness and does not come at the expense of her other identifications. In *Bastard Out of Carolina*, Allison presents such an alternative model of neighbourliness and community, and intersects these practices by moving beyond the idea of a white trash identity.

In the novel, Bone's aunt Raylene is presented to the reader as a fiercely independent 'reclusive old woman' (*Bastard* p. 180) who had been 'kind of wild' (p. 179) in her youth, and 'kept her gray hair cut short, and wore trousers as often as skirts' (p. 179). Raylene is the best cook in the family, and supports herself by selling her canned vegetables and fruit. Raylene lives alone, her 'shotgun house' positioned 'on a little rise of land' (p. 178) that gives her a clear view of the highway and the Greenville River, as well as imbuing her with a broader perspective and a symbolically elevated view of the countryside (and world) around her. Raylene resists the determinism of the white trash label: she lives outside the city limits, is self-sufficient, and she repurposes the reclaimed trash that Bone finds in the river: 'baby-carriage covers, tricycle wheels, shoes, plastic dishes, jump-rope handles, ragged clothes, and once the headlight off a Harley-Davidson motorcycle', all items that in symbolise either decay (plastic dishes, ragged clothes) or travel, movement, or escape (wheels, shoes, a motorcycle part) (p. 181). Raylene's view of trash in the river is valuable because it allows Bone to envision (and Allison to present) the possibility of a world beyond the determinism and fixity of the white trash label. According to Raylene: 'Trash rises ... out here where no one can mess with it, trash rises all the time' (p. 180). Raylene's comment is a reminder of the ideological and interpellative effects of society: what is labelled as 'trash' has the potential to 'rise' and be refashioned as long as it is undisturbed by the social, political, and class forces that named it as trash in the first instance.

While in the novel Raylene is perhaps Allison's clearest depiction of an alternative way of living in the world, the other women in her family also work – though sometimes unsuccessfully – to undermine the forces that work to label them all as trash. As Baker notes, 'Working in an almost subterranean, matrilineal network on the margins of patriarchy and capitalism, these women enable Bone to resist subjection to mutually reinforcing class and gender ideologies that define her as trash because she is both poor and a woman'.[56]

At the end of the novel, recovering from Daddy Glen's last but most brutal sexual assault, Bone is left to live with Raylene and is ultimately abandoned by her mother, Anney, who finds herself unable to choose Bone over her husband. Despite not choosing Bone over Daddy Glen, Anney's leaves Bone a parting gift: a new birth certificate, one that is blank where previous copies had certified Bone a bastard. The novel closes with Bone, now legitimate, leaning against Raylene, 'trusting her arm and her love' (p. 309), suggesting that Bone will adopt Raylene's approach to being marginalised and rejecting the ideologically motivated label of white trash as her defining characteristic. Instead, she would be like Raylene, 'a Boatwright woman' (p. 309). In the act of naming Bone as part of a community of women, Allison's character achieves self-realisation. As Lippard notes, 'Naming is the active tense of identity, the outward aspect of the self-representation process, acknowledging all the circumstances through which it must elbow its way'.[57] Bone ultimately 'renames herself by writing a story that forces the reader to reevaluate names such as "bastard," "poor white trash," and "ugly"' and provides for readers an alternative way of thinking about community belonging, one that thrives in spite of being interpellated and marginalised by both capitalism and patriarchy.[58]

For her part, Anzaldúa works to interpellate her readers into the new *mestiza* community she advances in her writing. In the poem 'To live in the Borderlands means you', Anzaldúa makes the function of the pronoun 'you' entirely ambiguous from the very outset (*Borderlands* pp. 216–17). By boldly phrasing the title as she has, Anzaldúa suggests that the 'you' is the reader who, unbeknownst to her, lives in the borderlands and is thus already involuntarily pushed to the periphery. The multiplicity of meanings becomes evident as the reader moves to the first line of the poem, which completes the title's fragment, becoming:

> To live in the Borderlands means you
> are neither *hispana india negra española*
> *ni gabacha*.

In this stanza, Anzaldúa essentially informs the reader of what she is *not*, forced into denying identifications she does not even know that she has, followed by another list of what identities she *is allowed* claim to:

> *eres mestiza, mulata*, halfbreed
> caught between the crossfire between camps
> while carrying all five races on your back
> not knowing which side to turn to, run from;

In the poem Anzaldúa uses a semi-colon as end punctuation, emphasising the lack of closure and frustration that she suggests comes with inhabiting the space of the borderlands. The piece continues as a list poem, progressing to a concluding moment of resolution: 'To survive the Borderlands / you must live *sin fronteras* / be a crossroads.' Despite the hopeful tone, these last lines are still fraught with ambiguity: to survive the borderlands, you must live without borders / be a crossroads. Once again, the 'you' is used to great effect: for the reader to survive the borderlands – because it is a matter of life and death – she must live without borders, a contradiction in terms. Instead, the reader must be a crossroads, an intersection. In so doing, Anzaldúa sets up the site of the subaltern counterpublic at which the reader can resist the system that pushes her (and Anzaldúa) to the periphery. This is an excellent example of how the act of reading can become an act of resistance, and ultimately an act that queers citizenship.

Such acts give the reader a model around which she may be able to foster 'partnerships between strangers and friends'. Using a language of resistance governed by what Lionnet would call 'a politics of solidarity', it is through the process of reading that subjects are able to identify with friends and strangers and in so doing transgress the borders of traditional understandings of community and citizenship. Both Anzaldúa and Allison's autobiographical acts work as strategies for personal healing, but also as sites at which their readers can identify with the social, political, and, crucially, civic marginalisation faced by both writers (and the fictional characters they craft). Reading

Anzaldúa and Allison together allows for a revision of the history of feminist activism and amplifies their feminism. It also identifies in their work the advancement of what this book calls a queered citizenship that has at its core a reading practice that follows the principles of intersectionality and solidarity, across racial, gender, and international borders.

Notes

1. Dorothy Allison, interview by Kelly Anderson, transcript of video recording, 18–19 November 2007, Voices of Feminism Oral History Project, Sophia Smith Collection, p. 6. www.smith.edu/libraries/libs/ssc/vof/transcripts/Allison.pdf (accessed 12 February 2017).
2. Gloria Anzaldúa, 'To(o) Queer the Writer – *Loca, escritoria y chicana*', in *Inversions: Writings by Dykes, Queers & Lesbians*, ed Betsy Warland (London: Open Letters, 1992), pp. 249–263, at p. 250.
3. Gloria Anzaldúa, *Borderlands/La Frontera: The New Mestiza* (San Francisco: Aunt Lute Books, 1997 [1987]), p. 82. All subsequent references will be included in parentheses in the main body of the text.
4. 'Presenters 1979–2011' (n.d.). https://womenwriters.as.uky.edu/presenters-1979-2011 (accessed 15 June 2017).
5. Anzaldúa's personal papers are held at the University of Texas' Library. Allison's essay 'Growing Up Different' (n.d.) is categorised as 'Collected Materials/Others' Work'. Gloria Evangelina Anzaldúa Papers, Benson Latin American Collection, University of Texas Libraries, the University of Texas at Austin, Box 183, Folder 2.
6. Sidonie Smith and Julia Watson, 'Introduction', in *Interfaces: Women/Autobiography/Image/Performance* (Ann Arbor: University of Michigan Press, 2002), pp. 1–46, at p. 11.
7. Dorothy Allison, *Trash: Short Stories* (New York: Plume, 2002 [1988]), p. vii. All subsequent references will be included in parentheses in the main body of the text.
8. Nisha Agarwal, 'This Bridge Called My Back: A Retro Look at Women of Color and Power' (25 May 2011). www.huffingtonpost.com/nisha-agarwal/this-bridge-called-my-bac_b_418196.html (accessed 30 June 2011).
9. Dorothy Allison, *Skin: Talking about Sex, Class, and Literature* (Ithaca, NY: Firebrand Books, 1994), p. 115. All subsequent references will be included in parentheses in the main body of the text.
10. Alma M. García, ed., 'Introduction', in *Chicana Feminist Thought: The Basic Historical Writings* (New York and London: Routledge, 1997), pp. 1–16, at p. 1.

11 Alurista, 'Cultural Nationalism and Xicano Literature during the Decade of 1965–1975' *MELUS* 8:2 *Ethnic Literature and Cultural Nationalism* (1981): pp. 22–34, at p. 22.
12 Luiz Valdez, qtd in ibid., p. 23.
13 Ibid., p. 24.
14 García, 'Introduction', p. 2.
15 Ibid., pp. 4 and 6.
16 Ibid., p. 3.
17 Dorothy Allison, *Bastard Out of Carolina* (New York: Plume, 1993), pp. 2–3. All subsequent references will be included in parentheses in the main body of the text.
18 Dorothy Allison, *Two or Three Things I Know for Sure* (New York: Penguin Books, 1995), p. 32. All subsequent references will be included in parentheses in the main body of the text.
19 John Hartigan, 'Who Are These White People? "Rednecks," "Hillbilly," and "White Trash" as Marked Racial Subjects', in *White Out: The Continuing Significance of Racism*, ed. Ashley W. Doane and Eduardo Bonilla-Silva (New York: Routledge, 2003), pp. 95–111, at p. 105.
20 Matt Wray, *Not Quite White: White Trash and the Boundaries of Whiteness* (Durham, NC: Duke University Press, 2006), p. 1.
21 Kelly L. Thomas, 'White Trash Lesbianism: Dorothy Allison's Queer Politics', in *Gender Reconstructions*, ed. Cindy L. Carson, Robert L. Mazzola, and Susan M. Bernardo (Burlington: Ashgate, 2002), pp. 167–88, at p. 169.
22 Wray, *Not Quite White*, p. 2.
23 Katherine Henninger, 'Claiming Access: Controlling Images in Dorothy Allison', *Arizona Quarterly: A Journal of American Literature, Culture, and Theory* 60:3 (2004): pp. 83–108, at p. 93.
24 William Byrd, *Histories of the Dividing Line Betwixt Virginia and North Carolina* (New York: Dover, 1967 [1929]), p. 184.
25 W. J. Cash, *The Mind of the South* (New York: Knopf, 1941), p. 25.
26 David Reynolds, 'White Trash in Your Face: The Literary Descent of Dorothy Allison', *Appalachian Journal* 20:4 (1993): pp. 356–66, at p. 365.
27 Moira P. Baker, ' "The Politics of They": Dorothy Allison's *Bastard Out of Carolina* as Critique of Class, Gender and Sexual Ideologies', in *The World is Our Culture: Society and Culture in Contemporary Southern Writing*, ed. Jeffrey J. Folks and Nancy Summers Folks (Lexington: University Press of Kentucky, 2000), pp. 117–41, at p. 137.
28 Sharon Monteith, *Advancing Sisterhood? Interracial Friendships in Contemporary Southern Fiction* (Athens and London: The University of Georgia Press, 2000), p. 56.
29 Anzaldúa, 'To(o) Queer the Writer – *Loca, escritoria y chicana*', p. 257.
30 Ibid., p. 255.

31 Carolyn E. Megan, 'Moving Toward Truth: An Interview with Dorothy Allison', *The Kenyon Review* 16:4 (1994): pp. 71–83, at p. 74.
32 Ibid., p. 78.
33 Albert E. Stone, *Autobiographical Occasions and Original Acts: Versions of American Identity from Henry Adams to Nate Shaw* (Philadelphia: University of Pennsylvania Press, 1982), p. 7.
34 Ibid., p. 4.
35 Anzaldúa, 'To(o) Queer the Writer – *Loca, escritoria y chicana*', pp. 255–6.
36 Sidonie Smith and Julia Watson, *Reading Autobiography: A Guide to Interpreting Life Narratives* (Minneapolis: University of Minnesota Press, 2001), p. 69.
37 Sidonie Smith, *A Poetics of Women's Autobiography: Marginality and the Fictions of Self-Representation* (Bloomington and Indianapolis: Indiana University Press, 1987), p. 50.
38 Lourdes Torres, 'The Construction of the Self in U.S. Latina Autobiographies', in *Women, Autobiography, Theory: A Reader*, ed. Sidonie Smith and Julia Watson (Madison: University of Wisconsin Press, 1998), pp. 276–87, at p. 279.
39 Ibid., p. 279.
40 Shelley Fisher Fishkin, 'Crossroads of Cultures: The Transnational Turn in American Studies', *American Quarterly* 57:1 (2005): pp. 17–57, at p. 20.
41 Gita Rajan and Rahdhika Mohanram, eds. 'Introduction: Locating Postcoloniality', in *Postcolonial Discourse and Changing Cultural Contexts: Theory and Criticism* (Westport and London: Greenwood Press, 1995), pp. 1–16, at p. 5.
42 Courtney George, '"It Wasn't God Who Made Honky-Tonk Angels": Musical Salvation in Dorothy Allison's *Bastard Out of Carolina*', *The Southern Literary Journal* 41:2 (2009): pp. 126–47, at p. 127–8.
43 Scott Romine, *The Narrative Forms of Southern Community* (Baton Rouge: Louisiana State University Press, 1999), p. 2.
44 Kimberlé Crenshaw, 'Mapping the Margins: Intersectionality, Identity Politics, and Violence Against Women of Color', *Stanford Law Review* 43 (1991): pp. 1241–99, at p. 1297.
45 Suzanne Bost, *Mulattas and Mestizas: Representing Mixed Identities in the Americas, 1850–2000* (Athens and London: University of Georgia Press, 2003), p. 22.
46 Carsten Schinko, 'Why Trash? Thirteen Ways of Looking at Poor (White) Folks', *Amerikastudien / American Studies* 55:1 (2010): pp. 143–64, at p. 153.
47 Matt Wray and Annalee Newitz, eds, 'Introduction', in *White Trash: Race and Class in America* (New York: Routledge, 1997), pp. 1–12, at p. 11.
48 Gabriela F. Arredondo, Aida Hurtado, Norma Klahn, Olga Nájera-Ramírez, and Patricia Zavella, eds. 'Introduction', in *Chicana*

Feminisms: A Critical Reader (Durham, NC and London: Duke University Press, 2003), pp. 1–18, at p. 2.
49 See for example work by Rudolfo Anaya and Rolando Hinojosa Smith.
50 Vincent King, 'Hopeful Grief: The Prospect of a Postmodern Feminism in Allison's *Bastard Out of Carolina*', *The Southern Literary Journal* 33:1 (2000): pp. 122–40, at p. 125.
51 Henninger, 'Claiming Access', p. 85.
52 Françoise Lionnet, *Autobiographical Voices* (Ithaca, NY and London: Cornell University Press, 1989), p. 13.
53 Ibid.
54 Renato Rosaldo, *Culture and Truth: The Remaking of Social Analysis* (London: Routledge, 1993), pp. 149 and 217.
55 Anzaldúa, *Borderlands/La Frontera*, p. 102.
56 Baker, '"The Politics of They"', p. 121.
57 Lucy Lippard, *Mixed Blessings: New Art in a Multicultural America* (New York: Pantheon Books, 1990), p. 19.
58 King, 'Hopeful Grief', p. 136.

3
Métis and two-spirit vernaculars in the writing of Gregory Scofield

Writing from the peripheral positions of hybridity at the US–Mexico borderlands and white poverty in the United States, Gloria Anzaldúa and Dorothy Allison's feminist autobiographical acts offer readers models for intersectional queer communities of belonging beyond the bounds of state citizenship. Across the 49th parallel, Canadian Métis poet Gregory Scofield similarly disrupts the relationship between the status and performance of citizenship, writing poetry that calls the notion of Canadian citizenship into question.

In its discussion of Scofield's writing, this chapter examines a range of Scofield's poetry, exploring his treatment of the history of the Métis in Canada, the aesthetic and political implications of his identification as two-spirited, and his code-switching, and exploring in particular how reading his work contributes to the practice of queering citizenship through the civic act of reading. Writing in what I call his Métis and two-spirit vernaculars, Scofield's vernacular texts become vehicles for his critique of Canadian citizenship in the case of the Métis.

Gregory Scofield was born in 1966 in Maple Ridge, British Columbia, and was raised by his mother, Dorothy Scofield, and aunt, Georgina Houle Young, both of whom identified as Métis. He also lived in several foster homes around British Columbia, Saskatchewan, and the Yukon. Scofield never knew his father, having met him just twice as an infant. The absence of Scofield's father features heavily in his work, as do the experiences of his youth; in fact, much of Scofield's writing is autobiographical in nature. To date, Scofield's oeuvre spans eight collections of poetry and one volume of his prose memoirs.[1] His first collection, *The Gathering: Stones for the Medicine Wheel* (1993) won the Dorothy Livesay Poetry Prize that year. In his writing,

Scofield critiques and subsequently revises Métis history in Canada, focusing especially on Louis Riel. Scofield strategically uses what he sees as his role of mediator as well as issues of sexuality to deal with the crucial questions of history and language in the Métis context. He engages with these themes while addressing other personal issues, which include his relationship with his mother and his absent father, whom he later tracks down and in so doing discovers his own Jewish heritage. Scofield never knowingly meets his father, as the latter dies just months before Scofield travels to England to be reconciled with him for the 2006 documentary on his life entitled *Singing Home the Bones: A Poet Becomes Himself*.[2]

Scofield's work is overtly political, tackling the history and future of the Métis. His writing also features frequent switches in code, as he writes in both in English and Cree, having learned the latter from a young age.[3] In his later work, once he discovers his father's Jewish heritage, he also writes in transliterated Hebrew. I show that what makes Scofield's critique of citizenship powerful is his choice to write in what Cindy Patton has called 'dissident vernaculars', which she understands as those terms that move 'away from the model of pristine scientific ideas which need "translation" for people lacking in the dominant culture's language skills or concepts'.[4] Patton's theorisation of dissident vernaculars also implies that 'meanings created by and in communities are upsetting to the dominant culture precisely because speaking in one's own fashion is a means of resistance, a strengthening of the subculture that has created the new meaning'.[5] The concept of dissident vernaculars has currency both in the ways in which Scofield engages with his identification as a two-spirited person, and in my discussion of how this engagement can be linked to questions of citizenship. In this vein, the notions of Patton's dissident vernaculars and Holloway Sparks' dissident citizenship bear more than semantic similarities to what Françoise Lionnet and Shu-Mei Shi call 'theorizing', a practice that 'challenges Eurocentric theories' claims while at the same time not giving in to naïve empiricism and documentarity with assumptions of transparent representation of reality'.[6] By working to critique and rewrite history (as is the case with, for example, his work on Louis Riel), Scofield interrupts ongoing dominant discourse about Indigenous people who identify as queer or two-spirited while simultaneously resisting and undermining the exclusionary discursive practices that prevent them from having full membership in the polity. Indeed, much of Scofield's oeuvre has interrogated the mainstream Canadian narrative – specifically that of the Canadian Métis – offering scathing and sarcastic critiques of the way history has been written and mis/remembered.

Patton's notion of dissident vernaculars provides a useful framework to analyse Scofield's writing on and rewriting of hegemonic history and languages. Scofield's unique dissident vernacular has as its purpose the reassertion of the Métis into the Canadian political sphere. Scofield, who can trace his roots back to the Métis' Red River settlement, sees himself as a physical and literal embodiment of colonial (and now neo-colonial) history in Canada. This is most certainly a dialogic process; as he writes he is mindful of the fact that he literally embodies history, enacting a reminder of the injustices done to the Métis since they came into being. At the same time, this same history has also been systematically *inscribed* onto his body, enacting a reminder of the feelings of inadequacy and inferiority cultivated by the mainstream against the Métis. In this way, 'the body [operates] as both mode and object of knowing' and reflects Scofield's theoretical view that the body can be a source of self-knowledge.[7] In this context, as the 'Other', Scofield finds himself, as Diana Fuss describes, 'Forced to occupy, in a white racial phantasm, the static ontological space of the timeless "primitive" ... [and] is disenfranchised of his very subjectivity'.[8] This disenfranchisement manifests in different ways; one important way that is clearly seen in Scofield's writing is the self-hate and lack of self-worth attached to being Indigenous in general and Métis in particular. As I will show, neither white nor legally recognised Indigenous groups readily welcome the Métis, even in light of recent legislation that goes a little way towards recognising the Métis as having 'Indian' status.[9] In Scofield's case, this led to first the denial of and then feelings of shame by his Métis ancestry. He describes his own skin as too pale, his hair too light and fine, and his blue eyes too light to ever pass as 'full-blooded' Indigenous person, sentiments echoed in a range of Métis writers and academics. This is linked to a systemic preoccupation with using whiteness as a reference point for defining the self, even for 'full-blooded' Indigenous people:

> For the white man, the considerable cultural capital amassed by the colonization of subjectivity amounts to nothing less than the abrogation of universality. While the 'black man must be black in relation to the white man,' the converse does not hold true; the white man can be

white without any relation to the black man because the sign 'white' exempts itself from a dialectical logic of negativity.[10]

Scofield's focus on writing a silenced voice is also crucially influenced by his identification as two-spirited. According to Sue-Ellen Jacobs, Wesley Thomas, and Sabine Lang, the term *two-spirit* (or *two-spirited*) was embraced in 1990 by Native American individuals during the third Native American/First Nations Gay and Lesbian Conference in Winnipeg.[11] The term *two-spirit* was agreed upon as an alternative articulation to its predecessor, *berdache*. The latter term carries significant controversy, given its historical roots in Western anthropological traditions. Pat Califia is adamant that the term *berdache* 'is not based on a word from any Native American language' and goes on to note that in the case of the 'corresponding' terms Native Americans used (and in some cases, continue to use), 'it seems the focus is on gender difference rather than on homosexual activity', the latter having been the main focus of early European observers of Native groups at the time.[12] Sara Jamieson notes that 'The Two-Spirited individual is neither male nor female, but combine[s] with him or herself elements of both genders'.[13] Elsewhere, the term *berdache* is said to have its origins in Persian, which spread to the Spanish through Arabic, and subsequently from Spain to France. Its passage to North America from there can be easily traced.

The main critique lodged against the use of the term is that it signifies an imposition of non-Indigenous heteronormative discursive frameworks onto Indigenous socio-sexual traditions and relations in order to make the gender variances of certain members of Indigenous groups more familiar to non-Indigenous observers, instead of recognizing that, as Lang suggests, 'terms referring to two-spirit people in Native American languages usually indicate that they are seen as combining the masculine and the feminine'.[14] Crucially, Lang observes that 'the fact that two-spirit females and males are seen as a mixture of the masculine and the feminine, and not something completely different from both, does not imply that they are not seen as separate genders different from both men and women'.[15] The implication here is that two-spirited men, for example, constituted a different (social and personal) gender identity in which sex with other non-two-spirited men *does not* constitute homosexuality. Gary Kinsman is quick to emphasise that '[t]hese cross-dressing/ cross-working or alternate-gender people who were called berdache cannot simply be interpreted as a form of institutionalized homosexuality'.[16] On the contrary, two-spirited people cannot be simply wedged into contemporary dominant discourses of sexuality entirely due to the sheer complexity of how gender identification operates.

From his perspective, Scofield notes that two-spirited people tread 'a fine line in-between' the Indigenous community and the gay community. It is a line he sees as having been 'walked by Two-Spirited people throughout generations ... that very sacred role of Two-Spirited people'.[17] As Jamieson puts it, 'Scofield's references to Two-Spirits enable his work to be positioned in relation to much broader theorizations of queer Indigenous identities'.[18] For Scofield, writing becomes what Morag Shiach would term 'a privileged space for the exploration of such non-hierarchally arranged [bi]sexuality'.[19] This writing is characterised by its polyphony and use of linguistic play to unbalance the relationship between the reader and the writer. The figure of the two-spirit presents a threat to mainstream understandings of gender and sexuality in the same way that homosexual desire is considered a threat. In this case, however, it is seen as multiply threatening since it also presents itself in an Indigenous framework. It is at this point that identifying as both two-spirited and Métis begins to allow questions of solidarity to emerge in Scofield's work; that is, his 'status' as multiply excluded and multiply threatening poses an almost impossible situation to mainstream society, particularly since, according to Sabine Lang, 'The two-spirit identity seems to be basically pan-Indian', which emphasises the potential of solidarity along these lines.[20] To continue to exclude him and those like him strengthens his potential to instigate change from the outside; to include him is to enact a shift in the very manner of how both the Métis and those who identify as two-spirited are conceptualised.

Who are the Métis?

In a provocative but short article 'Métis, Halfbreeds, and Other Real People: Challenging Cultures and Categories' (1993) Jennifer S. H. Brown provides a survey of the historiography of the Métis.[21] Over the course of the piece she laments the lack of acknowledgement of the Métis in academic scholarship and historiography. Writing to a US audience, she suggests that the 'seemingly invisible existence of the Métis on the United States side of the [Canada-US] border presents a continuing challenge to the historiography of the American West'.[22] The omission of the Métis in US historiography is mirrored by the same lack of US academic engagement with the Canada–US border, which until very recently had represented a significant scholarly lacuna. There have only been two significant historical accounts of the Métis prior to 1980 – Marcel Giraud's *Le Métis Canadien: son role dans l'histoire des provinces de l'Ouest* (1945) and Joseph Kinsey Howard's *Strange Empire: A Narrative of the Northwest* (1952).[23] Brown notes a steady increase in scholarship since 1980 on the Métis, both within and outside Canada.

In their more expansive *The New Peoples: Being and Becoming Métis in North America* (1985), Jacqueline Peterson and Jennifer S. H. Brown explain that the term 'Métis' follows the 'English-language usage for national identities', while the 'lower-case usage' evokes the 'original French term'. According to the Métis National Council, when 'written with a small "m", métis is a racial term for anyone of mixed Indian and European ancestry. Written with a capital "M", Métis is a sociocultural or political term for those originally of mixed ancestry who evolved into a distinct indigenous people during a certain historical period in a certain region in Canada'.[24] Crucial to understanding this difference is the phrasing 'mixed ancestry'; historically, the distinction between métis and halfbreed groups is the difference in their mixed ancestry. Halfbreed groups had English and Scottish roots, while many métis groups could trace their ancestry to French traders. As such, the group appellations were either Anglicised or used adaptations of French, depending on group ancestry. This becomes complicated, however, with the emergence of the Métis as a distinct entity with aspirations for national recognition, both as a Nation and for recognition within Canada. Chris Anderson identifies a further issue with this categorisation of Métis people when he suggests that 'understanding "Métis" in political terms of historical, peoplehood-based relationships – rather than in post-colonizing terms of mixedness – should profoundly alter how we understand the use of biological mixedness rather than peoplehood as a basis for Métis claims to recognition'.[25] This book uses the term 'Métis' inclusively and alongside the term 'Indigenous', which, as Anderson puts it, 'carries less ... conceptual baggage' than a term like 'Aboriginal', which in Canada is constitutionally and administratively loaded.[26]

Considered a comparatively new group, John E. Foster suggests that 'the métis [Foster's terminology here refers to both métis and halfbreed] were unique among Indigenous peoples in the sense that as distinct entities they did not antedate the fur trade. They alone could look to the fur trade for their origins and not simply for significant formative influences'.[27] That is not to say that there were no people of mixed ancestry *before* the fur trade; rather, it refers specifically to the people who later developed into a distinct Indigenous group that does not identify with or see itself as a subsumable part of other Indigenous or First Nations groups. Indeed, a significant sum of Métis, who have also been called the 'new people' of Red River, the Halfbreeds, the Road Allowance People, the Tortured People, and *Katipamsoochick* (the People Who Own Themselves), consider the designation 'First Nations' as 'part of the imperial vocabulary' which 'assumes there are second or lesser nations'.[28] For his part, Scofield also does not use the appellation 'First Nations', opting instead to use 'Native', 'Indigenous', or 'Aboriginal'. The lengthy but relevant list of appellations for the Métis above is evidence of both the group's rich history and of how significant naming can be for the identity of a group; certainly 'The Tortured People' or 'The Road Allowance People' are not names that inspire self-worth. Indeed, historically, the Métis have generally been described by historians or anthropologists as 'doomed and deficient' in a striking similarity to the figure of the tragic mulatto/a in the nineteenth-century United States.[29] For the sake of clarity, this book follows Monika Kaup's definition of the Métis as 'landless, non-status native peoples without aboriginal rights', though in 2016 the Canadian Supreme Court ruled that the Métis could be considered 'Indian' so that Métis and unregistered Aboriginals, and 'non-status Indians' will now be able to negotiate for new rights and benefits.[30]

As such the métis and halfbreed people (irrespective of whether they identify as Métis) have existed on the fringes of 'native' and 'settler' identity. In many cases, the only space for métis communities would have been on a border – on either side of road lines and roads – literal borderlands. Not legally recognised as 'true' or 'authentic' 'Indians' – by the state, the métis group that would later be known as the Métis was not present when, as Maria Campbell puts it, 'the treaty-makers came'. As a result, they are not considered status Indians.[31] This means they had no treaty rights to the land they had been living on, and were not provided for when the reservations were being drawn up; nor were sufficient provisions made for these groups when the government made homesteading laws.[32]

Scofield identifies as Métis, which to him is also a political and nationalist affiliation. For him, this entails the endorsement of a radical re-evaluation of mainstream understandings of education, history, nationhood, culture, and citizenship. His writing highlights the Métis struggle to be recognised as a distinct Indigenous group not only by the Canadian government but also by other Indigenous groups. To him, as for Peterson, the Métis are:

> not merely biracial, multilingual and bicultural, but the proud owners of a new language; of syncretic cosmology and religious repertoire; of distinctive modes of dress, cuisine, architecture, vehicles of transport, music, and dance; and after 1815 of a quasi-military political organization, a flag, a bardic tradition, a rich folklore and a natural history.[33]

Regardless of Peterson's lyrical tone of nostalgia, the distinctive character of the Métis is clear. However, it has not been as clear in legal terms. Indeed, as Robert K. Thomas has put it, 'In Canada, the legal definition and status of the métis are ambiguous, at best. In the United States, the courts do not at present even recognize the existence of métis in law. Moreover, most North Americans do not have a conceptual place for the métis in their view of the world'.[34] Brown echoes this since, according to her, 'No legal status based on mixed descent is available' to people who combine two or more ancestries through the US court system.[35] Writing more recently, Anderson reminds us that 'the power of colonial/racial classification in the positioning of both self-identifying and classifying Métis as irreducibly hybrid or mixed is deeply entrenched', and for him, the focus on hybridity is unhelpful, because it 'is based on an unstable and thus flexible set of criteria that are, at least in a Canadian historical context, arbitrary, ad hoc, and even in some cases iterated after the racial classification had already been made'.[36]

The very idea of the absence of *a conceptual place* for the Métis is troubling, not least because they clearly comprise a group that is at this moment *in existence*. Obviously it is far simpler to call something into question in legal terms than to introduce a conceptual place in the mind of the mainstream. Crucial to the survival of the Métis, then, is the recognition that as a group, it must retain its distinct Indigenous identity. In this sense, to Scofield, it is of the utmost urgency that the Métis maintain their connections with their history and this politics of recognition seeks, as Glen Sean Coulthard puts it, 'to "reconcile" Indigenous assertions of nationhood with settler-state sovereignty via the accommodation of Indigenous identity claims in some form of renewed legal and political relationship with the Canadian state'.[37] Scofield's writing engages with both the legal understanding of the Métis and the more conceptual issues that exist when discussing the group, including, for example, issues of stereotyping and questions of purity. I ultimately show that Scofield uses the name Métis, as Brown has it, 'in a strategic fashion, as a hybrid racial and ethnic identity that involves a complex set of identifications, while making room for new kinds of self-articulation'.[38] These new kinds of self-articulation can also include situating the Métis within the context of 'a growing literature on "stateless" or "minority" nations'.[39] These strategies are exemplified in Scofield's 'Answer For My Brother (Who Are The Métis?)' (*The Gathering* p. 82). In this poem, Scofield exposes his own stance on the history and identity of the Métis. According to the poem, it is Scofield's brother (in reality he does not have a biological brother) who asks the question as 'a clever way to get me thinking where is my place' (line 2).

The seven-stanza poem, in this case relatively short, is difficult to digest since Scofield does not use punctuation. Rather, he uses extra spacing on the line which serves to separate each idea. This extra spacing also serves as a connecting node between related ideas or sentences, so that the following stanza can be understood in different ways:

> There is so little written about the Métis because we
> are not one or the other but a shaded combination
> that is easier to figure out lumping all of us
> together because some Halfbreeds look like they have a
> dark past which to (lines 11–15)

When confronted with these seemingly unnecessary spaces, the reader is forced to create her own syntax. Here, the act of reading allows for a multiplicity of meaning, so that the stanza could also be read: 'There is so little written about the Métis because we are not one or the other but a shaded combination', followed by 'That is easier to figure out: lumping us all / together because some Halfbreeds look like they have a / dark past'. The reader here is put in a position of inhabiting Scofield's 'we' so that she too has been 'lumped together' with those Halfbreeds who 'look like they have a dark past'. This dark past also obviously refers to an 'Indian' past.

The next stanza completes the dangling line so that on the surface it reads 'some Halfbreeds look like they have a / dark past which to / The outsider appears an Indian past & then there are / some so white you wouldn't think twice' (lines 14–17). However, imposing a different internal logic to the sentence yields: 'The outsider appears: an Indian past. & then there are / some so white you wouldn't think twice they have an immigrant history.' In this version, the reader must make a decision about how to understand the referent of 'some' and whether 'some' refers to the (presumably European) outsider or the Halfbreed. 'White' also carries its own symbolic undertones, referring simultaneously to racial 'status' as white, the physical complexion of 'whiteness', and the notion of 'innocence'. In both cases, the underlying meaning provides a reminder about the immigrant nature of contemporary Canada and the history of its colonisation. Scofield points to this next: 'even tho they have birth to the / Province Manitoba' (lines 18–19). Again, changing the emphasis of the poem's rhythm allows the emergence of: 'the / Province Manitoba getting the short end of the stick / because greedy land / Grabbers wanted the whole damn country.'

What stands out about this poem is that a superficial reading will often not capture its nuances. It contains spelling mistakes and twenty-first century contractions; its tone is defiant but not – at first glance – particularly *powerful*. It is written, in a sense, as a stream-of-consciousness response to Scofield's 'brother'. However, closer inspection renders it an entirely different piece of writing: Scofield cleverly veils powerful ideas in an almost childlike writing style, simultaneously making the poem *more* and *less* readable. This is an implicit connection to racist ideas of the illiteracy and naivety of indigenous people, undermined by the fact that the poem constitutes Scofield's revised version of the history of the Métis. As he puts it, those who were not 'dark enough' ended up 'being written / right out of history except for / Brief mention of our leaders who were a thorn in the / government's ass they made it to the N section in the / encyclopedia under the "North West Rebellion"' (lines 28–32).

The final line of the poem is preceded by and ends with a full stop, Scofield's only use of punctuation throughout. This deliberate employment of punctuation serves to emphasise the unambiguous nature of the sentence: 'If anything, we are Katipamsoochick' (line

37). The Cree word *Katipamsoochick* translates to 'The People Who Own Themselves' and is one of the 'names' of the Métis. This is an act of self-determination on Scofield's part, an insistence that the Métis are in fact a distinct group deserving of the rights owed to them. Part of this process involves the revision of Métis history – a process that is important to the reclamation of the past in order to re-envision the future.

Revisi(ti)ng Métis history

Howard Adams' work on revisionist histories provides a useful framework to understand the process of revising Métis history. Adams, himself a prominent Canadian Métis academic, was one of the first intellectuals to theorise and articulate the Métis political, cultural, and social positions from an academic perspective. Widely viewed as the alternative to mainstream accounts of the history of the Métis, Adams' *Prison of Grass: Canada From a Native Point of View* (1975) was considered groundbreaking in its uncompromising depiction of what Adams describes as the colonisation of and subsequent institutionalised racism in Canada.[40] His second book, *A Tortured People: The Politics of Colonization* (1995) brings to light the Aboriginal perspective on the effects of colonisation while also introducing his thoughts on the challenge of decolonisation.[41] Both of Adams' texts are important because they provide both the historical backdrop to the Métis struggle and a critique of the status quo, in addition to presenting areas where practical progress can be made. Both of these books begin with the recounting of personal experiences from which he extrapolates the broader themes and arguments of his work.

Adams' principal aim over the course of *Prison of Grass* and *A Tortured People* is the reclamation of what he sees as a hijacked history of Indigenous–white relations by '[providing] a theoretical framework for analyzing Aboriginal history and culture'.[42] Adams asserts the potential of the reclamation and retelling of history to change the injustice of the status quo:

> Honesty for Indian and Métis history and culture is more than a quest for decolonization and a national identity; it is a pursuit to transform imperial structures of the state. History, as told by authentic Aboriginal historians, does more than retell establishment history. It explains the

struggles for self-determination and promotes efforts to overcome present colonization.[43]

Indeed, as I have indicated, Métis people were systematically convinced that they were nothing but 'no good Halfbreeds', a process Adams picks up on in the opening pages of *Prison of Grass*: from a young age, Native children are 'conditioned to accept inferiority as a natural way of life'.[44] From a personal perspective, Adams recalls actively working to dissociate himself from his 'halfbreed' community because in his mind, to be halfbreed was to be 'ugly and shameful'.[45] According to Adams, the authoritative white gaze looked at halfbreeds/métis only through racial stereotypes that were then internalised, until he too 'began to see [himself] as a stupid, dirty breed, drunken and irresponsible'.[46] To reconnect briefly with the previous chapter, Gloria Anzaldúa clearly theorises the *mestiza* figure with the intention that a new community, characterised by its *mestizaje*, be formed, challenging all borders and thinking with a logic of 'and' rather than 'or'. Adams feels he has a responsibility to tell a Métis story. In the preface to his *Prison of Grass*, Adams provides his personal and intellectual rationale for writing his revisionist history: 'Since colonized, indigenous people are deterred from compiling records on the history of their nation and from writing their own history, documentary material is scarce. Furthermore, some government documents that have been represented as authentic, official historical documents apparently were invented by officials of the federal government and are therefore misleading', with the purpose of distorting what Adams calls the 'true history of the Métis and Indian people of the plains'.[47] As he puts it, 'Since I am a Métis, I have developed the historical discussion as much as possible from a Native viewpoint'.[48] Adams' hope, expressed in the closing lines of *A Tortured People*, is that all Indigenous peoples in Canada 'shatter the bureaucracy and structures of capitalism that imprison [them] under colonialism' and achieve liberation.[49] This is consistent with Scofield's focus on unbalancing and retelling both personal and national (in the Canadian and Indigenous sense) history, as is evident in the poem 'When It Come to Your Turn' (*The Gathering* p. 31).

In the poem, Scofield speaks to an unknown white 'you' whose 'stink mouth shows / I'm the history lesson / You flunked at school' (lines 1–3). Although it is unclear which history lesson Scofield is referring to – it could be that of the colonisation of Canada and its impact on Indigenous groups in general, or the history of the Métis in particular – the accusation of racism and violence against Indigenous groups is unmistakable, while the reader is confronted with the possibility that she might be the 'you' to whom he speaks. The poem sheds light on the verbal and physical abuse, discrimination, and the extreme poverty that characterise the lives of many people of indigenous ancestry in Canada and the United States. Scofield notes that it '[w]ould be pointless for me to move / Even to Utopia / My job would be the same' (lines 8–10), highlighting the social and economic stagnation experienced by the Indigenous people of Canada. The poem also exposes what Scofield sees as a racist educational system; in his view, people of Indigenous ancestry are considered mere history lessons – lessons that for white people can be 'flunked' with no serious consequence.

The poem ends with what could be interpreted positively or negatively, as either a promise or a threat: 'So when it comes to your turn / Come to Indian country / Pull up a beer – start that / White mouth running / Guaranteed / You'll leave speechless' (lines 14–19). In either case, Scofield's point is that the verbal and physical violence against Indigenous people goes on in 'white' society, which does nothing to prevent it. 'When It Come to Your Turn' deals with important themes of speech and silence, both of which recur throughout the entirety of Scofield's writing. Scofield's reference to the Canadian education system here is an indictment of what he considers to be the silenced and repressed history of the Canadian Métis. Even at school, upon being assigned to read Maria Campbell's *Halfbreed* (1973), Scofield remembers wanting to dismiss it completely, as he believes it 'irrelevant to who we were as Indians' (*Thunder* p. 116).[50] But having read it, Scofield's dismissal turns to rage: 'Her life seemed so hopeless, so full of misery and suffering. I felt as if she was somehow describing Mom and Aunty Georgie, even me, and I hated her for it ... An inexplicable rage at everything – at Mom, at Aunty, our poverty, my grandfather's shame, my own shame' (p. 116). Even then, Scofield shelves his Métis heritage, unable to deal with the reality of who he is: 'I was Cree, not some forgotten half-breed who didn't belong anywhere' (p. 117). Later, as a young adult in Vancouver, unable to find work, and fast running out of money, Scofield's last resort is to go to the welfare office, where for the first time, he articulates his identity aloud: '"Half-breed," I whispered, unsure whether or not I had actually said it' (p. 156). Despite the negative reaction of the woman at the welfare office, the fact that Scofield has admitted to himself that he is in fact Métis is a crucial step in his own personal trajectory. Very soon after this incident Scofield starts writing seriously for the first time.

Scofield's self-equivalence with a 'history lesson' could also be read as a gesture towards Jeannette Armstrong (Okanagan), whose poem 'History Lesson' is well-known for its presentation of a dark alternative to the mainstream accounts and history of European hegemony in North America.[51] Armstrong's 'History Lesson', which is not preceded by an article (definite or indefinite) shows Christopher Columbus and his men as violent and barbaric buffoons chaotically 'running in all directions', mutilating and killing animals for their fur (a reference to the fur traders who would later gain control of Indigenous territory), and 'Shooting each other / left and right' (lines 6–7). Armstrong accuses these men of 'waiting to mutilate / whole civilizations / ten generations at a blow' (lines 36–8) all in the name of religion, development, and progress. Indeed, as she puts it, 'Civilization has reached / the promised land' (lines 19–20). Armstrong's focus on reformulating and reclaiming history, while told from a First Nations perspective, is particularly significant in the case of the Métis. According to Alan Lindsey McLeod, 'through its polemics, [Armstrong's poem] emphasizes the trajectory of an alternative history while parodying/countering the Western hegemonic version, which tends to view colonization and conquest as civilization and progress'.[52] Scofield's poem 'Making New History' effectively continues this trajectory, resisting dominant versions of history which, as he sees it, aim to shame Métis people by using 'Those better-than stares / Looking down on us' (*The Gathering* p. 84, lines 13–14). In the same vein, Scofield also gestures towards those individuals who can be characterised using the Uncle Tomahawk stereotype. In this scenario, Uncle Tomahawk can be read as the 'Indian' version of the 'Uncle Tom' stereotype. According to the stereotype, Uncle Tomahawk types are self-hating Indigenous people who are in denial about their ancestry, or else assimilate into the structure and mindset of mainstream white society. Scofield's Aunty describes them as 'da worse kinda Indians ... Apples! Red on da outside and white on da inside' (*Thunder* p. 49). A complementary reading of the meaning of Uncle Tomahawk is provided by Scofield himself, who defines the term in the glossary of the *The Gathering* as: 'a corrupt native organization and its administrators' (*The Gathering* p. 91). Scofield also engages with 'the blood quantum' that must be met in order for an

Indigenous person to be given legal 'status' as an 'Indian'. This is an instance where we see the Canadian legal system operating a classification system that is (inversely) comparable to the 'one-drop rule' (when it was applicable) in the United States. Since as I have noted, 'halfbreeds' were not present at any treaty signings, they were never legally considered truly 'Aboriginal' and as such were not entitled to 'status' rights.

Within this denial of a distinct halfbreed or Métis nation (which, again, is based on the assumption that the Métis comprise a distinct community rather than simply existing as a racial 'mix') is the expectation that Métis-identifying individuals 'support your [collaborating Native politicians'] constitutional demands' ('Making New History' line 8) despite being evicted from Métis territory and not being eligible for state benefits or welfare in the same way as those with 'status' are. Forced off the land on which they had lived for generations, Métis families were often forced into 'squatting / on road allowance' (lines 11–12). Scofield clearly identifies the state as responsible for the situation in which the Métis find themselves today, despite Bill C-31 being passed by the Canadian Parliament in 1985 (109 years after the original Indian Act was passed) which was intended to bring the original Act into line with the provisions of the Canadian Charter of Rights and Freedoms. Although C-31 has been effective in allowing over 100,000 previously non-status individuals to gain status, it still continues to operate what the Congress of Aboriginal Peoples (CAP) understand to be a wholly integrationist strategy. The CAP and other Aboriginal and Métis groups have criticised C-31, not least because, as Harry W. Daniels, former president of the CAP puts it, 'The federal government has no business telling Indian people who is and who is not an Indian'.[33] Indeed, while C-31 does much to reinstate 'Indian' status to many disenfranchised 'Indians', it does not eliminate the category of 'non-status'; in fact, it laid the groundwork for the non-status group to become even larger than before.

The lack of 'status' is a theme effectively demonstrated in Scofield's autobiographical *Thunder Through My Veins: Memories of a Métis Childhood*, which traces Scofield's childhood and early adolescence, his coming-out process, his development as a Métis community activist, and the trauma and abuse he experienced. One of the reasons he felt compelled to write his autobiography is once again related to the issues of voice and silence: Scofield engages with the popular version of Louis Riel and the Northwest Rebellion (also popularly known as the Riel Rebellion) of 1885, an event that brought the Métis as close as they have ever come to national independence. He describes how he felt when he was taught the history of Canada in his social studies class:

> By the time we got to the settling of the West and the Northwest Rebellion, I was humiliated ... Louis Riel was crazy and a traitor to the Canadian government. The Métis weren't Indians at all, but Frenchmen pretending to be Indians. They had no culture or language and nothing to be proud of. At least the Indians, no matter how ragged and poor, had an interesting culture. (*Thunder* p. 64)

Scofield's account of how the Métis are represented in mainstream history is more common than one would expect. In 'Answer for My Brother (Who Are the Métis?)' Scofield describes this 'Brief mention of our leaders who were a thorn in the / government's ass' as one of pure over-simplification and political exercise: 'they made it to the N section in the / encyclopedia under the "North West Rebellion" / which more or less infers we needed to be put into our / proper place' (lines 26–30). In this view, the over-simplification is designed to cast the Métis as primitive and unsophisticated Indigenous figures while continuing to deny them both status rights and the rights of 'white' Canadians.

In keeping with his critique and subsequent reclamation of Métis history, Scofield has most recently taken on the figure of Louis Riel, who is an important figure in terms of Scofield's role as a cultural mediator. In recent scholarship, Riel himself has been 'increasingly seen as "the potential mediator between red and white cultures." He is the go-between whose "mystical visions led him to dream of a peaceable kingdom in the west and himself as a prophet of the new world"'.[54] In *Louis: The Heretic Poems*, Scofield writes a poetic biography of Riel, adding his voice to the many of who have written on Riel in the last century.[55] This reimagining of Riel is divided into four sections: 'The Boy', 'The President', 'The Spokesman', and 'The Statesman' and Scofield deliberately draws attention to the facets of Riel's life and personality that are not often considered in mainstream Canadian historiography.

The collection begins with a statement from George G. Stanley, Head of the Department of History at the Royal Military College of Canada, who wrote of Louis Riel: 'To the Métis, the people whom he loved, he [Riel] will always be, mad or sane, the voice of an inarticulate race and the prophet of a doomed cause' (*Louis* p. 5). To suggest that Stanley's description of Riel is problematic would be a laughable understatement. Bearing this in mind, however, it is worth noting the structure of the sentence that Scofield has so cannily chosen to frame his poetic memorialisation of the Métis figure: 'To the Métis, the people whom he loved', reflects a clear appropriation of the Métis voice (an issue that continues to resurface in both Métis and Riel historiography). 'To the Métis, the people who he loved, he will always be, mad or sane' – here, Stanley speaks for the Métis, seemingly allowing the reader some deep insight into the mind of a people, suggesting that all that Riel did was because he loved the Métis – a particularly condescending notion relayed in a patronising tone. The grammar here also implicitly suggests that Riel *did not count himself* as Métis. Stanley did not write, for example: 'To the Métis, the people of whom he counted himself as part' or some other phrasing. Instead he sets up a relationship in which Riel is set apart from the Métis, as the only voice of an inarticulate race and as the prophet of a doomed cause. This kind of language is significantly clichéd – Riel as the 'only' leader, Riel as prophet, mystic, and madman. There can be no doubt that Scofield's use of Stanley casting Riel as '*the* voice of an inarticulate race' – *the* voice of a group that cannot speak is ironic on several levels, the most superficial of which is the fact that Scofield is clearly far more than merely articulate.

The poem that closes the collection is titled 'Epitaph' and Scofield draws attention to a side of Riel that is not often considered in historiography. Partly taken from a love letter Riel wrote to his wife in October 1885, Scofield's imagined 'Epitaph' for Riel reads:

> Be sweet to my words: and listen
> When I write you with a golden
> Pen
> Be not swayed: and give thoughtful pause
> when I speak to you with an iridescent
> Voice. (*Louis* p. 88, lines 1–6)

Here issues of voice, silence, and muteness are brought to the fore. Scofield sets line breaks between the words 'Pen' and 'Voice', making these more prominent, serving not only as reminders to Scofield's readers but also, perhaps, as reassurance to Scofield himself, that the power of the pen and the power of the voice live on after Riel, two tools that Scofield himself employs. Indeed, according to Albert Braz, 'most of the purported representations of the politician mystic are less about him than about their authors and their specific social reality'.[56] In significant ways, Scofield's social reality is connected to Riel and the consequences of the two Métis rebellions he led.

In 'Policy of the Dispossessed', Scofield deals with one of these consequences: the establishment of the province of Manitoba. Framing this poem are two epigraphs: the first is from the Manitoba Act of 1870, which established the province of Manitoba and set out – ostensibly – to provide some semblance of land rights for the Métis, and the second is from a speech by Sir John A. Macdonald, delivered at the House of Commons debates in July 1885, four months before Riel's execution (*Native Canadiana* pp. 53–5). By citing these two documents, Scofield allows the readers to come to their own conclusions about the government's evidently racist and essentialist views of the Métis, before launching his own critique of the policy. Ironically, one of the consequences of the Manitoba Act was 'the influx of newcomers' (line 9) that Scofield's 'great-great grandmother's people [who] refused to be pushed out' (lines 5–6) were forced to watch and powerless to resist, 'until one day / the prairie was completely taken over' (lines 10–11). Scofield punctuates each stanza of the poem with italicised words and phrases that emphasise the Métis' relationship with Canada in general and Manitoba in particular: '*our homeland*', '*our motherland*', '*our nation*', '*all public lands*', '*Canada*', and, finally, '*katipâmsôchik*' – this last term an alternate spelling of *Katipamsoochick*. In the absence of government recognition that the Métis are 'Indians' or 'whites' – Macdonald's claim that 'if they are halfbreeds they are whites, and they stand in exactly the same relation to the Hudson Bay Company and Canada as if they were altogether white' is especially ironic in this context – Scofield sees the Métis as having no choice but to own themselves, but ultimately, as the title of the poem suggests, they are dispossessed, their land all but stolen, and their relationship to this same land legislated as one of 'resident', as seen in the quotation from the Manitoba Act. As the closing lines of the poem suggest:

> In that part of the country
> *our homeland*
> I went back and dug in the prairie soil.

Métis and two-spirit vernaculars

> There among the buffalo bones and memories
> an ancient language sprang from the earth
> and wet my parched tongue.
> In that part of the country
> we were always *katipâmsôchik* –
> and our displaced history
> is as solid as every railroad tie
> pounded into place, linking
> each stolen province. (lines 46–57)

Scofield's use of the railroad imagery in this final stanza effectively juxtaposes the traditional narrative of the railroad as having built Canada and connected its provinces with images of exile and homelessness – the Métis would have used, as his grandfather did, to leave 'that part of the country' to head 'west to Saskatchewan'. Scofield's text thus, as Jennifer Andrews puts it, 'becomes a rewriting of government policy, authored by those people who have been dispossessed literally and disarmed linguistically'.[57] Andrews reads the reclamation of this Cree name as 'assert[ing] Métis individuality and giv[ing] insider status to those who know both Cree and English'. Indeed, according to Andrews, 'Scofield displaces the primacy of English and the words of Sir John A. Macdonald with his own policy document, a halfbreed account of the past and present that rejects institutionalised versions of history and memory'.[58] 'Policy of the Dispossessed' effectively demonstrates the process of reclaiming Métis history with Scofield's own personal account.

Multilingual dissident vernaculars

While Scofield's personal connections are made evident in his writing, he also intends his poetry to impact upon and teach the reader. The poem 'Mixed Breed Act' is an excellent example of how Scofield's dissident vernaculars operate in the text and on the reader (*Native Canadiana* pp. 56–8). The poem, composed of thirteen stanzas, begins with Scofield speaking as a single 'I'. It then moves on to speak for the Métis as 'we', before returning to his own 'I' voice in the last three stanzas, emphasising his reluctance to separate the private 'I' from the public 'I' or 'we'. The first line of the poem is composed of two statements than can be read in multiple ways: 'How do I act

I act without an Indian act' (line 1). The layers of meaning found here allow the reader to anticipate the tone of the poem to follow. By beginning the poem with 'How' but not using a question mark at the end of the first statement, leaving instead three extra spaces, Scofield invokes the stereotype that Indigenous people use 'How' as a greeting. The line can then be read differently, depending on how the reader herself punctuates, as: 'How / do I act I act without an Indian act.' The playfulness here is on the 'act' of Indian-ness, pushing the reader to ask and discover *how* Scofield acts as an Indigenous person and whether his 'act' is convincing. The word 'act' also provides the meter for the first line. Reading the line without the word 'act' yields the following: 'How do I I without an Indian' which further supports a reading that deliberately brings both performance of Indian-ness and the history of the emergence of the Métis to the fore of the discussion. Because of Scofield's own personal experiences of being Métis in Canada he is sure to be 'exact about the facts' to the point that he writes 'I act up when I get told I don't count / Because my act's not written' (lines 3–4). Scofield's gesture here is to the Indian Act's neglect of the Métis as well as the more positive affirmation that his act isn't written – his fate is not sealed due to the fact that he is not included in the legislative definition of an Indian. Not having his act written for him is thus empowering: 'No DIA director can pop me on a bus / Send me home' (lines 8–9). Despite this, they continue to 'act' 'Indian' (since they are). In fact, Scofield suggests that the 'status' of mixed-breeds or métis as 'outside' the remit of a legal system that does not recognise them allows them to 'act up' in protest against this same system – because the Department of Indian Affairs has no hold over them.

The third stanza again uses unconventional spacing to separate two powerful statements. The first, 'Send me home' can be read as a continuation of the previous line, affirming that the Canadian government cannot 'punish' him by putting him on a bus and sending him home (line 9). However, it can also be read as an imperative: 'Send me home homeless as I am.' This is the radical act he mentions two lines later, when confirming that he is so exact about the facts that, in his words, 'I act downright radical / Though never hostile unless provoked' (lines 11–12). Again Scofield mocks the image of the 'hostile Indian' and pits himself against it with the next line so that he is 'never hostile unless provoked to extract the truth' – in which case, his behaviour could be construed as 'hostile'. Scofield identifies with other 'rezless Indians' (recall that non-status Indians do not have land rights/the right to live on a reservation, so they are essentially homeless – and here it is worth considering his play on the homophone 'restless Indians') while simultaneously parodying the stereotypes about Indians, particularly in his acting 'downright radical / Though never hostile unless provoked' (lines 11–12). The truth he refers to after this line is that his 'treaty number's not listed' so he does not have to deal with the humiliating treatment that those 'listed' as Indians do 'from politicians breathing heavy in [their] ear' (line 16). That being said, the next line suggests that 'Still [he is] authentic enough to be counted' (line 18). The repeated use of the words 'counted' and 'listed' is Scofield's implicit accusation that Métis people are seen as mere statistics, nothing more than 'genuine artifacts' that are 'not so much precolumbian / But darn close' (lines 19–20). However, punctuated differently, the line takes on further complexity. If the reader understands 'Still' to be a modifier of 'I', then the meaning of the line changes so that Scofield is only authentic enough to be counted if he is *still* and unresisting rather than troublesome.

Scofield's play on the meaning of the word 'act' lies at the heart of 'Mixed Breed Act', interrogating and undermining how 'just' and 'representative' the Indian Act is as a whole. In the poem, Scofield repeats the word 'act' twenty-three times. Here we see a very clear insistence on three meanings of the word 'act': acting (as in performing, or as in a lie – referring to the multiple revisions of the Indian Act in order to repeal certain provisos), an Act (as in a piece of ratified legislation, such as the Indian Act) and taking action (which relates to political action and agency, and ultimately, freedom). With his defiant tone, Scofield questions the degree to which Bill C-31 has changed the system that continues to view and cast him as an outsider. This also introduces a discussion of how one can act 'Indian'. Is there a measure of 'Indian-ness' according to how well one acts the part or assumes the role? 'The fact is' that 'mixed-breeds' or Métis have little or no representation within the Canadian legal system. As he puts it: 'No DIA director can pop me on a bus' (line 8). As he parodies the stereotype of the savage, hostile Indigenous people who anthropologists would have described upon their first encounter with the inhabitants of the New World, he dismantles it, exposing its inherent racism and reminding his readers of the church father who came to the New World to 'civilize the savage heathen'. Once again, there is a definite connection to be made here with Armstrong's 'History Lesson', in which church priests are parodied for the way they spoke to Indigenous people in broken English, as if the latter were children. Armstrong's language highlights the paternalistic and patronising attitude of the church: 'Father mean well / waves his makeshift wand / forgives saucer-eyed Indians.'[59]

In addition to this broader theme of racism, 'Mixed Breed Act' also highlights the implicit assumptions about what it means to be Métis. With such a designation comes a tacit accusation of impurity and deception – the concept of a counterfeit, or even a simulacrum, is fitting here. Indeed, questions of authenticity plague Scofield, who is eager to assert his true Indigenous character: 'Still I'm authentic enough to be counted / a genuine artifact not so much pre-columbian / But darn close' (lines 18–20). Scofield's assertion that he, and by extension, the Métis, are 'darn close' enough to be 'aboriginal / even original' links to the national aspirations of the Métis. As a group, the Métis may not be old enough to be considered entirely original to Canada, but they are distinct enough to identify as a nation, because, as Scofield notes in 'Answer For My Brother (Who Are The Métis?), 'they gave birth to the / Province Manitoba' (*The Gathering* p. 82, lines 18–19). To confirm this in 'Mixed Breed Act', Scofield is clear: 'I mark my X for self-government' (*Native Canadiana* p. 56, line 21). Scofield accuses the first immigrants to Canada, fur traders or otherwise, of being 'too busy / playing hookey on our grandmothers / to notice they'd left behind a new nation' (lines 29–31) and emphasises the colonising nature of these immigrants, who in helping to create a new nation, created a group of people who were neither indigenous enough (at least by legal standards) or immigrant (white) enough (by virtue of their indigenous ancestry) to fit into society. Members of this group, not even qualifying to be considered non-status Indians, would, as Scofield describes the predicament, exist 'scrunched in between. / Suffocating ourselves to act accordingly' (lines 37–8). Here, Scofield exposes the physical and psychological difficulty experienced by the Métis in trying to fit into a society that does not recognise the validity of their existence. Once again, Scofield returns to his play on 'act', using what Mikhail Bakhtin would call a double-voiced discourse to '[act] out for equality' (line 44). This is a common use for double-voiced discourse since using 'act' in this way allows, as Bakhtin puts it, 'the author [to speak] through another person's word ... [introducing] a semantic direction to the word which is diametrically opposed to its original direction'.⁶⁰ The role of the reader here is paramount: only she can realise – in the most literal sense of the word – the polyphonic imperative Scofield embeds in the word 'act'. Here, the act the reader is being asked to carry out (among others) is one of both identification and disidentification; specifically, the reader is asked to continue the resistance Scofield begins in his writing. To be sure, Scofield's writing is itself an act of resistance, not revenge. He writes:

> This is not some rebel halfbreed act
> I just scribbled down for revenge
> Besides
> I don't need to be hung
> For my mixed mouth blabbing
> How they used their act
> To cover up
> Dirty goings-on in our country. (lines 44–52)

Even these last lines contain powerful images: 'I don't need to be hung', the last line of the twelfth stanza, is not punctuated. The word 'hung' quite literally hangs at the end of the line, referring once again to both Riel's execution by hanging, but also, quite humorously, to a stereotype about the genital endowment of Indigenous men – connecting well to the 'dirty goings-on' he refers to in the very last line of the poem.

The reader's role also becomes of paramount importance for another reason – the survival of indigenous languages. In 'The Poet Leaves a Parting Thought' Scofield recognises the importance of his remaining attached to Indigenous languages: 'if I don't give my tongue / a native language mammogram / check it regularly / for English lumps and bumps / I run the chance of becoming / totally anglicized' (*Native Canadiana* p. 123, lines 24–9). It is also why Scofield switches codes in his poetry, frequently using Cree.⁶¹ His use of Indigenous languages can be attributed to more than just poetic licence: in presenting readers with these languages, he asks us to suspend our disbelief and enter his world. There is a practical aspect to this also, as the Cree remains untranslated within the actual poetry, with translations appearing separately, either alongside the poem itself, or in some form of footnote or endnote. This forces the reader into a decision: she must either only partially understand the poem or put some work into the way we read his poems. It also provides a means through which Cree can survive. Through this process, the reader becomes complicit in Scofield's agenda and become responsible for the survival and continuity of the language.

The poem 'kipocihkân' effectively begins this process (*Kipocihkan* pp. 11–19). As the inscription to the collection bearing a variation of same title explains, *kipocihkân* denotes 'a slang word for someone who is unable to talk; a mute' (p. 7). In this poem, Scofield switches seemingly effortlessly between English and Cree, and then for the first time, also writes in transliterated Hebrew. In this poem Scofield sings his personal and family histories using the structure of a Cree thanksgiving prayer song. He begins by describing himself as 'the boy / whose tongue at birth *kipahikan*' and 'the one whose mouth / *kipocihkân*' (lines 1–2; 7–8). Over the course of this 203-line poem, Scofield counts the names of his ancestors and those in his own story 'whose tongues' he 'calls to prayer' (lines 20–1). These include his great-great-grandmother, 'whose tongue was made homeless, / shame-shame / the day Riel slipped through the gallows' (line 26–8). Here is a clear assertion of Scofield's own Métis lineage. Next he thanks his great-grandparents Johnny and Ida Scofield, 'whose tongues, shame-shame / diluted the gene pool', a reference to the blood quantum which is used to determine Indian status, and in the case of Scofield, has been used to marginalise the Métis from legal 'status' as Indian (lines 35–6). Scofield names his grandfather George, 'whose tongue, at fifty-nine / burst, shame-shame, / an illiterate blood clot'; and his grandmother Avis, whose tongue 'kept the secret' of their Métis heritage (lines 44–6; 54). Until this point the poem's mood is sombre, asking for blessings from the Great Spirit of the Cree and what is presumably the Christian God, and giving thanks. However, this mood changes when Scofield speaks of his mother, 'whose tongue / swept the halls of psych wards, / her whore days made dead / by pills and wine. Whose tongue / at forty-eight / she gave back to God. Fuck you!' (lines 62–7). This sudden shift from shame to anger immediately precedes a shift from English and Cree code-switching to the addition of transliterated Hebrew. Significantly, the introduction of Hebrew into the poem takes place when Scofield writes of his father, Ron, blessing him and giving thanks to him despite the fact that they only met when Scofield was an infant. Recall that Ron, 'whose tongue was a shmatteh [a rag]/ too moth-eaten / to keep all his children' died before Scofield had the opportunity to meet him as an adult (lines 73–5). Instead, he met Ann, Ron's wife and Scofield's stepmother, 'whose tongue / half-charitable, half-grudging / held all these years [his] father's pardon' (lines 94–7). It is at this point that Scofield's 'own half-tongue', which had 'hungered its blood root' begins 'growing back in fragments' (lines 96; 3; 97). Crucially, it is also at this point in the poem that Cree and Hebrew, and to a lesser degree, English, are used together in a perfectly seamless moment of prayer:

â-haw kisê-manitaw	Oh, Great Spirit
mâmaw-ôhtawîmaw	Our Father
Ba-ruch A-tah Ado-nai	Blessed are you, Lord our God
E-lo-he-nu Me-lech Ha-olam	King of the universe[62]
Kinanâskomitin	I give thanks
Toda, Toda	I give thanks. (lines 82–7)

Note that the first, second, and fifth lines are Cree and that the third, fourth, and sixth lines are Hebrew. The balance of language here, which occurs both on the levels of page layout and translation and also in its lyricism, is remarkable. The combination of all three languages is presumably a reflection and representation of Scofield's own tongue that is now able to articulate and sing its stories and songs. Also of great importance here is that Scofield's writing within the song begins to move beyond 'shame-shame' as a refrain, substituting it with 'No shame, no shame' (line 136). This is particularly clear when he names other figures from his life, including his Auntie Georgina, the man who abused him, and presumably, his partner, 'the one [he] goes around with / whose tongue ... is a rattle ... chasing out *kipocihkân*' (lines 150–9). Finally, Scofield gives thanks to the figures of the ghost, the bitch, the beggar, the glutton, the mute, and the singer, all of whom make up his tongue. He also takes responsibility for these figures, entering 'a plea of guilty' (line 182). What the guilt refers to is not readily clear, but presumably Scofield is taking responsibility for his own history and own silence – and most importantly, his own future. In this way, the poem operates as a microcosm of Scofield's larger body of work and thus maps his journey from shame, muteness, and silence, to voice, song, writing, and pride. Scofield's use of synecdoche here is an effective strategy that briefly connects the personal autobiography with the Métis autobiography so that the reader is presented with the personal *as* the political.

Mediation, empowerment, and survival

Integral to appreciating Scofield's poetry is his use of synecdoche; he uses himself and his autobiographical experiences to speak for those Métis whose voices are not heard, with which he clearly identifies. His writing works to actively resist mainstream perceptions about the Métis. Indeed, as Janice Acoose puts it, 'Contemporary Indigenous writers positively and knowledgeably construct aspects of their cultures that have been previously misrepresented by outsiders who knew little about the cultures about which they wrote. In this way, Indigenous writers following the example of Maria Campbell's *Halfbreed* significantly challenge literary trends'.[63] Scofield challenges more than just literary trends, however. His writing also calls into question mainstream accounts of history, and problematises commonly understood definitions and implications of 'nation', particularly that of self-determination. His autobiographical writing also disrupts conventional (read Western, mainstream, and normative) paradigms of self-expression and self-representation (re-)creating a self in the text. His writing is an act of resistance against essentialist views and perceptions of Indigenous groups. As Acoose puts it: 'For many Indigenous writers, the act of writing thus becomes an act of resistance, an act of re-empowerment.'[64] Damm also notes that when Indigenous writers 'enter into the writing of their texts, [they enter into] the writing of them/selves with the purpose of creating a better future for themselves and the people around them'.[65] As a result, and in Scofield's case, Sidonie Smith and Julia Watson's assertions about 'the autobiographical occasion' are very apt. They see the autobiographical moment as it 'becomes a site on which cultural ideologies intersect and dissect one another, in contradiction, consonance, and adjacency. Thus the site is rife with diverse potentials'.[66] The potential here lies in Scofield's own personal healing; as he is able to overcome his past, by extension the Métis Nation is able to move beyond survival. Smith and Watson accurately note that in 'deploying autobiographical practices that go against the grain, [the author] may constitute an "I" that becomes a place of creative and, by implication, political intervention'.[67] To Scofield, as with many other Indigenous writers, writing 'is a means of affirming the cultures, of clarifying lies, of speaking truth, of resisting oppression, of asserting identity, of self-empowerment, of survival, of moving beyond survival'.[68] For Scofield, the turning point in his writing was, as he puts it, 'realizing that all of this stuff was the past. That it was gone. That I had captured it and here it was. But I had the whole rest of my life to make new memories. I have new things to write about'.[69] Writing thus becomes an integral part of his resistance to the dominant structures of thought which characterise mainstream thinking about the Métis and have, as Nancy Hartsock has written, the same marginalising effect as 'the transcendental voice of universalizing Theory'.[70] Scofield resists this marginalising thrust, noting of his autobiography:

> My greatest hope for the book is that any younger people coming out of the native community and any young people coming out of poetry or coming out of situations where there's any kind of trauma that they'd be able to find a book like this and be able to read it. Become inspired somehow. That the book would help them.[71]

Scofield's own hopes for his autobiography are consistent with his multiple positionalities. While he is a child, 'living in the slums on welfare' Scofield's friend Abby is the only person to whom he can relate. As he puts it:

> Abby was in the same class as me and had a real taste for trouble. She had a smart mouth and swore like a trooper. Like me, Abby didn't have a father and her mother was on welfare ... She had a pale and sickly looking brother named Billy ... Her mother was rough-looking and had an equally dirty mouth. Grandma called them 'poor white trash' but I never repeated it. (*Thunder* p. 45)

Scofield does not repeat it because he understands that the designation 'poor white trash' means nothing because he connects with Abby on a personal level. That being said, Abby does not know about Scofield's Indigenous heritage and most likely sees him as her equal because he is able to 'pass' as white – yet another characteristic of his Métis ancestry. In fact, Scofield experiences a mixture of shame and anger when, later, Abby tells him not to talk to Indians because, according to her grandmother, 'They're all drunks, you know'.[72] This incident exposes the layers of oppression that prevent marginalised groups, such as those considered 'poor white trash', 'Indians', or 'Métis' from identifying with each other and forming group alliances.

However, as I have shown, Scofield's writing is able to cut through these layers, exposing, articulating, and attempting to dismantle them. Despite the difficulties associated with identifying as Métis, Scofield is able to build community relations through his writing. As he puts it:

> It's like I've always said insofar as community and insofar as the native writing community, is that I've always considered myself very much one small voice out of a community of powerful singers. I always maintain that. Because, of course, there are many different voices. Many strong voices. What's important is that in each of those voices there is power that's being created and there's a whole sense of spirituality and a whole sense of reclaiming, which is really important because when you put it all together it becomes this kind of entourage of powerful words and powerful sentiments of things that are about healing.[73]

Indeed, healing is perhaps one of Scofield's earliest motivations for writing; his writing of the personal in order to heal is also an attempt to heal the political.

Scofield's identifications as both Métis and two-spirited hold a great deal of potential particularly because he stands outside the bounds of traditional articulations of representation. Through his writing he is also able to articulate his two-spiritedness and his Métis identification clearly and powerfully. Scofield's commitment to the personal as political is integral to understanding his work. Indeed, when asked whether his writing is written from a mainly personal perspective, Scofield himself is quick to clarify that he does not see the distinction. As he puts it:

> Well, no. That's not entirely correct. It is a political story. The whole history of my family. The whole history of denial. The whole history of Métis people. That's all about politics and it's all about histories of shame. Histories of denial. Histories of poverty and coming out of a disadvantaged environment. This book is the contemporary – if you will – of those politics to date. The shame of my grandfather. The denial of my grandfather of being Native. That all comes from a political history. If people were afforded the opportunity and the human right of being allowed to be who they were, then maybe things would have been different. I was taught that everything you do from the way you brush your teeth, to the way you comb your hair to the way you

walk down the street is political. You're showing your politics and what you believe.⁷⁴

Part of the role of the two-spirit is the connection of communal or public history with the personal. In fact, 'a two-spirit person is seen as someone actively living, preserving, and honouring Native American cultures'. According to Lang, 'a number of formal and informal conversations with two-spirit people reflect their opinion that some of us continue to fill traditional roles in our tribal communities; others are artists, healers, mediators, and community organizers in urban areas; many of us are active in efforts to restore and preserve our cultural traditions'.⁷⁵ Scofield echoes this logic:

> I write from the perspective of my community. My political pieces, my political analysis, my political opinions, stem from that activism, if you will. They stem from being an Aboriginal person in this country and the things that need to be said about that, or the things I feel need to be said about that. So I write from that perspective, and not all the people in my community hold that perspective. For me it's very much a kind of camaraderie, to be able to have the freedom and the liberty to write our perspective of history and our perspective of colonization and the whole move towards the destruction of that colonization and the move towards self-government and self-determination.⁷⁶

Once again we see Scofield negotiating the personal and the political, this time using queer critical tools to advocate a lateral politics of solidarity. Along these lines, Jeannette Armstrong recognises and argues for 'the use of poetic form as a way to distil into symbolic imagery a perspective coming from our common experience of being Native in Canada'.⁷⁷ In this vein of self-articulation, Jennifer Brown notes that 'Métis people themselves are increasingly setting out their own concepts of their history and identities. They will come up with their own paradigms, old and new ... and they will perhaps be more liberated than we from some of our heavier and more troubling academic baggage. The really new paradigms are likely to come from them'.⁷⁸ Scofield's writing is part of these paradigms. Indeed, according to Kateri Damm, 'Already the voices of mixed-bloods play an important role in the breaking of silences, the telling of Indigenous perspectives, the dispelling of lies and stereotypes, the creation of Indigenous literature'.⁷⁹ However, what is significant about Damm's conception is that she seems to cast the 'mixed-blood' as a special figure that has unique abilities to cross cultural and racial borders. As she puts it:

> The power of the mixed-blood ... is to be able to see and speak the strengths and weaknesses of both Indigenous and non-Native cultures. Often the mixed-bloods ... become 'bilingual' interpreters, able to speak in the idiom of both 'White' and 'Indigenous' groups. Mixed-bloods see with two sets of eyes, hear with two sets of ears and those who write find the ability to assimilate and process all of this into a kind of tertium liquid: a blending or 'mingling' that cannot be completely ignored or discounted by either side.[80]

This is an interesting echo of W. E. B. Du Bois' work, whose 'double-consciousness' thesis strikes similar and familiar chords. More relevant to my project, however, is the parallel between Damm's characterisation of 'mixed-bloods' and Gloria Anzaldúa's formulation of the new *mestiza* consciousness, which I have already discussed at length. As Anzaldúa writes, in *Borderlands/La Frontera*:

> The *mestiza* faces the dilemma of the mixed breed: which collectivity does the daughter of a dark-skinned mother listen to? ... In attempting to work out a synthesis, the self has added *a third element* which is greater than the sum of its severed parts. That third element is a new consciousness – a *mestiza* consciousness – and though it is a source of intense pain, its energy comes from breaking down the unitary aspect of each new paradigm.[81]

Both Damm and Anzaldúa recognise the potential of mixed people to facilitate and increase communication between groups who would ordinarily be at odds with one another, particularly if power relations between these groups are asymmetrical, as in the case of the Canadian Métis.

Scofield's writing attempts to heal the injustices against the Métis by identifying as and allying himself with the Métis, despite the fact that his alliance is based on memories that he reconstructs rather than personally remembers, since the history of the Métis is one he learned and came to accept as an adult rather than having grown up with. As Scofield puts it in 'Answer For My Brother (Who Are the Métis?)': 'My writing is no comparison but I write to heal so I / find sacredness in the captured thought which brings / me to all the volumes written about Indians be that / pre-history or prophetic insights that will lead us into / the future' (*The Gathering* p. 82, lines 6–10). It is in this spirit that he writes about the Métis, attempting to create a history and the foundations for a future. As he does this, he consciously asserts his own Métis positioning. In this vein, Andrews usefully argues that Scofield uses 'a form of strategic essentialism to assert the ethnic/racial category of Métis but paradoxically couple[s] this assertion with irony'.[82] This allows Scofield to 'align [himself] with the very subjects who have been written out of conventional historiography' as he re-makes history.[83]

Scofield's 'Survival Poetry' provides a fitting transition to the next chapter, which explores how Guillermo Gómez-Peña's performance art and writing works in the queering of citizenship (*The Gathering* p. 34). 'Down here there is a different kind of poetry', writes Scofield:

Not classical poetry
With smooth & eloquent verse
Not even love poetry
Taking you to some far-off gazebo by crashing waves
But survival poetry
Raw, unflinching
Watching your back in some skid row bar
Down here
Each line will give you a day – or make it your last. (lines 1–10)

This poetry is neither what he calls 'classical' nor 'love' poetry, but one that is 'raw, unflinching'. Writing this kind of poetry, Scofield suggests, is tantamount to survival: 'Each line will give you a day – or make it your last.' Scofield leaves this last line with no end punctuation, leaving the reader with no closure and a distinct sense of danger and foreboding. There is a risk, he suggests, in writing poetry; in linking poetry and survival so inextricably, Scofield shows the urgency of our reading his poetry to his survival as two-spirited, as Métis, and as citizen.

Notes

1   Gregory Scofield, *The Gathering: Stones for the Medicine Wheel* (Vancouver: Polestar, 1993); *Native Canadiana / Songs from the Urban*

Rez (Vancouver: Polestar, 1996); *Love Medicine and One Song: Sâkihtown-Maskihkiy Êkwa Pêyak-Nikamowin* (Victoria: Polestar 1997); *I Knew Two Métis Women: The Lives of Dorothy Scofield and Georgina Houle Young* (Victoria: Polestar, 1999); *Thunder Through My Veins: Memories of a Métis Childhood* (Toronto: HarperCollins Canada, 1999); *Singing Home the Bones* (Vancouver: Polestar, 2005); *Kipocihkân: Poems New and Selected* (Vancouver: Nightwood Editions, 2009); *Louis: The Heretic Poems* (Vancouver: Nightwood Editions, 2011); and *Witness, I Am* (Gibsons, BC: Nightwood Editions, 2016). All subsequent references to these publications will be included in parentheses in the main body of the text.
2   *Singing Home the Bones: A Poet Becomes Himself*, DVD, directed by Hilary Pryor (Victoria, BC: May Street Group Film, 2006).
3   Interestingly, Scofield says he does not know Michif, the language of the Métis. The next section shows that those now known as Métis (comprised of those called métis and halfbreeds) were most often the offspring of Cree and Europeans; however, Michif is rarely spoken outside long-standing Métis communities. It is most commonly found in Métis communities in Saskatchewan and Manitoba in Canada and North Dakota and Montana in the United States.
4   Cindy Patton, *Inventing AIDS* (New York: Routledge, 1990), p. 148.
5   Ibid.
6   Françoise Lionnet and Shu-Mei Shi, eds, *Minor Transnationalism* (Durham, NC and London: Duke University Press, 2005), p. 12.
7   Susan Stewart, *On Longing: Narratives of the Miniature, the Gigantic, the Souvenir, the Collection* (Durham, NC and London: Duke University Press, 1993), p. 131.
8   Diana Fuss, 'Interior Colonies: Frantz Fanon and the Politics of Identification', *Diacritics* 24:2/3 (1994): pp. 20–42, at p. 21.
9   Chelsea Vowel, 'What a Landmark Ruling Means – and Doesn't – for Métis, Non-Status Indians' (16 April 2016). www.cbc.ca/news/indigenous/landmark-supreme-court-decision-Métis-non-status-indians-1.3537419 (accessed 20 April 2016).
10 Fuss, 'Interior Colonies', p. 23.
11 Sue-Ellen Jacobs, Wesley Thomas, and Sabine Lang, eds, 'Introduction', in *Two-Spirit People: Native American Gender Identity, Sexuality, and Spirituality* (Chicago: University of Illinois Press, 1997), pp. 1–18.
12 Pat Califia, *Sex Changes: The Politics of Transgenderism* (San Francisco: Cleis Press, 1997), pp. 123–4.
13 Sara Jamieson, 'Âyahkwêw Songs: AIDS and Mourning in Gregory Scofield's "Urban Rez" Poems', *Canadian Poetry* 57 (2005): pp. 52–64, at p. 60.
14 Sabine Lang, 'Various Kinds of Two-Spirit People: Gender Variance and Homosexuality in Native American Communities', in *Two-Spirit*

People: Native American Gender Identity, Sexuality, and Spirituality, ed. Sue-Ellen Jacobs, Wesley Thomas, and Sabine Lang (Urbana and Chicago: University of Illinois Press, 1997), pp. 100–18, at p. 103.
15   Ibid., p. 104.
16   Gary Kinsman, *The Regulation of Desire* (Montreal: Black Rose Books, 1996), p. 93.
17   R. W. Gray, '"…in my writing I see myself as a community worker": An Interview with Gregory Scofield', *Arc* 43 (1999): pp. 21–9, at p. 23.
18   Jamieson, 'Âyahkwêw Songs', p. 60.
19   Morag Shiach, *Hélène Cixous: A Politics of Writing* (London and New York: Routledge, 1991), p. 16.
20   Lang, 'Various Kinds of Two-Spirit People', p. 112. This becomes far more complicated with the rise of Queer Nation movements in Canada (for example the Two-Spirited Peoples of the First Nations). See Gary Kinsman and Patrizia Gentile, *The Canadian War on Queers: National Security as Sexual Regulation* (Vancouver: University of British Columbia Press, 2010) for more on this.
21   Jennifer S. H. Brown, 'Métis, Halfbreeds, and Other Real People: Challenging Cultures and Categories', *The History Teacher* 27:1 (1993), pp. 19–26.
22   Ibid., p. 19.
23   Marcel Giraud, *The Métis in the Canadian West*, trans. George Woodcock. 2 volumes (Lincoln: University of Nebraska Press, 1986 [1945]); Joseph Kinsey Howard, *Strange Empire: A Narrative of the Northwest* (New York: William Morrow and Co, 1952).
24   The Métis National Council, quoted in Jacqueline Peterson and Jennifer S. H. Brown, eds, 'Introduction', in *The New Peoples: Being and Becoming Métis in North America* (Winnipeg: University of Manitoba Press, 1985), pp. 3–18, at p. 6.
25   Chris Anderson, *'Métis': Race, Recognition, and the Struggle for Indigenous Peoplehood* (Vancouver and Toronto: University of British Columbia Press, 2014), p. 11.
26   Ibid., pp. 16–17.
27   John E. Foster, 'Some Questions and Perspectives on the Problem of Métis Roots', in *The New Peoples: Being and Becoming Métis in North America*, ed. Jacqueline Peterson and Jennifer Andrews (Winnipeg: University of Manitoba Press, 1985), pp. 73–93, at p. 73.
28   Howard Adams, *A Tortured People: The Politics of Colonization* (Penticton, BC: Theytus, 1995), p. 11.
29   Brown, 'Métis, Halfbreeds, and Other Real People', p. 23. See for example, Marcel Giraud, George F. G. Stanley, and W. L. Morton.
30   Monika Kaup, 'Constituting Hybridity as Hybrid', in *Mixing Race, Mixing Culture: Inter-American Literary Dialogues*, ed. Monika Kaup and

Debra J. Rosenthal (Austin: University of Texas Press, 2002), pp. 185–210, at p. 198.
31 Maria Campbell, *Halfbreed* (Lincoln: University of Nebraska Press, 1982 [1977]), p. 15.
32 The Manitoba Act of 1870, for example, makes provisions for the what it called 'residents' of the area now known as Manitoba – the Métis – however, the government continuously allowed settlers to take over the land until the Métis were, as I have noted, living on Crown Lands.
33 Jacqueline Peterson, 'Many Roads to Red River: Métis Genesis in the Red River Region, 1680–1815', in *The New Peoples: Being and Becoming Métis in North America*, ed. Jacqueline Peterson and Jennifer S. H. Brown (Winnipeg: University of Manitoba Press, 1985), pp. 37–72, at p. 64.
34 Robert K. Thomas, 'Afterword', in *The New Peoples: Being and Becoming Métis in North America*, ed. Jacqueline Peterson and Jennifer S. H. Brown (Winnipeg: University of Manitoba Press, 1985), pp. 243–51, at p. 247.
35 Brown, 'Métis, Halfbreeds, and Other Real People', p. 21.
36 Anderson, *'Métis'*, p. 58.
37 Glen Sean Coulthard, *Red Skin, White Masks: Rejecting the Colonial Politics of Recognition* (Minneapolis and London: University of Minnesota Press, 2014), p. 3.
38 Jennifer Andrews, 'Irony, Métis Style: Reading the Poetry of Marilyn Dumont and Gregory Scofield', *Canadian Poetry: Studies, Documents, Reviews* 50 (2002): pp. 6–31, at p. 7.
39 Anderson, *'Métis'*, p. 207.
40 Howard Adams, *Prison of Grass: Canada from the Native Point of View* (Toronto: New Press, 1975).
41 Adams, *A Tortured People*, p. 3.
42 Ibid.
43 Ibid., p. 1.
44 Adams, *Prison of Grass*, p. 9.
45 Adams, *A Tortured People*, p. 9.
46 Ibid., p. 11.
47 Adams, *Prison of Grass*, p. xi.
48 Ibid., p. x.
49 Adams, *A Tortured People*, p. 204.
50 Maria Campbell's *Halfbreed* (1973) is widely considered to be one of the most important and foundational texts in Canadian Métis literature. The novel sheds light on the every day life and struggles of living as a Métis in Canada during the 1940s. The word has been described by many as a bildungsroman; in the novel, Maria is described as being part of a community deprived of its pride, dignity and identity by dominant (white) Canadian culture.

51 Jeannette Armstrong, 'History Lesson', in *Native Poetry in Canada: A Contemporary Anthology*, ed. Jeannette C. Armstrong and Lally Grauer (Peterborough: Broadview, 2001), pp. 110–11.
52 Alan Lindsey McLeod, *The Canon of Commonwealth Literature: Essays in Criticism* (India: Sterling Publishers Pvt. Ltd, 2003), p. 83.
53 Harry W. Daniels, 'Bill C-31: The Abocide Bill', Congress of Aboriginal Peoples 1998. www.abopeoples.org/programs/C-31/Abocide/Abocide-3.htm#Membership (accessed 13 November 2009).
54 Albert Braz, *The False Traitor: Louis Riel in Canadian Culture* (Toronto: University of Toronto Press, 2003), p. 89.
55 Maurice Constantin-Weyer published a fictionalised biography of Louis Riel, *La Bourrasque* (1925). An English translation/adaptation was later published as *A Martyr's Folly* (Toronto: The Macmillan Company, 1930), and a further edition in 1954, *The Half-Breed* (New York: The Macaulay Company, 1954). Depictions of Riel's role in the Red River Rebellion include the 1979 CBC television film *Riel* (dir. George Bloomfield) and Canadian cartoonist Chester Brown's 2003 graphic novel *Louis Riel: A Comic-Strip Biography* (Montreal: Drawn and Quarterly Publications, 2003). Interestingly, Erín Moure, the subject of chapter 4, published a poem on Riel in her first collection of poetry, *Empire, York Street*, published in 1979.
56 Braz, *The False Traitor*, p. 3.
57 Andrews, 'Irony, Métis Style', p. 19.
58 Ibid., p. 20.
59 Armstrong, 'History Lesson', lines 8–10.
60 Mikhail Bakhtin, *The Dialogic Imagination: Four Essays*, trans. Caryl Emerson and Michael Holquist (Austin: University of Texas Press, 1981), p. 160.
61 Recall that Scofield's use of Cree is connected to his upbringing. Many Métis are not exposed to Michif, instead speaking Cree.
62 Just a note to clarify that the translation here is slightly misleading. 'Lord our God' is not on the line that it claims to be. This is most likely a cosmetic issue of layout and format.
63 Janice Acoose, 'Post *Halfbreed*: Indigenous Writers as Authors of Their Own Realities', in *Looking at the Words of Our People: First Nations Analysis of Literature*, ed. Jeannette C. Armstrong (Penticton: Theytus, 1993), pp. 27–44, at p. 31.
64 Ibid., p. 33.
65 Kateri Damm, 'Dispelling and Telling: Speaking Native Realities in Maria Campbell's *Halfbreed* and Beatrice Culleton's *In Search of April Raintree*', in *Looking at the Words of Our People: First Nations Analysis of Literature*, ed. Jeannette Armstrong (Penticton: Theytus Books, 1993), pp. 93–114, at p. 111.

66 Sidonie Smith and Julia Watson, 'Introduction', in *De/Colonizing the Subject: The Politics of Gender in Women's Autobiography* (Minneapolis: University of Minnesota Press, 1992), pp. xiii–xxxi, at p. xix.
67 Ibid.
68 Damm, 'Dispelling and Telling', p. 113.
69 'Interview with January Magazine', *January Magazine* (1999), n.p. http://januarymagazine.com/profiles/scofield.html (accessed 15 October 2009).
70 Nancy Hartsock, 'Rethinking Modernism: Minority vs. Majority Theories', *Cultural Critique* 7 (1987): pp. 187–206, at p. 204.
71 'Interview with January Magazine', n.p.
72 Ibid.
73 Ibid.
74 Ibid.
75 Lang, 'Various Kinds of Two-Spirit People', p. 113.
76 Gray, ' "…in my writing I see myself as a community worker": an interview with Gregory Scofield', p. 23.
77 Jeanette Armstrong, 'Four Decades: An Anthology of Canadian Native Poetry from 1960 to 2000', in *Native Poetry in Canada: A Contemporary Anthology*, ed. Jeannette C. Armstrong and Lally Grauer (Peterborough, ON: Broadview Press, 2001), pp. xv–xx, at p. xv.
78 Brown, 'Métis, Halfbreeds, and Other Real People', p. 25.
79 Kateri Damm, 'Says Who: Colonialism, Identity, and Defining Indigenous Literature', in *Looking at the Words of Our People: First Nations Analysis of Literature*, ed. Jeannette Armstrong (Penticton: Theytus, 1993), pp. 10–25, at p. 24.
80 Ibid., p. 19.
81 Gloria Anzaldúa, *Borderlands/La Frontera: The New Mestiza* (San Francisco: Aunt Lute Books, 1997 [1987]), p. 100 (my italics).
82 Andrews, 'Irony, Métis Style', p. 8.
83 Fuss, 'Interior Colonies', p. 31.

4

Performing the border and queer *rasquachismo* in Guillermo Gómez-Peña's performance art

Where Gregory Scofield's negotiation of the practice and habitus of citizenship in Canada is focused on the Métis, a group whose rights and identity have been debated and unjustly dismissed for centuries, this chapter recrosses the 49th parallel and returns to the border between the United States and Mexico, the site that features most prominently in work by Mexican-American and self-identifying Chicano performance artist and cultural theorist Guillermo Gómez-Peña. Like Scofield, Gómez-Peña's writing is concerned with survival and mediation, but from the perspectives of those whose lives are intersected by the US–Mexico border.

In the first poem from his '1992 Trilogy', Guillermo Gómez-Peña opens by consciously 'choosing to remember' Christopher Columbus' 'discovery' of the Americas.[1] The poem, entitled '1492 Performances', and the trilogy allude to pivotal moments in North American history: Columbus made first landfall in Hispaniola in 1492, and in 1992 the United States celebrated its 500th 'birthday' (or more accurately, the 500th anniversary of the 'discovery' of the Americas), to the consternation of many. Gómez-Peña's poem highlights the controversial side of this birthday, reminding his reader or listener that to assume the history of North America began in 1492 is to affirm and legitimise the colonial history and neo-colonial present of the United States, in addition to dismissing and ignoring the Indigenous peoples who stand dispossessed of their land. Indeed, Gómez-Peña confirms that 'five centuries of foreign domination' (line 4) led him to 'this stage' (line 3) – a reference here to both the chronological moment at which he writes, and the literal stage from which he ostensibly recites this poem. Gómez-Peña writes this piece on the occasion of his 1,492nd performance, which takes place in 1992, deliberately playing on the irony of these resonating dates. The author of several books and myriad performance texts, Gómez-Peña moved to the United States from Mexico in 1978 and received his MA in Post-Studio Performance from the California Institute of the Arts.[2] Since then he has been involved in a range of individual and collaborative projects, most notably the annual 'Border Arts Workshop' which began in 1984, and more recently with his performance troupe La Pocha Nostra. Gómez-Peña's writing and performances deal with contemporary issues of insider/outsider status, fragmented, hybrid, and multiple identities, in addition to calling for new ways of articulating the changing landscape, or as he calls it, the topography, of citizenship. This chapter examines how his work exposes the fractures inherent in what he calls a Manichean universe, his performances and writings posing a challenge to conventional understandings of citizenship. Through his melancholic yet humorous and satirical treatment of borders (physical and otherwise), identity politics, and citizenship, Gómez-Peña creates an alternative North America founded on a radically new understanding of citizenship. I show how, in allowing his audience entry into this alternative nation state, Gómez-Peña brings together a collective (if temporary) challenge to and re-evaluation of the role of the citizen. This process understands that performance art holds within it a distinct and special potential to sow the seeds of civic change.

This chapter investigates Gómez-Peña's use of what I call a queered *rasquachismo*. In his use of this practice, Gómez-Peña connects his audience and readers to a self-consciously Chicano aesthetic strategy. Embedded within this practice is the trope of the US–Mexico border. Whether textually or in a live setting, Gómez-Peña's performances unbalance the relationship between performer/writer and audience/reader.[3] His performances disrupt the status of citizenship so that the act of reading/spectating is one that exposes and then transgresses the border between the status and practice of citizenship.

This chapter's exploration of Gómez-Peña's work first considers the process by which he comes to identify as Chicano, before moving to an analysis of the *rasquache* aesthetic, focusing specifically on how Gómez-Peña employs such a practice to further his project of performing the US–Mexico border. In its reading of several performance texts, both by Gómez-Peña as a solo artist and by La Pocha Nostra as a group, the chapter then traces Gómez-Peña's ideological

Performing the border and queer *rasquachismo* 95

and performative development through an analysis of his work before and after 9/11, which triggered a civic crisis in the United States.[4] I use this date as a pivot around which to show a marked difference in his work, arguing that before the events of 9/11 he was primarily concerned with the US–Mexico border and its impact on continental and national identity and citizenship. After this date, however, his work is more concerned with building solidarity groups and alternative communities through his performance art and other cultural criticism, using the trope of the border in a more sophisticated way. Throughout, the reader of Gómez-Peña's work plays a key role in how the performance of text, both in a live setting and on the physical page, works to open up a site at which an alternative, queered citizenship can be developed.

Becoming a Chicano artist

While an earlier chapter offered a brief history of the Chicano movement to contextualise Gloria Anzaldúa's feminist Chicana theorisations, this chapter focuses on how understandings of *mestizaje* in Mexico can be used to contextualise the movement and, in particular, how, as a naturalised US citizen, Gómez-Peña comes to identify as a Chicano in the United States. Taunya Lovell Banks suggests that after first contact, 'Spanish colonialists, offspring from relations between Spaniards, Africans and Indigenous people in colonial Mexico, developed a complex set of rules creating a race-like caste system'[5] and this racial stratification is played out within the Chicano movement in important ways.

Born in Mexico in 1955 to an affluent family, Gómez-Peña describes himself as a *mestizo*, referring to the mixed-race group that constitutes the majority of Mexico's racial makeup. While it is beyond the scope of this book to provide an in-depth account of the history of Spanish and European colonisation in Mexico which resulted in a 'hybrid' group comprised of *mestizo/a* individuals, it is worth noting that this racial group is now perhaps the most powerful and dominant in Mexico, which on a state level prides itself on its hybrid character. This represents one of the earliest issues Gómez-Peña contends with; in a middle-class family in the Jewish quarter of Mexico City he became acutely aware of a crisis of representation in Mexico – people who identified as Indigenous were brushed aside by the state and simultaneously romanticised as Mexico's 'lost' history. Likewise, those of (visible) African descent were vilified and brushed aside. Banks traces the source of the glorification of *mestizaje* to 'The 1812 Spanish Constitution of Cadiz [which] abolished the *casta* system and accompanying racial laws'.[6] After this, identification as '*mestizo* ultimately becomes a source of pride rather than a stigma because much of the population was mestizo'.[7] Gómez-Peña notes: 'The millions of *indios*, the original proto-Mexicans, were portrayed as living in a parallel (and mythical) time and space outside *our* history and society' (*Ethno-Techno* p. 7). Banks argues this was an effective strategy in consolidating Mexico's identity: 'Mexico's policy of ennobling its indigenous population while simultaneously encouraging European migration is not inconsistent with the creation of a single national identity.'[8] Across the US–Mexico border since 1848, however, 'race issues among Latino/as get papered over in the celebration of Latino/a mestizaje. In discussing the concept of mestizaje in Latin American and U.S. society, it is essential to determine not only what mestizaje moves toward, but more importantly from what mestizaje moves away'.[9] The Chicano movement reflects the shifting emphasis of *mestizaje*'s influence.

The Chicano movement is generally considered to have had three goals: the restoration of land rights, farm worker rights, and educational reforms. In the late 1960s activists began to identify themselves as 'Chicano', a previously derogatory term that was reclaimed as a strategy of empowerment. The struggle for land was rooted in two things: first, the annexation of most of what had been northern Mexico by the United States as a result of the Treaty of Guadalupe Hidalgo in 1848; and second, a desire to return to the ancestral homeland of Aztlán. Despite the US government's promise that, as Banks put it, 'the original 1848 Treaty of Guadalupe Hidalgo signed by the President accorded Mexicans the status of "free white person(s)" and granted them citizenship "as soon as possible," Congress changed the language on conferral of citizenship to "at the proper time" as determined by Congress'.[10] The extent to which the former citizens of Mexico were treated as white 'was deferred to each state's constitution and pervasive social practices of racialization'.[11] In this way, a de facto system of quasi-segregation existed.

More relevant to this analysis, and as chapter 2 explores, an artistic dimension to *El Movimiento* also began to develop; in particular, Rodolfo 'Corky' Gonzales' 'Yo Soy Joaquín' [I am Joaquín] is considered a significant moment in the Chicano Literary Renaissance. Gonzales' poem became famous for its representation of Chicano history:

> Equality is but a word–
> The Treaty of Hidalgo has been broken
> And is but another treacherous promise.
> My land is lost
> And stolen,
> My culture has been raped.[12]

Gonzales' poem reflected the general mood of the time and was intended to represent *la raza* [the race] – the people of the movement. The Chicano movement was specifically sited and comprised primarily of Mexican-Americans who identified with *la raza*. The poem was a powerful call to action and resistance with an emphasis on the particularly *mestizo/a* character of Chicano/as. 'Yo Soy Joaquín' effectively signifies the power of art in a moment of civic awakening. Today, the US Census classifies Mexican Americans as 'Hispanic', an ethnic group. Individuals checking this category also have six racial options: American Indian or Alaska Native, Asian, Black or African American, Native Hawaiian or Other Pacific Islander, White, or some other race.[13]

According to Gómez-Peña, then, performance art is a medium that not only reflects his own personal reality, but also leaves space for him to construct a new reality once the performance is over. In this way, performance itself is not mimesis, as conventional theories of the theatre might assert. Indeed, as Gómez-Peña puts it, 'Performance is about presence, not representation; it is not (as classical theories of the theatre would suggest) a mirror, but the actual moment in which the mirror is shattered' (*Dangerous* p. 9). It is in this mirror-shattering moment that the power of performance comes to light: in this understanding, instead of perceiving a performance as an act which is simply repeated and repetitive, Gómez-Peña sees it as an act that *constitutes* reality rather than re-presenting it, running in parallel to the act of reading as constituting civic subjects theorised in chapter 1.

In the remainder of the poem '1492 Performances', with which I opened the chapter, Gómez-Peña calls his audience's attention to his body, which plays an integral role in his performances. As he puts it, during his performances, he has 'cut [his] hair / sliced [his] wrists /

farted & eaten on stage' (lines 8–10). This focus on his corporality on stage serves to heighten the shock value and the effect here is to call attention to the 'problematic' Latino body he and almost fifty-seven million other people of Latino descent in the United States inhabit.

Gómez-Peña's focus on the 'singular journey' which brought him to the stage where he now finds himself also relates to the personal journey he undertook when he moved to the United States from Mexico. As he puts it, when he crossed the border, he 'unwittingly started [his] irreversible process of *Pocho*-ization or de-Mexicanization' (*Ethno-Techno* p. 6). Derived from Spanish, where it can be used to describe fruit that has become rotten or discolored, Gómez-Peña's use of the complex term '*pocho*' is significant here. When used in the context of US–Mexico relations, it has uses that are both pejorative and neutral. In some situations, the term can be used to describe a Mexican person who 'acts' American; in other situations, it is a pejorative term used by Mexicans to refer to Chicanos who seem to have forgotten or moved away from their Mexican roots. Gómez-Peña uses the term to refer to yet another meaning, a person who frequently crosses the US–Mexico border and feels equally at home and displaced on both sides of this border.[14] This interpretation is further bolstered by Gómez-Peña himself, who notes that 'We are interstitial creatures and border citizens by nature – insiders/outsiders at the same time – and we rejoice in this paradoxical condition. In fact, in the act of crossing a border, we find temporary emancipation' ((*Ethno-Techno* p. 23). That said, despite this positive interpretation, Gómez-Peña's use of '*pocho*' is most certainly inflected with the other less empowering meanings of the word, rendering the celebration of his paradoxical personal identity also as a lament.

Gómez-Peña must therefore negotiate the positive and negative impacts of the border on his identity, and this negotiation plays an integral role in his performances and writing. Gómez-Peña received American citizenship in 1988, ten years after he first crossed the border as an immigrant, making him a dual citizen of both the United States and Mexico and the theme of dual citizenship continues to feature heavily in Gómez-Peña's writing and performance. His citizenship status gives him a dual perspective that places him in a productive position from which he is able to simultaneously understand and critique the complexities of the US–Mexico border. He offers: 'Often the work of performance artists becomes a blank screen for people to project their own agendas, personal struggles, and tribulations, especially when it opens infected wounds. That may be where the power of performance lies' (*Dangerous* p. 162). This understanding allows the audience or reader to share in his experiences, if only for the duration of the performance. As Roger Bartra has put it, 'Gómez-Peña invites us to live on the border, to convert ourselves into permanent exiles, into nostalgic and melancholic beings, and to undergo the dangers that take us to the discovery of the infected wound'.[15] The repeated return to particular images or metaphors – in this case, the trope of the infected wound that recalls Anzaldúa's famous description of the US–Mexico border – is one that features prominently in the *rasquache* method, which I discuss below.

Queered *rasquache* as methodology

The *rasquache* aesthetic is not uncontroversial. Since its theoretical formulation by Tomas Ybarra-Frausto and Amalia Mesa-Bains in the mid-1990s, the idea of a specifically Chicana/o aesthetic sensibility has been both glorified and vilified.[16] The aesthetic principles of *rasquachismo* were famously put forward by Ybarra-Frausto in 'Rasquachismo: A Chicano Sensibility'.[17] In the piece, Ybarra-Frausto posits two ways by which *rasquachismo* is translated into specific approaches to art-making and formal elements of Chicano/a art through 'recuperation and recontextualizations of vernacular sensibilities ... It can be sincere and pay homage to the sensibility by restating its premises', or it can be evoked through self-conscious manipulation of materials or iconography. Mesa-Bains articulated *rasquache* from a feminist viewpoint in her article 'Domesticana: The Sensibility of Chicana Rasquache'. She sees *rasquachismo* 'as a survivalist irreverence (based on sustaining elements of Mexican tradition and lived encounters in a hostile environment) that functioned as a vehicle of cultural continuity'.[18]

In Gómez-Peña's work, the *rasquache* aesthetic is characterised by his use of recycling, the prominence of the US–Mexico border, his use of reverse ethnography, and strategies of defamiliarisation, like drag. According to Robert Neustadt, Ybarra-Frausto specifically notes that Gómez-Peña manipulates 'rasquache artifacts, codes, and sensibilities from both sides of the border', emphasising the 'cultural particularities of the Chicano/a lived experience as primarily working class, bicultural, bilingual, and resistant to assimilation within the United

States'.[19] For José Anguiano, 'rasquache aesthetics have always been a mechanism of survival and resistance'. Similarly, Gerald Vizenor's concept of survivance, an Indigenous trope that foregrounds survival and resistance in the Native North American context, is relevant here. Vizenor suggests that '[s]urvivance is an active resistance and repudiation of dominance, obtrusive themes of tragedy, nihilism, and victimry'.[20] If, as Rafaela Castro suggests, *rasquachismo* is 'an underground perspective – a view from *los de abajo* [the underdog], an attitude rooted in resourcefulness and adaptability', appropriating the concept of survivance – as both resistance *and* survival – enriches the *rasquache* aesthetic and allows for a more complex framework through which to analyse how Gómez-Peña deploys it.[21]

Underpinning much of what I call Gómez-Peña's use of *rasquache* is a particularly self-reflexive process. Ramon Garcia's controversial 'Against *Rasquache*: Chicano Identity and the Politics of Popular Culture in Los Angeles' provides a theoretical basis for this queered *rasquache*.[22] Garcia argues that an uncritical *rasquache* is 'an inadequate model for framing Chicana/o art and literature ... because it didn't recognize the complexity and sophistication of the kind of work that was out there, on the streets'.[23] Garcia believes that it is crucial to 'be self-critical, and to correct ourselves just like any intellectuals in the universe. That is necessary in order for us to evolve and grow intellectually and artistically'.[24] Gómez-Peña's queered *rasquachismo* is even more complex.

Neustadt suggests that 'Gómez-Peña elaborates a kind of double border *rasquachismo*. He appropriates and merges Chicano poetics with Mexican and "Gringo" counterparts to engender an intertextual conflation of transnational signs'.[25] One aspect of this is Gómez-Peña's use of drag, which he uses to 'underscore and efface' the US–Mexico border. According to Marjorie Garber, transvestism can indicate a cultural 'category crisis' where there is 'a failure of definitional distinction, a borderline that becomes permeable, that permits of border crossings from one (apparently distinct) category to another'.[26] Neustadt suggests that Gómez-Peña 'transgresses categories precisely in order to draw into question the existence of clearly delineated cultural classifications'.[27] Along the same lines, Butler asserts that 'drag fully subverts the distinction between inner and outer psychic space and effectively mocks both the expressive model of gender and the notion of a true gender identity'.[28] The consequences for Gómez-Peña's drag performances are significant, for, as Butler notes, 'if the anatomy of the performer is already distinct from the gender of the performer, and both of those are distinct from the gender of the performance, then the performance suggests a dissonance not only between sex and performance, but sex and gender, and gender and performance'.[29] Gómez-Peña's use of drag highlights the dissonance within and between the categories of race, ethnicity, and gender that he wishes to undermine. This process of undermining is visible in Gómez-Peña's own theorisation and commentary on his artistic and performance practice, and he claims to be 'critical of the way indigenous and ethnic identities are portrayed by mainstream cultural institutions and commodified by pop culture, tourism, and self-realization movements' (*Dangerous* p. 81). In order to resist these portrayals and commodifications, he utilises 'humor, multilingualism, and surprising performance strategies to fight back' along with 'melancholic humor and tactics of "reverse anthropology" as strategies for subverting dominant cultural projections and representations of Mexicans and Native peoples' (p. 81).

Particularly challenging for scholars of Gómez-Peña's work has been his tendency to publish his performance scripts in written form. Jill S. Kuhnheim, for example, asks whether the concrete publication of performance pieces that are, by virtue of their very ontology, intended to be ephemeral, is a productive decision, especially since Gómez-Peña's work is so focused on a live, immediate reaction from an audience. On the other hand, Peggy Phelan believes that '[t]his textualization goes against the ephemeral ontology of performance art which becomes itself through disappearance'.[30] Phelan writes that performance is 'representation without reproduction',[31] and, as Kuhnheim puts it, 'its duplication and distance from the "live moment" makes it something else – a product that participates in a reproductive economy'.[32] Gómez-Peña suggests that these texts are hybrid, suffering, like him, 'from an identity crisis. Are they spoken word poetry, performance "monologues," pop philosophy, art theory, post-colonial thought, or Chicano stand-up comedy?'[33] If these texts are, as he terms them, 'open texts, works in permanent progress', what are the implications of forcing them into stasis on the page ('El Mexorcist' p. 5)?

According to Gómez-Peña, publication 'merely preserves them in one phase of their ongoing development', assuring his reader that in performance, these texts are conveyed in different combinations, with a '15–20 percent margin for improvisation' ('El Mexorcist' p. 6).

However, as readers we are compelled to read the text in the order presented to us – linearly – and there is no scope for improvisation on our part. Gómez-Peña seems to be aware of this, reminding his readers that

> Not one performance art piece is ever the same. In performance, whether text-based or not, the script is just a blueprint for action, a hypertext contemplating multiple contingencies and options, and it is never 'finished.' Every time I publish a script, I must beware the reader: 'This is just one version of the text. Next week it will be different'.[34]

It is important to note that although Gómez-Peña and his collaborators primarily use performance as their dominant medium, their work is not considered here using a theatre studies framework. Instead, owing to the nature of his performances and writing, my treatment of his work consists primarily of textual analysis. I am interested in how performance art can, as Kuhnheim wonders, 'function as literature, an aesthetic experience defined by reading words and images on the page'.[35]

For his part, Gómez-Peña believes the power of performance art is in its ephemeral nature. He emphasises the importance of repetition in his performance art, affirming the recycled and reclaimed nature of his performances. This repetition and recycling operates in the same way myth-making practices do, effectively serving to create new myths. It also functions to represent what Gómez-Peña calls 'the multiplicity of mythologies and perceptions of Mexicans and Chicanos in the U.S.' (*Dangerous* p. 170). In so doing, audience members witnessing the performance are confronted with physical manifestations of their own perceptions of Chicanos/Latinos in the United States regardless of their own identifications. Gómez-Peña himself acknowledges the 'hidden civic goal' in his work, which is 'to create an ephemeral community of artists, technicians and activists in which [his] texts become a mere blueprint for action. This collaborative work is consensual by nature. It gets made in constant dialogue with others' (*Dangerous* p. 172).

Working within a queered *rasquache* allows Gómez-Peña and La Pocha Nostra to sidestep more pressing questions about and critiques of their work. Indeed, one criticism of Gómez-Peña and La Pocha Nostra is that in their attempt to recuperate the ways in which their audiences think about borders, identity, and solidarity, they have been co-opted into dominant structures of performance art. This question of normalisation is one that resurfaces over the course of this book, particularly when considering a methodology that has queer studies at its core. The issue in the context of Gómez-Peña, for example, is whether being within the ideological and institutional system that created and perpetuates exclusionary practices is effective. Here, I argue that instead of simply being merely co-opted, Gómez-Peña has been able to enact shifts in the political character of performance art practice. Jill Kuhnheim is more sceptical, noting that '[b]oundaries are inherent to the definition of subject positions, and a border identity is no exception. Gómez-Peña must inevitably participate in the activity that he is critiquing in order to make his critique'.[36] Neustadt supports this: 'Aware that there is no escape from representation, Gómez-Peña constitutes his critique from the *inside*.'[37] While this may well be the case, it does not preclude the possibility of instigating civic change in readers.

In an important way, the structure and composition of La Pocha Nostra mirrors the kind of community that Gómez-Peña is interested in building. As he notes: 'The fact that we are this ephemeral community that keeps reinventing and reshaping itself over and over again, almost from one project to another, is what makes us last so long. We are an open system, not a clan or an ensemble. But there are some difficulties.'[38] The openness of this artistic community is its key to survival and continuity. Gómez-Peña sees the troupe as 'a global collective, in the best sense of the term "global"', noting that 'it took us many years and lots of stupid mistakes to discover this fluid model of concentric circles and ephemeral communities'.[39] La Pocha Nostra is a small, intimate troupe with a few core members, comprising Gómez-Peña and including, at various stages, performance artists such as Balitrónica, Roberto Sifuentes, Violeta Luna, Michele Ceballos, James Luna, Gabriela Salgado, Emma Tramposch, Dani D'Emilia, and Erica Mott, in addition to a number of other collaborators. The troupe's name is a Spanish neologism that translates as either 'our impurities' or 'the cartel of cultural bastards'.[40] Gómez-Peña has noted that as a troupe, 'We love this poetic ambiguity. It reveals an attitude toward art and society: Crossracial, poly-gendered, experi-mental' (*Ethno-Techno* p. 78). Another translation for of the troupe's name is 'bleached', a 'derogatory term used by Mexicans for Chicanos, implying they're bleached to whiteness by living in the United States. Within Chicano artistic and cultural circles, *pochismo* also designates an in-your-face style, very ironic, that appropriates dominant cultural motifs and materials in order to make fun of them'.[41] George Lipsitz notes that 'Chicano art also constitutes a process of art-based community-making, [as well as] community-based art-making'.[42]

This perhaps partially explains Gómez-Peña's ability to consistently attract (generally white) audiences, without being entirely co-opted by the mainstream industry and art community, and expose – in controversial and unsettling ways – these audiences to realities they would not ordinarily experience as a result of their privilege. As Amanda Morrison notes, 'For Gomez-Peña, it is a political necessity that he performs in spaces on the "inside" of the art establishment, to reach this sort of audience. Yet he performs in alternative spaces as well, successfully reaching as broad a range of people as he depicts in the works themselves'.[43] Exposing mainstream audiences to the queered *rasquache* aesthetic works to defamiliarise the audience from the material, allowing for different understandings of the work and opening up a space for Gómez-Peña's 'hidden civic' processes to operate.

Crossing the border as a 'brujo'

As I have demonstrated, much of Gómez-Peña's work draws attention to the US–Mexico border as an example of a site at which many contemporary issues and injustices in and between the United States and Mexico originate. That said, he also sees the border as an opportunity for understanding and collaboration. As he has put it, in one of his open letters to the national arts community: 'La Frontera es lo unico que compartimos/The border is all we share.'[44] This focus on the border as a positive site for cooperation and collaboration represents an interesting and productive (if in some ways, conservative) shift in the discourse surrounding the US–Mexico border. As I noted in my previous treatment of Gloria Anzaldúa's work and the Chicano movement, the literature and criticism surrounding the US–Mexico border tends to focus on the border's history and the implications and consequences of its imposition. While it is important for these aspects to be studied and discussed, Gómez-Peña's approach can be seen at times as far more conciliatory. Recall that Anzaldúa characterised the US–Mexico border as '*una herida abierta* [an open wound] where the Third World grates against the first and bleeds';[45] in Roger Bartra's reading of Gómez-Peña's work, 'the border is no longer a wound whose pain serves to reaffirm identity, but rather a place where Anglos and Latinos confront one another'.[46] Gómez-Peña's position works towards an understanding of this border as contamination, in both its positive and negative connotations.

Gómez-Peña mirrors his personal movement across the US–Mexico border in his performance texts and other critical writing, attempting to recreate the crossing of a border for his audience to experience. To do this he code-switches between English, Spanish, Spanglish, and Nahuatl (in the latter case, he speaks in both actual Nahuatl and what he calls gibberish Nahuatl, or essentially, in tongues). This guarantees that at any one time, a significant portion of his audience or readership does not fully understand what is being said. This continuous recreation of the border that will be crossed multiple times over the course of one performance allows Gómez-Peña and his audience – an ephemeral but nevertheless present nation state – to resist the political structures that impose such borders in the first place. In a sense, then, Gómez-Peña takes on the role of the *coyote*, smuggling 'innocent' audiences across one of the most famous borders in the world. Not only does Gómez-Peña assist the audience's passage – he also performs the role of a cultural *coyote*, an intercultural community broker who is able to manipulate his audience through visual and verbal performances. This connection between Gómez-Peña's work and the trope of the US–Mexico border is crucial, argues Neustadt, to comprehending his 'discursive positionality'.[47] Read this way, the transgressive nature of Gómez-Peña's work is undeniable. More recently, however, he has been keen to question what is meant by transgression and radicalism, particularly in the context of performance art: 'In this time and place', he asks, 'What does it mean to be "transgressive"? / What does "radical behavior" mean [...] Who can artists shock, challenge, enlighten?'[48]

'Border Brujo' is the earliest performance text explored in this chapter. Taken from the performance series 'Documented/Undocumented', this piece was written in 1989 and a version was later published in 1991. Dedicating the text to his son, Guillermo Emiliano, Gómez-Peña expresses the hope that when his son 'grows up, most of these words will be outdated and unnecessary'.[49] The trope of the border clearly plays a central role in this performance text; in the preface to the performance text proper, Gómez-Peña notes that the text is 'a ritual, linguistic, and performative journey across the U.S.-México border', emphasising the meaning of 'Border Brujo' – in Spanish, 'brujo' can mean 'shaman', 'witch', and 'clown' – all appropriate in this context and certainly relevant when considering Vizenor's notion of the trickster ('Border Brujo' p. 49). The preface continues to symbolically construct, erect, and then dismantle the US–Mexico border in the form of other binary relationships; according to Gómez-Peña, '*Border Brujo* unfolds into 15 different personas, each speaking a different border language. And the relationship between these personas is symbolic of the one between North and South; Anglo and Latin America; myth and social reality; legality and illegality; performance art and life' (p. 49). In putting these terms into binary pairs, Gómez-Peña also draws connections within and between each binary relationship, such that 'North' is also linked to 'Anglo', 'myth', 'legality', and 'performance art', while 'South' relates to 'Latin America', 'social reality', 'illegality', and 'life'. In doing this Gómez-Peña textually presents the logic of the US–Mexico border as being arbitrary (all of these terms could be read as connected in various other permutations). This is reflected in the structure of the performance poem, which he describes as 'disnarrative and modular, like the border experience'.[50] At this point it is possible to identify a trace of trickster discourse here, particularly as Gómez-Peña notes that the border brujo crossed the US–Mexico border in costume, which could be read in two ways: in disguise and in drag. Continuing in this vein, Gómez-Peña signs off at the end of the preface as follows:

> Gómez-Peña
> desde la herida infectada
> toward 1992. (p. 50)

The approximate translation of the second line is 'from the infected wound', directly invoking Gloria Anzaldúa's 'open wound' imagery from *Borderlands/La Frontera*. In shifting the description of the border as 'open wound' to the border as 'infected' Gómez-Peña emphasises the crisis of the US–Mexico border in the late 1980s. Later in the text Gómez-Peña provides more insight into his description of the border as 'infected':

> the day I was born
> September 23 of 1955

eternity died
& the border wound became infected
the day my father died
February 17 of 1989
my last tentacle with México broke
& I finally became a Chicano. (p. 54)

Becoming a Chicano is therefore connected with the passing of Gómez-Peña's last familial connection in Mexico. As a result, he notes, he 'finally became a Chicano'. Gómez-Peña's becoming, or identification as a Chicano was thus contingent on becoming an orphan and seeking out a new home. Here, we see Gómez-Peña playing with the meanings of 'documented' and 'undocumented' in the context of the US–Mexico border and immigration and despite being a citizen of the United States he suggests 'I haven't been documented yet/ I'm still an illegal alien'. The poem also refers to the stereotypes projected onto Mexican immigrants (legal or otherwise), as diseased sexual predators involved in drug-smuggling and other crime, apparently maliciously intending to take advantage of the 'welfare' system and determined to destroy the United States. This sarcasm is countered after the first scripted 'Pause' by a more 'genuine' tone, with which Gómez-Peña relinquishes his authority in these matters: 'don't listen to me / I'm just a deterritorialized *"chillango"* / who claims to be a Chicano' (p. 58). Gómez-Peña prefaces his identity – a deterritorialised *chillango* who claims to be a Chicano – with 'just', a sarcastic commentary on how these complex identifications are simplified or dismissed by those who do not understand them. In this context, the term *'chillango'* is a derogatory term used to describe someone who is from Mexico City. In describing himself as a deterritorialised *'chillango'* Gómez-Peña makes no mention of *how* he became deterritorialised – through his deliberate, legal act of crossing the US–Mexico border – instead focusing on his 'claim' to being a Chicano. Gómez-Peña continues in his mockingly self-pitying tone, telling his audience that he is 'not even eligible for amnesty' – the amnesty he refers to here is most likely the 1986 Immigration Control and Reform Act which granted amnesty to 2.7 million people 'without' legal status in the United States – because he never documented his work.[51] This double talk about both legislative concerns and a commentary on the ephemeral nature of performance art is subtle but effectively calls attention to the 'work' done by people illegally working in the United States. He then asks the audience to 'take a photo of this memorable occasion' in order that it may be added to the annals of 'the archives of border culture' and 'the history of performance art', both contested narratives in their own right (p. 58). Sarcastically, he pleads with his audience to photograph him 'to authenticate his existence' (p. 58). This request can be read in two ways: first, it is a critique of how illegal immigrants in the United States are legally classified as undocumented in order not to exist in legislative terms (in the sense of having any rights whatsoever); and second, as an artist, he is asking for his performance to be validated by the act of taking a photograph. The crucial role of the reader/spectator here cannot be overstated. Gómez-Peña draws attention to the fact that the performance cannot exist without documentary proof, yet the audience itself lends existence to the performance, too. In the same way, the stereotypes he takes on and parodies cannot exist without the reader/spectator, showing our complicity with the system he critiques.

Another ironic iteration of the need for authentication of the performance installation is Gómez-Peña and Roberto Sifuentes' *Temple of Confessions*. Premiered in Arizona in 1994, this piece combined the 'pseudo-ethnographic diorama' with more 'traditional' religious dioramas in which Gómez-Peña and his Pocha Nostra colleague Roberto Sifuentes were on display in plexiglass boxes. The space was split into three sites: the Chapel of Desires, the Chapel of Fears, and an in-between morgue-like area between them. Sifuentes sat at an altar in 'the Chapel of Desires' posing as 'El Pre-Columbian Vato' – a 'holy gangmember', sharing his plexiglass box with live cockroaches, an iguana, and random gadgets which included 'a spray can, a whip, realistic weapons, and drug paraphernalia' (*Temple* p. 15). In his box in the Chapel of Fears, Gómez-Peña posed as 'San Pocho Aztlaneca', sitting on a toilet, 'a hyper-exoticised curio shop shaman for spiritual tourists'. Gómez-Peña's costume can best be described as 'Tex-Mex Aztec' and he shares his box with live crickets, taxidermied animals, and 'witchcraft-looking' artifacts (p. 18). After wandering around the spaces, visitors are encouraged to 'confess' in the appropriate temple. They can do so either by kneeling in front of one of the plexiglass boxes and speaking into a microphone, depositing their written confession into an urn, or call a 1-800 number after they have left the event.

The *Temple of Confessions* installation is appropriate to this book's theorisation of reading as queering citizenship as it effectively exhibits one of Gómez-Peña's most intriguing practices: what he calls reverse ethnography. Visitors to the *Temple of Confessions* approached the installation as a whole and Gómez-Peña and Sifuentes in particular as 'authentic' representations of Latino-ness or Mexican-ness. This is of course deliberately perpetrated by Gómez-Peña in order to confront visitors with the realisation of their own racist and exoticised expectations. As Gómez-Peña puts it: 'The installation functions simultaneously as an elaborate set design for a theatre of mythos and as a melancholic ceremonial space for people to reflect on their own racist attitudes towards other cultures' (p. 22). Gómez-Peña deliberately and elaborately stages this in order to elicit spontaneous and honest reactions to examples of extreme and bizarre cultural otherness from visitors. Indeed, Gómez-Peña confirms that the *Temple of Confessions* 'is more about America's cultural projections, and its inability to deal with cultural otherness than about the Latino "other." And in this sense, it is a project of reversed anthropology' (p. 23). Here, Gómez-Peña's inversion of 'anthropological' practices is a thinly veiled but intelligent critique of early Eurocentric anthropological fieldwork carried out by white academics to 'study' other non-white, 'primitive' indigenous cultures. In the *Temple of Confessions*, the power dynamic of the visitors' white gaze is reversed. The visitors are 'asked to swallow their fears and to question any ethnocentric assumptions they might have about otherness, Mexico, Mexicans, other languages, and alternative art forms' (*New World Border* p. 7). In this way, the installation is as much the work of the visitors as it is the work of the artists.

The confessions themselves represent yet another facet of this process. Not only do Gómez-Peña and his collaborators present visitors with their own bizarre projections of 'otherness' but they also then ask (non-coercively) that the visitors record a confession. These confessions, some of which are shared in *Temple of Confessions* and other books authored by Gómez-Peña, add another dimension to this process of reverse anthropology and are symptomatic of what Gómez-Peña understands to be 'America's obsession with public and private confession' – in other words, another facet of reality television (*Temple of Confessions* p. 14). What many of these confessions have in common is their brutal honesty, something that Gómez-Peña and his collaborators did not actually expect: 'The kind of recorded and written confessions we obtain through this [type of] project, I believe, couldn't possibly be obtained through fieldwork, direct interviews, or talk radio', notes Gómez-Peña (*Temple of Confessions* p. 22). The confessions' themes ranged from sexual fantasies, to articulations of fear, anger, and pseudo-intellectual attempts at understanding the *Temple of Confessions* installation.

Gómez-Peña's performances discussed above do more than just present a critique of citizenship; they also encourage the visitor, audience member, or reader to rethink their position on citizenship based on their personal experiences of the performance, installation, or text. One of the ways in which Gómez-Peña does this is by defamiliarising his performances and texts. This works to unbalance the viewer's or reader's expectations, eliciting a more spontaneous thought process and reaction. Once again, the *Temple of Confessions* cannot exist without the reader/spectator and Gómez-Peña actively seeks out language and images that can prompt his reader/spectator: 'The ultimate goal is to look for images that will create a disturbing sediment in the consciousness of the spectator, images that the audience cannot easily escape from, that will haunt them in dreams, in conversations, in memories' (*Dangerous* p. 168). This is the crux of the matter; Gómez-Peña sees performance art not only as a medium, but as a language. As he puts it, describing his very first public performance piece after moving to the United States: 'The strong emotional responses from my involuntary audiences made me realize what an ideal medium performance was to insert my existential and political dilemmas into the social sphere ... in my new language, performance art' (*Ethno-Techno* p. 6). Gómez-Peña's experience with audiences is what leads him to theorise the impact of his performances:

> You walk out of a performance feeling troubled and perplexed. The performance triggers a process of reflexivity that continues through days and sometimes weeks, creating sediments in the consciousness of people. People slowly begin to come to terms with the images and make up their minds about what they saw, but it takes them weeks, even months. Sometimes people think they are offended because they don't want to face certain realities or certain feelings they harbor. (*Dangerous* p. 169)

Here, Gómez-Peña has clearly presented his articulation of the process I call the civic act of reading using the language of his performance practice. This identification of realities that need new languages and vocabularies to be represented or articulated is something that

Gómez-Peña grapples with: 'one of the many jobs of an artist is to look for new, fresh metaphors and symbols to help us understand our ever-changing realities and fragmented cultures' (*Dangerous* p. 168). In *Travels in Hyperreality*, Umberto Eco engages with what he sees to be America's fixation with reality and reproduction. Specifically, he focuses on how this need to 'experience' reality is so great that it ultimately results in the creation, or rather, the simulation, of what reality is perceived to be. As he puts it, in order to attain 'the real thing', the 'American imagination ... must fabricate the absolute fake'.[52] The marketing and commodification of this simulated reality serves to further perpetuate the illusion of this real hyperreality. As this becomes accepted by the mainstream, this simulated reality becomes reality, which in turn is perceived as 'not real enough', triggering the cycle once again. Eco's analysis is useful here as another articulation of what Gómez-Peña describes as 'the mainstream bizarre'. For Gómez-Peña, the mainstream bizarre is the most accurate way to describe how people experience reality and the world today. To him, the mainstream bizarre is 'this superficial fascination that the media has with everything "extreme"' (*Ethno-Techno* p. 249). This obsession with extreme reality has implications for performance art and radical thinking, in that very little is considered 'revolutionary' or 'radical'. Indeed, the current work of Gómez-Peña and La Pocha Nostra must negotiate this issue. In this vein, Gómez-Peña asks: 'What do words like "radical," "transgressive," "rebellious," and "oppositional" mean after 9/11?' (*Ethno-Techno* p. 93). Indeed, a very simple way to explain this phenomenon is to consider the events of 9/11. Having been witness to such horror, he believes that people now seem immune to anything less horrifying. In addition, the world order that came into existence in the aftermath of 9/11 does not faze people as one would expect. To illustrate this point, Gómez-Peña gives the example of airport security, suggesting that a practice such as racial profiling, while not actively endorsed by the general population, is seen by the same group as a necessary evil rather than racism.

As part of his study of simulation, Eco also analyses the museum as a site of reproduction and recreation of reality; this too is of interest in the context of Gómez-Peña's work, particularly with regard to his living dioramas (including for example, the *Temple of Confessions*). In the living diorama/performance *The Museum of Fetishized Identities* (2000), Gómez-Peña and his La Pocha Nostra collaborators enact a critique of the corporate multiculturalism they call the 'mainstream bizarre' by posing and performing as extreme personas. Some performance artists played characters including 'Evil Other #27846: El RoboWarrior' and 'The Samoan Cyborg', for example.

One important aspect of a performance piece such as *The Museum of Fetishized Identities* is the role it can play in decolonising the body. With the current fixation on the bizarre and its inevitable focus on the human body, Gómez-Peña is very aware of the how the body is rendered powerless and meaningless by implication. According to Gómez-Peña, in his performances, the 'body is also the very center of our symbolic universe – a tiny model for humankind – and at the same time, a metaphor for the larger sociopolitical body. If we are capable of establishing all these connections in front of an audience, hopefully others will recognize them in their own bodies' (*Ethno-Techno* p. 23). However, given the widespread, almost clichéd spectacle of bizarre bodies, Gómez-Peña and his collaborators ask: 'what prevents us from becoming the very stylized freaks we are attempting to deconstruct or parody?' (*Ethno-Techno* p. 52). As a result, their 'formidable challenge in this respect is how to rehumanize, repoliticize, and decolonize our own bodies wounded by the media and intervened upon by the invisible surgery of pop culture, and to do it in such a way that our audiences are not even aware of it' (*Ethno-Techno* p. 60). Given that 'the mainstream bizarre has effectively blurred the borders between pop culture, performance, and "reality"', Gómez-Peña counteracts this process by cautiously embracing the development and utilising it to his own ends – appropriate to his queered *rasquache* practice (*Ethno-Techno* p. 51).

If the queering of citizenship as I understand it takes place at the theoretical site of the subaltern counterpublic, then in Gómez-Peña's case, the location of this counterpublic is at the intersection of the stage or performance space, upon which he forces the US–Mexico border, the reader/spectator, and his body, both of which function as performance texts. The stage and the body form a nexus at which the public self and the private self intersect and intervene in dominant discourses of citizenship. As Gómez-Peña's performances (both solo and with La Pocha Nostra) progress, they blur and ultimately erase the boundaries between the public and the private self by challenging members of the audience to reconsider the polity and their relationship to the state. For Gómez-Peña, the performance space is a civic site at which the 'goal is to create situations in which people get to exercise their civic will, in which audience members face democratic dilemmas they must resolve in situ'.[53] In pushing members of the audience to make these decisions, Gómez-Peña disrupts their ordinary decision-making processes. The performance area thus becomes a 'safe' space at which civic responsibility can be performed differently.

Inextricable from this discussion is Gómez-Peña's project of recuperating the voice of the artist. The artist occupies a position that is both inside and outside the dominant structures of power – and for this book, citizenship – and as such inhabits a site that allows for a critique of the state while also operating within the vague parameters which allows such a critique to be heard. In the case of Gómez-Peña, this is the site of performance; in the case of citizenship, this is the site at which queering can take place. This is also the site at which solidarity movements can form. As Gomez-Pena himself puts it: 'There is another kind of global culture – not imposed from above but emerging organically from within grassroots communities and the streets. I'm talking about a kind of borderized proletarian *transcultural*, a hybrid culture that often resists, consciously or unconsciously, the "legitimate" forces of globalization.'[54] The 'transcultural' he means here can also be found in the work of Cuban poet Nancy Morejon, for whom

> [t]ransculturation signifies constant interaction, transmutation between two or more cultural components, whose unconscious end is the creation of a third cultural whole – that is, culture – new and independent, although its roots rest on preceding elements. The reciprocal influence here is determining. No element is superimposed on the other; on the contrary, each one becomes a third entity. None remains immutable. All change and grow in a 'give and take' which engenders a new texture.[55]

While Morejon's comments resonate with Homi K. Bhabha's formulation of the 'third space' it is more apt in this context to briefly consider the similarities between the idea of the transcultural and the process of transculturation in the context of Gloria Anzaldúa's work. For Anzaldúa, the new *mestiza* is the embodiment of the process of transculturation in action, as is the process by which the new *mestiza* reaches out to other minority communities to form coalitions. In Gómez-Peña's context, the transcultural becomes a crucial concept, particularly after 9/11.

Performing citizenship, *juntitos* [together]

After 9/11, Gómez-Peña's work shifts in important ways, with a sustained acute focus on the role and responsibility of the artist. As he sees it, his role as an artist has shifted:

> My job may be to open up a temporary utopian/dystopian space, a 'demilitarized zone' in which meaningful 'radical' behaviour and progressive thought are allowed to take place, even if only for the duration for the performance. In this imaginary zone, both artist and audience members are given permission to assume multiple and ever-changing personalities and identities. In this border zone, the distance between 'us' and 'them' self and other, art and life, becomes blurry and unspecific. (*Ethno-Techno* p. 24)

The blurring of 'us' and 'them' is crucial to Gómez-Peña's work as it allows for the oscillation of identifications necessary for the civic action to take place.

In 'America's Most Wanted Inner Demon' from 2003, Gómez-Peña deals with the question of the enemies of the United States, performing three 'enemy' personas (*Ethno-Techno* p. 221). First, El Archeotypal Greaser babbles in tongues before introducing himself as the 'great-great-grandson / of Cortes y La Malinche, / l'enfant de la chingada da-da', a clear allusion to the history of Mexico and the emergence of the *mestizo* race that now constitutes a large proportion of the population of Mexico (*Ethno-Techno* p. 221). Over these three lines of text, Gómez-Peña uses three languages, English, Spanish, and French, to make a point about the colonisation of Mexico and Cortes' colonisation of La Malinche, also known as La Chingada (the fucked one). In describing himself as 'l'enfant de la chingada da-da' El Archeotypal Greaser gives himself a Messiah identity – in French, Jesus is described as 'l'enfant de la bonne Vierge' – and places La Malinche in a position occupied by the Virgin Mary. This move to cast La Malinche as a virgin or a whore, while not innovative or novel, is more a commentary by Gómez-Peña through this persona of how La Malinche has been portrayed since the sixteenth century. The seemingly innocent 'da-da' in that sentence is a reference to Dadaism, about which Gómez-Peña has been vocal. As Robert Alan Neustadt has noted, Gómez-Peña has argued against 'Eurocentric art historians who trace the roots of performance art to Dada' since he sees 'the Mexican *carpa* tradition and Latin American popular theatre as primary influences that developed independently from the Western avant-garde'.[56]

Gómez-Peña then has El Archeotypal Greaser reference 'I am Joaquín', Rodolfo Corky Gonzales' famous epic poem, but changes the words to read: 'Soy yo Joaqin, pero el otro / El que se perdió when crossing the border' [I am Joaqín, but the other one, the one who was lost when crossing the border] (*Ethno-Techno* p. 221, my translation). This play on one of the most famous pieces of Chicano literature, written in slang – Gómez-Peña uses 'Soy yo' rather than the more formal 'Yo soy' of the poem – serves to emphasise the destabilising effects that the (US–Mexico) border has on identity and language. Next in Gómez-Peña's line-up of America's inner demons is 'El Mad Mex'. This pop culture reference to Mad Max is also a reference to another of Gómez-Peña's works, *El Mexterminator*. In this sketch, El Mad Mex provides scathing commentary on Mexican artists (including Gómez-Peña himself): 'all Mexican artists were made in Taiwan; / our body parts assembled by German curators / to perform X-treme art functions / at expos, festivals and TV ads' (*Ethno-Techno* p. 222). This critique of the commodification and mass production of performance art is one that runs throughout Gómez-Peña's work.

Finally, Gómez-Peña transforms into the third persona of the piece: 'El Allatola Whatever'. This persona is complex. Gómez-Peña is performing an 'Arab' character, who states 'Arabs and Latins are / as hard to distinguish from one another / as a Hutu from a Tutsi / or an Irish from a Scot' (*Ethno-Techno* p. 225). According to El Allatola Whatever, 'at this point in time, /outside of Bush's inner circle / we all are "Arabs," or rather / all Arabs are Latin'. As a result, El Allatola suggests, 'I am, I can be, I could be / America's most wanted inner demon' (*Ethno-Techno* p. 225). But Gómez-Peña is doing far more than drawing together the 'otherness' of Arabs and Latinos – he is in fact casting himself as America's most wanted inner demon, using the personas of El Archeotypal Greaser, El Mad Mex, and El Allatola Whatever to mirror the trajectory of his own development as an artist and of his personal identity. As Neustadt notes, it is 'through the embodiment of stereotypes, [that] Gómez-Peña *inhabits* (and de-naturalizes) the dominant images of social contradiction'.[57] As Gomez-Pena puts it:

and my only privilege here is
to be allowed to cross
the many many forbidden borders that exist
between my mouth and your fears.
And now, with your permission,
I will cross the border between 'I' and 'we'. (*Ethno-Techno* p. 226)

Once again Gómez-Peña erases the distinction between the audience (and in this case, reader) and himself. In doing this he momentarily creates a moment in which 'I' and 'we' are the same. Perhaps this moment is best described as solidarity, but it is initially unclear who is showing solidarity with whom, and for what purpose. In crossing the border between 'I' and 'we' Gómez-Peña momentarily becomes the 'you' he addresses on stage. Conversely, crossing this border also allows the 'you' to become the 'I' of the performer on stage. In this way, at some point during the performance, every single member of the audience has the potential to be America's most wanted inner demon. This in turn, Gómez-Peña would suggest, has the distinct potential to allow the 'sediment' to settle in people's minds, making them engage with these ideas and perhaps even changing their minds about, in this case, some aspects of the fear-mongering of the 'War on Terror'. This strategy allows the reader/audience to identify with Gómez-Peña and disidentify with the political process to which he refers.

Gómez-Peña goes further in 'A declaration of poetic disobedience from the new border' from 2004, which echoes the 'We, the People' format of the United States Declaration of Independence (*Ethno-Techno* pp. 227–36). Gómez-Peña continues to blur the I/we distinction. He recites: 'I say, we say: / We generic brown and black males who fit all taxonomic descriptions' thus aligning himself with all people of that group – 'Yes, we are equally scared of one another [...] I speak therefore I continue to be part of "us"' (*Ethno-Techno* p. 227). Gómez-Peña's invocation of the most famous of the United States' founding documents consolidates his argument, undermining the 'we' so that the reader does the same, drawing a line of alliance between herself and the 'other'.

Along these lines, an anonymous 'Cyber-communiqué' from 2003, republished in *Ethno-Techno*, outlines 'The Post-9/11 "rights and privileges" of a U.S. citizen' (*Ethno-Techno* p. 237). This list of ten rights and privileges uses irony to recall the US Bill of Rights which sets out the original ten Amendments to the US Constitution. This list engages directly with social and political fallout that occurred as a (direct or indirect) result of 9/11, such as, for example, number 5, in which Gómez-Peña affirms, 'I have the right to a prompt trial by jury, if I should be accused of a crime, so long as I am not Arab or Arab-looking' – which critiques the Fifth and Sixth Amendments. Number 2 suggests that citizens 'may speak or write as [they] please, so long as [they] do not interfere with the patriotism and intolerance of others', while number 9 asserts that citizens 'have the right to worship a Christian god'; both here speak directly to the First Amendment, which famously states that 'Congress shall make no law respecting an establishment of religion, or prohibiting the free exercise thereof; or abridging the freedom of speech, or of the press; or the right of the people peaceably to assemble, and to petition the Government for a redress of grievances'.[58]

Gómez-Peña also suggests strategies for the creation of solidarity groups and movements; while these are for the most part humorous, they also quietly shed light on the absurdity of the post-9/11 United States. For example, in a Cyber Communique from 2001 that was banned by National Public Radio, Gomez-Pena and Elaine Katzenberger provide a list of 'Helpful performance tips on how to avoid xenophobia and express solidarity with innocent Arab-Americans after 9/11' (*Ethno-Techno* p. 235). In this list they suggest that '[i]n order to avoid misled racist attacks, all Arab-Americans should wear a mariachi hat and a Mexican *zarape* when going out in public. All Arab-looking Latinos and South Asians should follow suit' (*Ethno-Techno* p. 235). On the surface this seems to be a humorous but well-intentioned solidarity tactic; upon closer inspection it illustrates the shifting nature of 'Otherness' in the United States. Gómez-Peña and Katzenberger's suggestion that the current 'Other' (Arab-American) don the apparel of the stereotype of former (or at least less immediate) 'Others' (Latinos/Mexicans, South Asians, or Native Americans) in order to pass as non-threatening is unequivocally ironic. Indeed, the assertion that one can be phenotypically 'Arab-looking' is deliberately inserted into the text so that when read, can seem ridiculous but is effective in provoking a response. However, and most significantly, this is a list of 'helpful performance tips' that provides additional proof that passing as non-threatening (read: white) in the United States after 9/11 requires a performance and an act rather than a reliance on legal, inalienable rights.

The final performance piece explored in this chapter is Gómez-Peña's 'El Mexorcist (A Performance)'. This performance was published in 2006 but is in fact a collection of poetic prose pieces dating back over the five years preceding its publication, further evidence of Gomez-Pena's reliance on *rasquache*.[59] Gómez-Peña begins by exclaiming: 'Today is an extremely special day for humankind' because 'War is over' ('El Mexorcist' p. 13). The clearly sarcastic but simultaneously utopian tenor of these remarks set the tone for the rest of the performance: 'We are all extremely happy, no shit [...] War is over my dear contemporaries ... at least for the duration of this performance' (p. 13). Immediately the performance text displays its own self-reflexivity – we are *reading* a performance that has given itself an expiration date. For the duration of the performance, war is over; is this the same duration as reading the same text? Without providing an answer, Gómez-Peña immediately regrounds the reader/audience by turning to the theme of his own body, and retelling an incident that he has written about in several other texts: the infliction of his 45th scar. Years earlier he handed a dagger to a member of the audience, offered her his abdomen and said: 'Here ... my colonized body ... My solar plexus ... your moon-like madness' – and the woman 'went for it' (p. 6). This reminder of the full corporeal commitment of the performance artist is necessary as it assists the audience in their suspension of disbelief. About midway through the text, Gómez-Peña informs the audience of his 'main subject matter: Mapping' (p. 11). This trope resurfaces continually in his work on topography and cartography, and in this instance he is:

> Mapping the immediate future
> so you and I can walk on it
> without falling inside the great faults of history.
> You & I, verbally walking together,
> You & I, an ephemeral community
> You & I, a tiny little nation-state
> You & I, a one-hour-long utopia titled 'You & I'
> Alone on stage
> Fighting together the World Bank,
> the WTO & Bush Cartel,
> Fighting Avant-garde desire & the Patriot Act
> *Tu y yo, juntitos.* [You & I, together][60]
> Fighting isolation and isolationism

But who are you, really? (p. 11)

Most evident in this sketch is the creation of a relationship between the reader(s)/audience member(s) and Gómez-Peña himself. Significantly it is unclear whether the 'you' he addresses is singular (one audience member, or one reader) or plural (the entire audience, or the community of readers) – and this ambiguity is emphasised by his refusal to use the pronoun 'we'. More crucially, however, he defines the parameters of this 'You & I' relationship: in this performance Gómez-Peña sees himself as 'mapping the immediate future' in order that 'you and I can walk on it / without falling inside the great faults of history'. There are at least two layers of suggestion here, first that history is at fault, and that these faults inevitably impact the future – part of Gómez-Peña's larger critique of dominant histories – and second, that the future, in the alternative world inhabited by this performance, is unclear, is characterised by fault lines of seismic proportions to which 'You & I' could lay victim. What will happen in this immediate future, Gómez-Peña asks, given that for the duration of this performance, there is no war?

In utilising 'you' synecdochically, Gómez-Peña is able to convincingly show the various iterations of what 'You & I' can do: 'verbally [walk] together', in order to form 'an ephemeral community' that functions as 'a tiny little nation-state'. This coupled with the ambiguity of to whom 'you' refers suggests that the singular 'you' can effectively signify the entire audience/readership. The common usage of 'you' to signify the third person singular augments its synecdochic value by suggesting a broader, quasi-universal audience. Significant here is the role that language plays; 'You & I' walk *verbally* – a clear indication that conversation and dialogue are crucial to the formation of the utopian community and nation state Gómez-Peña aspires to forming. The utopian performance entitled 'You & I' sees Gómez-Peña and his interlocutor 'Alone on stage / Fighting together the World Bank, / the WTO & Bush Cartel' – an example of how this pairing has the potential to resist the powerful institutions that quietly control our everyday lives. Alternatively, given that 'El Mexorcist' is a performance script and is intended to be read aloud by Gómez-Peña, the same lines could read: ' "You & I" alone on stage / fighting'. This simple shift reflects the ease with which even a utopian community and 'a tiny little nation-state' can implode and be overwhelmed by both internal and external factors. However, the poem can be read as going even further to accuse the World Bank, the WTO and the Bush Cartel – three 'institutions' that control key factors, including money and currency, trade regulation, and oil economies – of 'Fighting Avant-garde desire'. The ambiguity of the text only becomes readily clear once the reader has been reminded that it is intended for performance, which Gómez-Peña provides with the stand-alone phrase 'Alone on stage'. He then reiterates the need for '*Tu y yo, juntitos*' to combat 'isolation and isolationism' – these are considered hallmarks of the United States since the Patriot Act, recalling the signature character of the United States: exceptional. Finally, as if to unravel all of this work, Gómez-Peña closes by asking: 'But who are you, really?' Again the verbal and performance nature of this piece becomes significant, as this question can be asked in two differing ways: first, it asks who the 'you' of the 'You & I' couple is – is it a single audience member, the entire audience, or the reader? Second, it asks a more personal question of the reader or audience member: 'Who are you?' As Kuhnheim has noted, 'Gómez-Peña continually utilizes this inclusion/exclusion strategy to aggressively position his audience in performance and text. He creates his "other" in the process of creating his "self" (both discursive stances), demonstrating the mutual dependence and antagonism between these positions'.[61] Once again, the reader is pushed to engage in the processes of identification and disidentification.

Immediately after this section of the performance, Gómez-Peña inserts a 'Harsh Pause' before addressing the audience directly, asking: 'Does anyone have anything to say about my text / at this point? / I said my text, not my performance skills, / Not my looks, or my voice, / just my text ...' (p. 11). The irony here lies in the fact that, as I have shown, Gómez-Peña's body is itself a text, as made evident by his many scars. After taking notes on the audience's answers, he confirms, 'I am writing down / your words will change my next performance' (p. 11). Once again, the line break is intended to be manipulated to unbalance readerly interpretations, perhaps to suggest: 'I am writing down your words / [which] will change my next performance.' In either scenario, the suggestions and feedback of the audience serve to change Gómez-Peña's body, which functions as a performance text in the same way the literal performance script does.

Over the course of this chapter I have shown how through his use of a queered *rasquache* Gómez-Peña is able to embody and perform the US–Mexico border, exposing the reader to its complexity and enacting a shift in readerly engagement with the border itself.

Formally, Gómez-Peña's writing and performances allow for readings that draw open sites for multiplicity and contradiction, impelling multivalent engagements by the reader. In each of the performance texts analysed here, Gómez-Peña calls attention to the flawed principles behind dominant understandings of what citizenship is in the first place. While much of his criticism is aimed at the United States and its conception and application of citizenship, it is important to note that Gómez-Peña's focus on the United States is productive because it can be used to consider other situations of domination and privilege. In the next chapter, I show how Erín Moure's *O Cidadán* exposes the figure of the citizen – her *cidadán* – as an enactment across boundaries, constituted by and of her readers.

Notes

1 Guillermo Gómez-Peña, '1492 Performances', in *Dangerous Border Crossers: The Artist Talks Back* (London and New York: Routledge, 2000), p. 3. All subsequent references to this collection will appear parenthetically in the text.
2 Guillermo Gómez-Peña, *Warrior for Gringostroika* (St. Paul: Graywolf Press, 1993); *The New World Border: Prophecies, Poems, and Loqueras for the End of the Century* (San Francisco: City Lights Books, 1996); *Ethno-Techno: Writings on Performance, Activism, and Pedagogy* (London and New York: Routledge, 2005). With Roberto Sifuentes: *Temple of Confessions: Mexican Beasts and Living Santos* (New York: Powerhouse Books, 1997). All subsequent references to these collections will appear parenthetically in the text.
3 In the remainder of this chapter I use the terms in each of the following groupings interchangeably: performer/writer and reader/audience/spectator.
4 See, for example, 'Top Ten Abuses of Power Since 9/11' (n.d.). www.aclu.org/other/top-ten-abuses-power-911 (accessed 18 July 2016).
5 Taunya Lovell Banks, 'Mestizaje and the Mexican Mestizo Self: no hay sangre negra, so there is no blackness', *Southern California Interdisciplinary Law Journal* 15 (2006): pp. 199–234.
6 Ibid., p. 214.
7 Ibid. For more on this, see Martha Menchaca, 'Chicano Indianism: A Historical Account of Racial Repression in the United States', *American Ethnologist* 20:3 (1993): pp. 583–603; Moisés González Navarro, 'Mestizaje in Mexico During the National Period', in *Race and Class in Latin America*, ed. Magnus Mörner (New York: Columbia University Press, 1965), pp. 145–69.

8   Ibid., p. 220. For more on this, see Reginald Horsman, *Race and Manifest Destiny: The Origins of American Racial Anglo-Saxonism* (Cambridge, MA: Harvard University Press, 1981), p. 208 and Mónica Russel y Rodríguez, 'Mexicanas and Mongrels: Policies of Hybridity, Gender and Nation in the US-Mexican War', *Latino Studies Journal* 11:3 (2000): pp. 49–73.
9   Ibid., p. 232.
10 Banks, 'Mestizaje and the Mexican Mestizo Self', p. 218.
11 For further clarification of this last point, see The Treaty of Guadalupe Hidalgo (1848).
12 Rudolfo 'Corky' Gonzalez, 'Yo Soy Joaquín'. http://americanwiki.pbworks.com/w/page/12595270/I%20am%20Joaquin%20(Yo%20Soy%20Joaquin (accessed 2 September 2012).
13 Banks, 'Mestizaje and the Mexican Mestizo Self', p. 224. For more on this, see Laura E. Gómez, *Manifest Destinies: The Making of the Mexican American Race* (New York: New York University Press, 2007).
14 It is also worth noting here that *pocho* is also the title of an early Chicano novel by José Antonio Villarreal (1959).
15 Roger Bartra, 'Introduction', trans. Coco Fusco, in Gómez-Peña, *Warrior for Gringostroika*, pp. 11–14, at p. 12.
16 Tomás Ybarra-Frausto, 'Rasquachismo: A Chicano Sensibility', in *Chicano Art: Resistance and Affirmation, 1965–1985*, ed. Teresa McKenna, Yvonne Yarbro-Bejarano, and Richard Griswold del Castillo (Los Angeles: Wright Art Gallery, 1991), pp. 155–62; Amalia Mesa-Bains, 'Domesticana: The Sensibility of Chicana Rasquache', in *Distant Relations: A Dialogue among Chicano, Irish, and Mexican Artists*, ed. Trisha Ziff (New York: Smart Art Press, 1996), pp. 156–63.
17 For more on this, see José Esteban Muñoz, 'Choteo/Camp Style Politics: Carmelita Tropicana's Performance of Self Enactment', *Women and Performance: A Journal of Feminist Theory. New Hybrid Identities: Performing Race/Gender/Nation/Sexuality* 7:2–8:1 (1995): pp. 39–51.
18 Mesa-Bains, 'Domesticana', p. 158.
19 Robert Neustadt, 'Guillermo Gómez-Peña: Dragging Representation'. http://fuentes.csh.udg.mx/CUCSH/Sincronia/neustadt.html (accessed 12 June 2012).
20 Gerald Vizenor, 'Aesthetics of Survivance: Literary Criticism and Practice', in *Survivance: Narratives of Native Presence*, ed. Gerald Vizenor (Omaha: University of Nebraska Press, 2008), pp. 1–24, at p. 2.
21 Rafaela G. Castro, *Chicano Folklore: A Guide to the Folktales, Traditions, Rituals and Religious Practices of Mexican-Americans* (New York: Oxford University Press, 2001), p. 2.
22 Ramon García, 'Against Rasquache: Chicano Identity and the Politics of Popular Culture in Los Angeles', *Critica: A Journal of Critical Essays* (1998): pp. 1–26.

23 Ramon García, 'Session Three: Staking the Claim: Introducing Chicana/o Cultural Studies', in *The Chicana/o Cultural Studies Forum: Critical and Ethnographic Practices*, ed. Angie Chabram-Dernersesian (New York: New York University Press, 2007), pp. 54–132, at p. 125.
24 Ibid.
25 Ibid.
26 Marjorie Garber, *Vested Interests: Cross-Dressing and Cultural Anxiety* (New York: Harper Perennial, 1993), p. 16.
27 Neustadt, 'Guillermo Gómez-Peña: Dragging Representation', n.p.
28 Judith Butler, *Gender Trouble: Feminism and the Subversion of Identity* (New York: Routledge, 1999 [1990]), p. 174.
29 Ibid., p. 175.
30 Peggy Phelan, *Unmarked: The Politics of Performance* (New York: Routledge, 1992), p. 146.
31 Ibid., p. 11.
32 Jill S. Kuhnheim, 'The Economy of Performance: Gómez-Peña's New World Border', *Modern Fiction Studies* 44 (1998): pp. 24–35, at p. 27.
33 Guillermo Gómez-Peña, 'El Mexorcist (A Performance)', *Journal of Visual Culture* 5:1 (2006): pp. 5–15, at p. 5. All subsequent references to this performance text will appear parenthetically in the text.
34 Guillermo Gómez-Peña, 'In Defense of Performance Art' (n.d.). www.pochanostra.com/antes/jazz_pocha2/mainpages/in_defense.htm (accessed 5 April 2010).
35 Kuhnheim, 'The Economy of Performance', p. 25.
36 Ibid.
37 Robert Neustadt, *(Con)Fusing Signs and Postmodern Positions: Spanish American Performance, Experimental Writing, and the Critique of Political Confusion* (New York: Garland Publishing Inc., 1999), p. 134.
38 Guillermo Gómez-Peña and Lisa Wolford, 'Navigating the Minefields of Utopia: A Conversation', *The Drama Review* 26:2 (2002): pp. 66–96, at p. 69.
39 Ibid., p. 79.
40 Ibid., p. 68.
41 Ibid., p. 68.
42 George Lipsitz, 'Not Just Another Poster Movement: Poster Art and the Movimiento Chicano', in *Just Another Poster? Chicano Graphic Arts in California*, exh. cat., ed. Chon A. Noriega (Santa Barbara: University Art Museum, University of California, Santa Barbara, 2001), pp. 71–87.
43 Amanda Morrison, 'Performance Review: Guillermo Gomez-Peña brings Borderland Aesthetics to the Avant-Garde', *Text, Practice, Performance IV* (2003): pp. 133–8, at p. 136.
44 Gómez-Peña, *Warrior for Gringostroika*, p. 47.
45 Anzaldúa, *Borderlands/La Frontera*, p. 25.

46 Bartra, 'Introduction', p. 12.
47 Neustadt, (Con)Fusing Signs and Postmodern Positions, p. 135.
48 Guillermo Gómez-Peña, 'Excerpt from Philosophical Tantrum, 2005' (n.d.). http://hemisphericinstitute.org/hemi/en/e-misferica-81/gomez-pena (accessed 20 February 2013).
49 Guillermo Gómez-Peña, 'Border Brujo: A Performance Poem (from the series "Documented/Undocumented")', The Drama Review 35:3 (1991): pp. 48–66, at p. 49. All subsequent references to this performance poem will appear parenthetically in the text. Gómez-Peña regularly recounts an incident when he and his son (who is blond) were out for lunch at a restaurant in Los Angeles. Other patrons of the restaurant grew suspicious of Gómez-Peña because, despite being Guillermo Emiliano's father, did not look like he could be, because he was not white. Gómez-Peña was arrested for ostensibly kidnapping his own son. In the piece, he discusses the humiliation he endured, despite being a legal alien, simply because of his appearance.
50 Ibid.
51 The Immigration Reform and Control Act, 1986 – Public Law 99–603. www.uscis.gov/ilink/docView/PUBLAW/HTML/PUBLAW/0-0-0-15.html (accessed 9 April 2013).
52 Umberto Eco, Travels in Hyperreality, trans. William Weaver (London: Pan, 1987), p. 8.
53 Gómez-Peña and Wolford, 'Navigating the Minefields of Utopia', p. 95.
54 Guillermo Gomez-Pena, Guillermo Gomez-Pena: Conversations Across Borders, ed. Laura Levin (London: Seagull Books, 2011), p. 111.
55 Nancy Morejón, 'Race and Nation', in AfroCuba: An Anthology of Cuban Writing on Race, Politics and Culture, ed. Pedro Perez Sarduy and Jean Stubbs (Melbourne: Ocean Press, 1993), pp. 227–37, at p. 228.
56 Neustadt, (Con)Fusing Signs and Postmodern Positions, p. 147.
57 Ibid., p. 34.
58 Ibid., and The United States Bill of Rights. www.ourdocuments.gov/doc.php?doc=13&page=transcript (accessed 20 February 2016).
59 I saw Gómez-Peña perform the piece in 2008, and while the 2006 written text bears striking similarities to the 2008 performance, it is by no means the 'same' work.
60 My translation.
61 Kuhnheim, 'The Economy of Performance', p. 29.

5
The antianaesthetic and 'a community of readers' in Erín Moure's *O Cidadán*

Each of the previous chapters has discussed how the work of a 'peripheral person' can be mobilised to push readers to blur the boundaries of the status and performance of citizenship, enacting a queering of the concept. I have explored how Anzaldúa and Allison create alternative queer communities of belonging, while Scofield and Gómez-Peña use, among other strategies, synecdoche as a device to position the reader as occupying the place of the 'other' (whether singular or plural). These acts of reading unbalance the relationship between 'self' and 'other', working to destabilise both terms. In the context of citizenship, the reader is then equipped to envision and practise new civic acts.

This chapter examines the strategies used by queer Canadian language poet Erín Moure in her 2002 collection *O Cidadán* to do the same. The analysis of Moure's poetry in this chapter is markedly different from that of Anzaldúa, Allison, Scofield, and Gómez-Peña's work, first in its focus on one particular text, but principally because the multiple layers of intertextuality in Moure's writing preclude static or linear readings. The readings here locate several entry points to *O Cidadán* and weave them together, while being aware of the innumerably different possible permutations of any interpretive strategy. In its discussion of *O Cidadán*, this chapter also relies heavily on Moure's *My Beloved Wager*, a 2009 collection of her own critical essays in which she provides essential commentary on her own work.

This chapter explores *O Cidadán*'s critique of established ideas of citizenship and its formulation of an alternative narrative of citizenship and community building, with Moure's figure of the *cidadán* at its core. Embedded within Moure's narrative are specific writing and reading practices that challenge the reader to act on the text, constituting the reader as a civic subject *within* this alternative narrative. Equally crucial in *O Cidadán* is Moure's focus on destabilising language.

The argument is structured along several intersecting lines. It begins by contextualizing Erín Moure, briefly considering *O Cidadán* within her larger oeuvre. It then outlines her critique of conventional citizenship before moving to an extended definition of the *cidadán*. Briefly moving away from the thematic dimension of *O Cidadán* the chapter discusses Moure's writing and reading practices in order to clarify how they both inform and are informed by her theorisation of the *cidadán*. Finally, the chapter examines how the reader engages with *O Cidadán* in terms of the act of reading and its implications for the constitution of a civic reading subject in the North American context.

Born in 1955 in Calgary, Alberta, Erín Moure moved to Vancouver in 1974 and began writing poetry soon after. Her first collection, *Empire, York Street*, was published in 1979 and since then she has published forty-five volumes of poetry, critical essays, translations, and collaborations with other poets.[1] With a career spanning over three decades, a series of pseudonyms and alteregos – Moure changes the spelling of her name regularly– and the multilingual character of her work – she writes in English, French, Galician, Portuguese, and Spanish, and has collaborated in Romanian – Moure's poetry is distinctive in its content, form, and style.

O Cidadán is the last in a trilogy of collections dealing with themes of language, feeling, responsibility, and identity within the spaces occupied by peripheral peoples.[2] It is a radically dialogic text in which Moure melds her poetry with the work of a range of other writers, critical, cultural, and political theorists, and philosophers. In terms of its structure, *O Cidadán* is composed of three series of distinct 'forms': 'Georgette' love poems, numbered 'document' prose poems, and individually titled 'Catalogue of harms' poems. While each series is distinct from the others, Moure deftly connects them through a sustained focus on different dimensions of the theme of citizenship. In addition, Moure experiments with type, type size, orientation, and seemingly handwritten notes, and uses shapes, symbols, crosswords, fractions, and computer-generated images to emphasise the difficulty of her project to rethink borders and citizenship. According to Johanna Skibsrud:

Moure draws attention to borders by literalizing them on the page – not just metaphorically but *literally* exceeding the boundaries she has drawn – and thus calls into question the notion of exteriority and interiority in terms of both social and personal constraints that define what must be 'kept in' and what should remain outside.³

These notions of interiority and exteriority and the related issues of inclusion and exclusion abound in *O Cidadán* and can be seen as early its opening pages. Moure's dedication of the collection is to, among others,

> *two young Africans who tried to call out to Europe,*
> *with the body (mortos) of writing (escridas nos seus petos):*
> *Yaguine Koita and Fodé Tounkara.*⁴

Such a dedication compels active and attentive readers to research and discover the identities of Koita and Tounkara, who were 'found in the cargo hold of a plane in Brussels in August 1998'. Their deaths 'tried to call out to' governments, 'Excellencies, gentlemen, and responsible citizens of Europe', a call as relevant now as it was then, shedding light on the ongoing struggles of refugees across the globe. Moure's inclusion of Koita's and Tounkara's story is an indictment of the political systems that are complicit in events that 'end' with the desperate acts (and deaths) of people such as Koita and Tounkara. Framing *O Cidadán* in such a way immediately positions her work in opposition to those European states whose immigration policies forced Koita and Tounkara to stow away in the cargo hold of a plane rather than have the opportunity to be 'legally' included within Europe.

A few pages previously, opposite the beginning of the contents pages, is an uncited passage in faded typescript taken from Titus Livy's comments in *The History of Rome*. These comments, 'The subjects to which I would ask each of my readers to devote their earnest attention to are these – the life and morals of the community', can be found in Livy's 'Preface to the Founding of a City', in which Livy sets out his approaches and methodology – a convention at the time.⁵ It is also in this section of his *History* that Livy points out that his narrative is but one version of the history of Rome, and focuses on the founding principles as well as what he calls 'these modern days in which the might of a long paramount nation is wasting by internal decay'.⁶ More to the point, Livy asks his readers to pay 'earnest' attention to '*quae vita, qui mores*' (the life and morals of the community) for these are the true foundations of Rome (and by extension, the Roman Empire). This last comment can be directly connected to Moure's own agenda in *O Cidadán*. Indeed, her critique of community and citizenship in the contemporary context has much in common with Livy's observation that the nation 'is wasting by internal decay'. Like Livy, in using this passage at the very start of the collection, Moure addresses her readers, requiring them 'to devote their earnest attention' to 'the life and morals of the community', a community she calls for and creates over the course of *O Cidadán*, and one that she believes can be brought into being and nurtured through the communal reading and writing of poetry.

Moure's critique of democracy in *O Cidadán* is grounded in her understanding of the (modern) *polis* as 'a social organization'.[7] According to Moure, 'we live in an age of civic despair' in which the *polis* is 'entropic' (p. 59). Indeed, she insists that 'entropy is the organizing law of the City' (p. 60). Moure sees poetry as key to unsettling and, ultimately, undoing the law, 'because it both precedes and passes through that Law: it precedes it, for poetry is yet unsettled and passes through it, for even poetry can't avoid the Law' (p. 60). Even memory, according to Moure, cannot avoid the Law since that too 'is mediated by language, by the conceptual frameworks buried in language, as use values' (p. 60). Poetry has this potential to undermine the Law because its 'sound precedes the forms acceptable to the law: representation, meaning, codification'. But Moure warns against using poetry simply to oppose the Law, as it runs the risk of either being defined using the Law's terms or being contained by it: 'Sometimes to threaten the civic order only makes the order more pernicious and invasive' (p. 60). Accordingly, Moure asks that 'our voices [...] leak out *before* the Law settles, or have to keep unsettling it' (p. 61). What Moure is advocating can also be recognised as the processes of queering citizenship that is explored over the course of *Crossing borders and queering citizenship*. Her comments shed light on what she sees as strategies used by the Law (in this case, Law refers to the patriarchal, heteronormative, and neo-colonial character of the modern nation state) to pre-empt and counteract resistance and dissent. In this sense, Moure's call to continue unsettling the Law is the promise of queer studies' call to persist in interrogating the status quo rather than normalising it. Likewise, there are useful parallels to be made when Moure advises her readers to '[a]void falling into difference as mere opposition. It's the *same* thing. And one reinforces the other. Perpetuates the civic order, the Polis' (p. 61). To reconnect briefly to the context of the framework set out in a previous chapter, Moure's words are echoes of Gloria Anzaldúa's, who writes:

> It is not enough to stand on the opposite river bank, shouting questions, challenging white, patriarchal conventions. A counterstance locks one into a duel of oppressor and oppressed [and] all reaction is limited by, and dependent on what it is reacting against. But it is not a way of life.[8]

Both Anzaldúa and Moure insist that those groups merely *reacting* to the Law run the risk of being 'recuperated as marginal into the social order', a strategy of containment that gives the illusion of subversion and transformation but in actuality reinforces the very Law it rejects and works to overcome (*My Beloved Wager* p. 65). This is also reminiscent of Muñoz's understanding of disidentification as positive action rather than simple reaction.

Before moving further into Moure's critique of citizenship, it may prove useful to recall my broader definitions of citizenship and community in order to more fully appreciate the depth and breadth of Moure's critique and her articulation of an alternative narrative. At the beginning of this book, when setting out my theoretical model and methodology, I used T. H. Marshall's definition of a citizenship as a starting point for my analysis. According to Marshall, citizenship is 'a direct sense of community membership based on loyalty to a civilization which is a common possession'. As I noted then, this concept of citizenship is contingent on a community that on the ground and in our lived realities translates as the nation state. In this framework, the citizen is bound by national and state borders, that is, implicitly and explicitly tied into narratives of territory, belonging and some notion of a shared history (or to use Marshall's words, a 'civilization that is a common possession'). By definition this citizen is (ideally) capable of engaging and identifying with this common civilisation and culture, co-creating a sense of national belonging with other citizens. The principal and underlying assumption in this relationship is its basis in the idea of sameness and the notion that all citizens engage with this 'common' culture in the same way. Since to be a citizen one enjoys this shared attachment to a civilisation that is a common possession, the logical implication is that this dynamic is the same for all. However, it does not account for those citizens who do not see this culture as 'common' to their experience. What then of difference, Moure wonders, in 'document17 (sainte terre)': 'Where difference is founded upon a model of the "same," we are in the / realm of Law, serving only what has been previously established' (*O Cidadán* p. 47, lines 1–2). Frameworks such as Marshall's imply that citizens are seen by the state as the same, that is, interchangeable. This assumption of sameness connects to the various other assumed characteristics of the citizen (in the dominant framework). In addition to attachment to a nebulous (and loaded) concept such as civilisation, the citizen is bound by an attachment to the physical territory occupied by this civilisation (which in turn clarifies the citizen's attachment to the state), that is, one is a citizen or the smallest unit of a discrete entity, the state, which itself necessitates the physicality of territory. A further implication here is the expectation of loyalty to the state; indeed, dominant thinking about citizenship equates this feeling of belonging to civilisation that Marshall takes for granted to loyalty to the state engendered by this civilisation. What emerges most clearly from this discussion is the need not only to clarify the relationship between the citizen and the state, but also to examine the concept and role of the state as an entity that defines and represents citizens.

In *O Cidadán*, Moure is interested in identifying the mechanism through which the state exercises its authority and regulates its citizens. Certainly the state is founded on one variation of a social contract, which casts the state as an immutable yet organic organism rather than an entity that imposes laws, for example. Legal processes such as voting and elections lend legitimacy to the state as an organism, and in such a scenario citizens are seen as integral to legislative processes. It is here that Moure takes issue with traditional understandings of the citizen and the relationship between the citizen and the state. Indeed, this is one of the relationships she hopes to 'unmask' in her writing. Part of this process of unmasking is identifying what Moure calls the anaesthetising tendencies of ideology, language, and representation. In fact, Moure goes so far as to advocate what she calls 'the anti-anaesthetic', which is crucial to her view that the true relation of the citizen to the state is masked. This is most evident to Moure in the way that the word 'citizen' is played out in language. Moure makes this clearest in her preface to *O Cidadán*, in which she remarks that the word 'citizen' has a masculine inflection with only a feminine supplement. It is for this reason that

Moure uses the term *'cidadán'*, which is able to 'intersect' the word and concept of 'citizen'. The preface foreshadows Moure's own methodology and theoretical approaches and assumptions in her poetic study of the citizen, and writing in general: 'If', she asks, 'a names [sic] force or power is "a *historicity* ... a sedimentation, a repetition that congeals," can the name be [...] set in motion again' (p. v, lines 12–14). The issue here is one of language: Moure also argues that 'language itself is ideology and dominance and oppression ... Poems that say poetry is not political are usually just reinforcing the dominant order without questioning or acknowledging that it is there'.[9] Moure's work takes the masculine-generic word 'citizen' and the feminine word for 'citizen' in Galician and enacts a semantic pandemonium to both in order to create a new generic form of citizen: 'o *cidadán*'. This is in line with what Eugenia Sojka sees as a function of language writers, who she says 'believe that political structures are informed and supported by particular verbal structures; when they are questioned and dismantled they open as space for social transformation'.[10]

Moure's writing acts transform the very language used to discuss the citizen, and are transgressive, for '[i]f women writers choose the standard genres they also implicitly agree to the status quo and hence to the invisibility of woman in a literary discourse. To avoid this, women writers opt for a dialogue with the patriarchal tradition. They engage in multiple acts of transgression, in multiple acts of subversive translation/transformance'.[11] Moure's entire writing practice works to undermine and call into question the more traditional and conventional understandings of poetry in general and language poetry in particular. This is evident in her use of space on the page, for example, which connects back to the influence of American and Canadian language poets such as bpNichol, Ron Silliman, Charles Bernstein, Susan Howe, Lyn Hejinian, and Carla Harryman. That said, an equally strong influence on Moure has been the work of Canadian feminist writers such as Nicole Brossard, Daphne Marlatt, Gail Scott, Lola Lemire Tostevin, and Betsy Warland whose work exposed her to language poetry that is simultaneously marked by gender. This Canadian (and specifically Québécois) articulation of gender-marked writing uses as its inspiration the decidedly French feminist *écriture féminine* (feminine writing). I argue that Moure's writing can be characterised by its engagement with the writing practice referred to in Québec as *écriture au féminin*, and as such can be considered an example of gender marked writing. Since the practice of *écriture au féminin* (also referred to as writing in the feminine) is to write '*through a feminist consciousness*', Moure's writing in O *Cidadán* traces the contours of a citizen who is not *automatically* gendered as male and not constrained by the boundaries of the state.[12]

As a text that practices a mode of *écriture au féminin*, Moure's O *Cidadán* argues for 'a notion of frontier or border as a line that admits filtrations, that leaks'.[13] At its core O *Cidadán* entails a radical questioning and requestioning of how borders work and what citizens do. Using the figurative *cidadán*, Moure's imagined citizen, the poetry in O *Cidadán* works to cross and recross the boundaries of reading practices, the state and society, and language in the same way *écriture au féminin* does. Moure writes: 'To push these boundaries is, I believe, to take up a civic responsibility, but also not to censor myself or accept old notions of the self and body, or of language, in personal relationships or in society. It is not a process of resistance, of an "antiaesthetic," but one of productive openings towards an *elsewhere*, beyond a dialectical norm – an *anti-anaesthetic*' (*My Beloved Wager* p. 161).

From the outset, *écriture au féminin* shows the influence of Hélène Cixous and Luce Irigaray, both of whom were instrumental in theorising what Cixous would later, in 'Laugh of the Medusa', call *écriture féminine* or feminine writing. *Ecriture féminine* is, in a general sense, a kind of writing that is anti-logocentric and anti-phallic. I use Cixous' theory in its broader sense; that is, I do not see it as a static theory that is limited to formulating a very specific kind of writing that is marked by gender. Instead, I deploy it as a theory that recognises writing as a powerful tool in the struggle for representation. It also recognises that language and representation are reflections of positions of privilege and are dominated by the heternormative, masculine, and binary-based structures of thought that are oppressive and exclude those considered 'other', alienating them from, among other things, their own bodies. Its strength as a theory lies in its understanding that writing can move beyond male-focused writing and its dependence on dualistic thinking. In moving past dualistic thinking *écriture féminine* undermines dominant structures and modes of representation, liberating the writer (and the reader) and allowing the writer to reclaim his/her body and desires. *Ecriture féminine* is a mode of communication that recognises and deals with the politics of location through engaging with a kind of writing that is not stifled by the need to justify and qualify in the language and economy of the dominant structures of thought. In this way, 'writing can be the site of alternative economies: it is not obliged simply to reproduce the system'.[14] It is because *écriture féminine* possesses such scope that it has effectively been able to travel from its original context in 1975 to become a powerful theory of gender-marked writing that is distinctively Québécois.

Indeed, writing in the feminine was a 'response to a historic moment of radical cultural re-assessment' in Québec.[15] According to Nicole Brossard, one of the Québec women writers instrumental in formulating *écriture au féminin* as a practice, writing in the feminine acts 'both as an imaginative site on which to construct new identities for women and as an indication of the emerging desire of contemporary women to transform themselves, both individually and collectively, into autonomous agents in the process of signification'.[16] As Gould notes, 'The process of rethinking the functions and transformational power of language from the point of view of women prompted writers in Québec to develop textual strategies that work to displace hierarchical thinking by dismantling conventional writing practices'.[17] In this way, *écriture au féminin* texts 'theorize on the nature of women's oppression in patriarchal culture which legitimize male authority by undermining the rigid, constricting forms of discourse'.[18] Moure's linguistic constitution of the *cidadán* is also a constitution of the *cidadán*'s body, which connects to another aim of writing in the feminine: 'In its quest for a gender-specific inscription in language, writing in the feminine recognised the necessity to reinscribe the female body (maternal, sexual – heterosexual or lesbian – and intellectual) in a symbolic order that had always been interpreted on masculine grounds.'[19]

The crucial question in relation to writing in the feminine as an alternative mode is whether or not it is actually effective in its project of re-inscribing the feminine into language that is dominated by patriarchal values. According to Marie Carrière, 'Writing in the feminine stems from the work on language; it is a form of writing that encodes a feminine generic'.[20] In a similar vein, France Théoret notes: 'Le langage au féminin n'est pas une [*sic*] langage nouvelle au sens où il faudrait parler d'un nouvel idiome. Le langage au féminin est déplacement du symbolique' ['Language in the feminine or feminine language is not a new language in the sense that a new idiom must be spoken. Language in the feminine is the displacement of the symbolic' (my translation)].[21] For her part, Teresa de Lauretis also notes that 'the only way to position oneself outside of [any given] discourse is to displace oneself within it – to refuse the question as formulated, or to answer deviously (though in its words), even to quote (but against the grain)'.[22] Another crucial aspect of writing in the feminine is its self-reflexive character and, as Moure's work suggests, its preoccupation with seeking out the other. Indeed, 'as first and foremost a self-conscious writing practice, writing in the feminine is also an ethical practice of excess, one that bears within itself its "other" that always exceeds it: reading'.[23] Moure's work most certainly qualifies here; as Susan Rudy notes, Moure 'writes in excess of signification; refuses conventional word order and usage; redeploys grammar, punctuation, syntax, and spelling; juxtaposes as many as ten versions of a poem; and ignores the conventions of pronominal and prepositional reference'.[24] Rudy's comments are particularly relevant when considering the reader's engagement with Moure's poetry.

Where Moure's poetry is an example of writing in the feminine and an attempt to displace the hegemonic force of language, it is the task of the reader to decrypt such an agenda. While it is a fairly straightforward task to outline the structure of *O Cidadán*, its governing principle remains the identification of the trace that constitutes language as exclusionary. Writing about the trace is a difficult task; writing about the trace in a way that is readable is even more difficult. Along these lines, William Large asks:

> How is it possible to write about the trace, when it is not a phenomenon which offers itself to thematization and conceptualization? To adequately portray, if such a thing is possible, this signifying prior to a system of signs, would it not require a different kind of writing which did not operate at the level of description, designation and objectivity?[25]

Interestingly, Jacques Derrida and Emmanuel Levinas, both of whom are referenced extensively in *O Cidadán*, identify poetry as this 'different kind of writing' which brings the borders of language to light. Indeed, Moure believes that '[t]o see the seams in language, we have to question our readerly selves. And, as writers, we have to expect our readers to desire the text, to be willing to read and let go of their fixities. We have to permit them to admit that more is accessible to them than they thought. It's accessible in a different way' (*My Beloved Wager* p. 55). This relates to perhaps the most significant challenge of this chapter, which has been to strike the balance between explaining and interpreting the poems in *O Cidadán*, a sizeable task in itself, and attempting to use the poems fairly seamlessly to illustrate my larger argument about Moure's work.

Indeed, this speaks to a larger issue related to Moure's poetry: accessibility, which has been the most common point of criticism of Moure's writing. Given that she believes that *O Cidadán* is, as the title of this chapter suggests, 'a reading practice in a community of others' (*O Cidadán* p. 141), the issue of accessibility is of utmost importance. However, Moure's stance on accessibility is not as clear-cut; she sees accessibility in a trade-off with subversion and displacement. To her, 'accessibility can be reductive: the lowest common denominator of the possible. Literalist uses of the accessible don't help women and working-class people for they act to reproduce their place in the social order that diminishes their capacities' (*My Beloved Wager* p. 67). Describing another perspective, Rudy is realistic in her assessment: 'Not all readers will be willing or able to meet [Moure's] high expectations.'[26]

Moure's challenge to readers began as a challenge to herself: 'I wanted a poetry that refused erasure. That clamoured [...] I wanted, and want, a poetry that could not be simply ingested. Not a consumer poetry. I wanted a poetry that lets us think' (*My Beloved Wager* p. 252). Moure's comments here find their roots in her own theoretical inclinations in relation to ways of reading. In advocating these reading practices, Moure invokes Gilles Deleuze's *Negotiations* (1997), which outlines two possible ways of reading a book: 'the first kind of reading', according to Moure, 'is the way reading is taught in classes in schools, in institutions. The second way of reading is what [she calls] writerly. It finds ways forward or sideways in what the book itself essays: without trying to box it into explanations, it finds ways out of the box' (*My Beloved Wager* p. 15). Reading *O Cidadán* out of the box, in a writerly way, must therefore attempt to conceive of the community of others with which Moure is preoccupied. However, how to start building this community? Indeed, in 'document9 (categorical resistance)' Moure asks:

> How to think along the edges of something that is not yet a thing, using one's own 'not yet' which is anterior to our 'our'ness, to any 'my' or any *sum* ... and which creates the 'our'ness too as a further (always further) 'not-yet' superimposed or perhaps coalescent with an

'our' that is tentative (but oh this is beauty) and urged up and forward by the 'not yet'. (*O Cidadán* p. 28)

Moure suggests that one crucial step to arriving at the community that exists in the 'not-yet' is a shift in the way we recognise and differentiate between self and other. For, 'clearly to keep the self intact, to *identify*, is in some way an acknowledgment of the otherness and multiplicity of the non-self, of what is outside the self, an acknowledgement the body makes automatically at a pre-social level to retain its own sense of body, of presence, of equilibrium ... This acknowledgment is the building block of community and self' (*My Beloved Wager* p. 28). What can be immediately gleaned from this is that this equivalence of reader, citizen, and subject position is based on a politics of inclusion and solidarity, which in turn reflects, to return to more practical matters, on Moure's use of space on the page: 'The result of this gesture toward inclusion is a tangible space of omission, of absence, on the page. It is the revelation of precisely this sort of gap at the "microcosmic" level of the text that allows Moure the space to explore the "contiguities and tangential contacts" at the level of the self, and nation.'[27] This ties in very well with the 'sense of body' Moure speaks of, particularly given that she sees, as I have already mentioned, the book as an extension of the body, or the body of writing. It is certainly worth arguing, in this case, that the spaces of omission on the page are complex reflections of the place of the other's body in a civic context. In this way, Moure not only draws our attention to the absence of otherness, by using 'this space of continual movement and intersection [to] establish for the reader a "contact zone"', but also allows readers to begin the process of re-inscribing absent bodies onto the page – and into community.[28] As Moira Gatens puts it, this requires us to address 'the other, the "thou" of our social relations' as Moure does in the first poem of *O Cidadán*.[29]

In fact, it is in the first (recognisable) poem of the collection, a 'Georgette', that Moure positions the intimate as the foundation of the *cidadán*'s civic relationships:

Georgette thou burstest my deafness
woe to the prosperities of the world
because I am not yet full of thee I am but a burthen
to myself. (*O Cidadán* p. 3)

Here, it is a physical relationship with Georgette that 'burst[s]' the speaker's 'deafness' – implying that it is the *cidadán*'s intimate relationship that instigates a critique of citizenship. Moure's use of traditional lyric poetry language is 'fitting' with the poem's formal demands while simultaneously overturning conventional understandings of the citizen whose legal status is the starting point for *his* relationship with the public sphere. In the Georgette poems Moure's *cidadán* is deliberately 'excessively' erotic, emphasising Moure's critique of the division between private and public spheres.

Despite opening *O Cidadán* with a lyric love poem, it is not only love and affection that moves Moure's *cidadán* to connect to others in a network of sympathy or intimacy, but also, it is harm that characterises her relationship to others, hence, her catalogues of harms. The 'Catalogue' poems represent a different facet to Moure's critique. These twenty poems, beginning with 'Catalogue of the Harms' and ending with 'Twentieth Century of the Festering of Harms' follow a trajectory that inextricably connects the *cidadán* to harm. In the 'Second Catalogue of the Substitution of Harms' Moure, in an asterisked note, clarifies these harms are represented 'in the form of functions' and then in a handwritten edit, crosses out 'functions' and replaces it with 'fractions' (*O Cidadán* p. 11):

harm	harm	harm	harm	harm
------	------	$\sqrt{}$	------	------
forms	term	devices	units	count

The relationships represented above are both functional *and* fractional, intended for the reader to determine the exact nature of the relationship: which term folds into which? Which are functions of which? However, it is the third relationship that is most telling, as instead of using a fraction, Moure uses the symbol for the square root: the radical. Thus, it emerges that devices are the root of harm, or harm is the root of (harmful) devices.

In the 'Fifth Topology of the Renaissance of Harms', Moure makes evident the idea that she shares the responsibility with her reader of making the poems in *O Cidadán* (p. 23). In this case, the poem is written in French; but it is only upon reading the words aloud that the reader can recognise French words. Beginning the poem with an epigraph, '*je le prends à l'enverse*' which (approximately) translates to 'I take the reverse' or 'I take the inverse', Moure attributes the epigraph to 'Engiatnom ed Lehcim' or Michel de Montaigne in reverse. The reader is left to translate and decipher the epigraph, before considering the main body of the poem:

aultres	vrayment	sçay	tousjours
-------	-------	√	-------
disoit	joyeulx	estoit	compaignon

Only reading these words aloud makes it clear that they are French words written using English phonetic conventions. Of course this recognition is only possible if the reader already has some knowledge of French; for a reader who does not, Moure offers a French lesson. Reading French words in such a way turns French on itself, creating a new dialect that only those reading the poem can speak. Such an enterprise is deliberate, as in 'document31 (la república)' (p. 78) where Moure criticises the nationalist tendencies of 'state' languages:

> All this, in the face of the French fright (spring '99) at signing a charter to protect regional European languages. Fear for its 'language of the republic.' Where did this fear come from, this republic? For such charters so often give the right to speak a language without the right to have anyone listen.

Moure's incredulity at a need to maintain 'the purity' of languages is an issue that resurfaces throughout *O Cidadán* and is made particularly evident in her use of Galician, a language that has continued to exist despite its censorship and dismissal by the Spanish state. The 'Fifth Topology of the Renaissance of Harms' draws attention to issues of censorship in language closer to 'home' for Moure – the linguistic and political relationship between Anglophone and Francophone Canada.

As the 'Catalogue' poems progress, Moure uses the 'document' poems as ciphers with which to read the catalogues. In 'document9 (categorical resistance)' she explains:

> As if, then, to exhibit harms is not to *describe* but to present exactly that rhetorical bind [excess] at which reading breaks. Thus: *fractions* as a visible/visual presentation, the line of the letter on an axis that is a will or intentionality.

Further, in 'document45 (words' relation)', given the fraction laboural,

>   -------
>   time

Moure shows the multiplicity of readings possible:

> readable here as 'laboural above time'
> 'laboural over time'
> 'laboural's portion of time'
> 'time into laboural'
> 'laboural divided by time'

or as 'indicated relations' <- -> various possibilities as syntaxes
punctuations
pronunciations,

Even here, providing a 'key' to reading the 'Catalogue' poems does not force the reader into a limited set of reading choices. Moure deliberately provides several possibilities and allows the reader to make 'other in-trusions and en-frontations possible on the page', such as 'time under laboural', perhaps (*O Cidadán* p. 115). Such readerly interventions, Moure argues, have an effect on the body of the relationships she sets out on the page, in turn affecting the human body, and ultimately, she hopes, leading to 'a citizen's alteration'. In this way, the 'Catalogue' poems not only serve as repositories for harms done to citizens, but the very act of reading them also enacts a shift in the reader, constituting her as an *altered* citizen.

Moure's *cidadán* (ostensibly Moure herself) is able to connect to other citizens through common experiences of harm. Although Moure and her *cidadán* have not experienced the same degree of harm listed above, in 'Sixth Catalogue of the Pubis of Harms', she writes: 'there were places where we were cast aside / our grip was cast aside[.]' (pp. 26–7). This exclusion, in which Moure's 'we' was 'cast aside' is enough to engender a network of sympathy and empathy through which the *cidadán* emphasises that any harm done to any citizen (whether exclusion, deportation, or murder) should be taken seriously instead of being prone to the 'irregular / justice' of the state.

> To see her as citizen is indeed to know citizen as repository of harm, where harm is gendered too. Myths of violability, inviolability, volatility,

utility, lability played out. In wars, women are territories, and territories are lieux de punition. (p. 79)

In the 'Catalogue' poems more than any other type in the collection, Moure's insistence on harm as a common experience of citizens (often at the hands of states) is clear: she cites Nazi concentration camps, the Dili massacre in East Timor, the Rwanda massacres – all of which evoke Koita and Tounkara once again. Yet if the reader does not know about the events Moure lists, a concerted effort must be made to interpret and understand these poems, fractions, and functions. The reader must bring their own attention to the kind of 'decay' Moure appropriates from Titus Livy's description of Rome mentioned earlier.

The 'Georgette' poems represent a counterpoint to the 'decay' exposed in the 'Catalogue' poems. The importance of sexual identity and erotic love are clearest in these poems, which are deliberately excessively erotic while simultaneously comical:

> O Georgette, is this my letter of adoration?
> If ecstasy is abrupt, I love you.
> So sexual a register by so public a village.
> Call out now to my turbine? (p. 110)

The importance of the Georgette poems can be found in considerations of sex and sexuality: to love and crave the other is to love something that is exterior to the 'self' of the *cidadán*, who Moure has already described as based on the recognition of the other in the first place. This in turn is based on the recognition and, ultimately, a rejection of the interior/exterior binary, for according to Moure, recognising the other involves recognising one's self, also. Moure's understanding of 'other' follows from this. The other is 'unknowable, nearly unlocatable, but also already part of us' in the same way that Diana Fuss sees identification as the detour through another that constitutes one's self (*My Beloved Wager* p. 163). The other here is not only other as individual or body, but also (and primarily) the other of language, as Moure notes: 'Rather than just turning endlessly around the "self" and "other," *O Cidadán* examines not so much the relation of other=*autre* but the relation with other=*autrui*, with those-others-outside-me-whom-I-do-not-know-but-in-whose-company-I-am-alive' (p. 163).

In 'document 2', Moure focuses on the relationship of the *cidadán* to the other; in particular, 'other she craves, the she she craves also a she' (*O Cidadán* p. 9). Clearly Moure refers to the *cidadán* as lesbian, but also once again the bodily, the somatic aspect of the *cidadán*, and her capacity to love. For as Moure reminds us in 'document27 (intelligibility's demure)', 'our bodies extend into the book' and 'as citizens we are sexual beings' (p. 70). The Georgette poems are included because they depict private desire played out in 'so public a village'. The citizen loves and desires the other – the Georgette poems tackle the *cidadán*'s relationship with the other whom she loves in both the private and public spheres.

The line between inside (self) and outside (other) becomes blurred and is further undermined by sex, as Moure notes in 'document30 (viable risk)'. As she puts it, 'Sex's relation: to "extend" the "boundaries" of such interiority. But even to / say "boundaries" implies a prior exercise of restraint upon belief (or / tabulation)' (p. 77). As I have noted, blurring of the traditional interior/exterior and self/other distinctions is crucial to Moure's own *cidadán* project:

> The view of the citizen that emerges from this work is, then, minoritarian and problematized. In *O Cidadán*, the cidadán is a woman and a lesbian, and not necessarily, or not only, 'a cidadá,' grammatically marked as female. And this citizen – who is all of us, because men too have to accept the reversal of their gender markings – is not marginalized, for the poems beckon beyond the dialectic of centre/margin, displacing that problematic formulation. They urge toward possibilities beyond reified notions of the body, for the bodily delineation of the individual also exists in *public* space, and our conceptions of this body and its extensionality affect the conceptions we are able to have of public life, and of the citizen, and thus of history. (*My Beloved Wager* p. 160)

Since, as Moure suggests, the figure of the *cidadán* is minoritarian, in that it attempts to inflect the generic, any language used for meaning to the *cidadán* must also be minoritarian. I have already indicated that Moure's unmasking of the relation with regards to citizenship takes place on the dual levels of language and writing. In the same way that Françoise Lionnet exposes the puritanical tendencies of the English language – recall that in chapter 1 I discuss Lionnet's critique of English for having no word for 'hybrid' or 'hybridity' without a pejorative tone or an inflection that lowers the process to the level of animal breeding – by setting it alongside the French term *métissage* and the Spanish *mestizaje*, Moure uses her *cidadán* to expose the inability of English, French, Castilian, and Galician (all languages she is fluent in) to speak for and represent her: 'a woman who [among other minority affiliations] bears a *policed sexuality*'. According to Moure she can only enact the unmasking if she writes it in 'a minor tongue' (*O Cidadán* p. v) a gesture here, of course, to Gilles Deleuze and Felix Guattari's notion of 'minor literature'.[30] In *Kafka: Towards a Minor Literature*, Deleuze and Guattari argue for an understanding of minor literature – one that is not written in the 'major' language (read: discourse). In the case of Moure, *O Cidadán* is certainly written in what Deleuze and Guattari have called a 'majoritarian' tongue – yet that detail continues to work in favour of this analysis, as Moure is able to defamiliarise English to itself and us by allowing it to be 'invaded or traversed in many ways, most visibly by other tongues – Castilian, Galician, Latin, Portuguese, [and] French' (*My Beloved Wager* p. 164). Another approach to reading *O Cidadán* as minor(itarian) literature is Moure's own location as a writer; a lesbian, writing from Québec in the five languages listed above, Moure can certainly be considered minoritarian:

> I who have made myself strange in the *arena* of country and, here, come to Québec where I bear a strange tongue (yet hegemonic), allowed to be foreign. As foreign, to be, paradoxically but sensibly, a part of the body politic. To be a stranger (hospes or advena) here is to faire partie de tout ce qui comporte le civis. (*O Cidadán* p. 82)

There is much to be gained by reading *O Cidadán* as a text written in a minor tongue, given Moure's relationship to Québec, but particularly in her use of Galician. One aspect as yet unexamined in this chapter is the very local and sited nature of Moure's *cidadán*. Despite its generic form, Moure clearly intends the *cidadán* to represent her, at least in the first place, in the face of institutionalised silencing of difference:

> In my own work, I thought at one time that the simplest line was best. Yet when I wrote anecdotal-conversational poems without reversal (which is to say, without the language confronting itself and its assumptions in the poem), I suppressed both my feelings as a lesbian

and my concerns as a woman. My poetry was supposed to reflect my life, especially my life as a worker, and these things were suppressed in that life. To write poems, then, perpetuated (unknowingly) my own pain at being invisible, and left my desire silenced or screened. As if I could belong, by force of will, to that *sameness*, that *anaesthesia*. (*My Beloved Wager* p. 65)

Sited as Moure is, the *cidadán* inevitably bears these same markings. Sometimes referred to as the *cidadán*, sometimes *cidada*, sometimes citizen, the figure in *O Cidadán* echoes the many appellations Moure uses for herself as a poet, including Erin Mouré, Eirin Moure, EM, and the alterego Elisa Sampedrin, with whom she co-authored *Little Theatres*.[31] As I noted in the introductory comments to this chapter, Moure's habit is to change her name with each new project, since 'each new spelling of the authorial name will sign off a new work while straining the social contract' and believes, as Julia Kristeva does, that 'social protocol views the multiplication of names as a series of repudiations, all of them inauthentic'.[32] Stephen Scobie suggests the signature 'offers the author twin possibilities: to re-sign the work, or to resign from the work'.[33] More importantly, 'signature, indeed all writing, reaches out towards the other', as if the act of writing or signature confirms the self – but only in a community that can read such a signature – a community of readers.[34]

In changing her name to resist what she regards as the prohibitive and restrictive behaviour of the social contract, Moure indirectly invokes the authoritative and regulatory position of the state in relation to the citizen, a perspective in keeping with that of Louis Althusser, who posits that society is essentially a set of ideological practices and apparatuses that interpellates or hails individuals as subjects of that society or system. As he notes, 'Ideology is the system of the ideas and representations which dominate the mind of a man or a social group'.[35] Given this definition, he theorises how ideology functions to subject individuals to its practices, thereby hailing them as subjects who both constitute and are constituted by it. In this way, the practice of interpellation is very clearly a strategy of containment for anything that is considered different, since, as Althusser suggests, 'ideology "acts" or "functions" in such a way that it "recruits" subjects among the individuals (it recruits them all), or "transforms" the individuals into subjects (it transforms them all)'.[36] As a result, 'individuals are always-already subjects', since all individuals will either be recruited or transformed into subjects, and that subjects are repetitively hailed over the courses of their lives. In fact, simply naming a child registers him/her into the system. It is useful here to briefly return to Scobie, who notes that

> the signature identifies, and the signature puts identity *en jeu* (in play/at risk). It is in the signature that the name (as *un nom de mort*) lives on, and the name lives on the signature. The signature comes at the end, as closure, but the signature always comes back, *revenant*, as a performative name. The signature is a sign that never ends.[37]

As the subject in Althusser's scenario grows older, s/he is exposed to the state's ideological practices, through what Althusser terms 'ideological state apparatuses'.[38] These ideological state apparatuses include the family, which is the primary purveyor of ideology, the school, and the church (meaning religion or spirituality in general). As a result, subjects' relationship to the real world can be characterised as 'imaginary', since 'Ideology represents the imaginary relationship of individuals to their real conditions of existence'.[39] Moure's understanding of the ubiquitous nature of ideology and the state is reiterated in her poetic attempts to undermine this anaesthetic with the antianaesthetic, as is clear when she asks: 'But how not to already "suppose" / the very thing we question?' (*O Cidadán* p. 47). The question of how to identify exclusion and exteriority without somehow normalising the interior force that excludes is also a crucial facet of queer studies, which also attempts to strike this balance.

Along these lines of exteriority and interiority, Moure believes 'poetic work [...] is civic work' (p. 1). This idea that poetry is not 'just' art or is always only accessible to a certain class or kind of people is a significant one – it is the idea that poetry can have civic, public value and utility. Also significant here is Moure's choice of calling poetic work 'civic' rather than 'political'. While it is without a doubt political, this is another way in which Moure exposes relationships her readers will likely tend to take for granted. In this case, the civic and the political exist as two distinct (and not necessarily intersecting) types of work. Moreover, Moure specifies *where* this distinction is valid: 'the poetic work, which is civic work, in my country' (p. 1). It is not automatically clear here that Moure means Canada as a whole; she could just as easily mean Québec, for example. It is most likely that the country she refers to gestures towards other landscapes or terrains such as language or philosophy, for, as she notes, 'the act of inhabitation can occur in language as well as in a place'.[40] Most importantly, Moure's 'country' is populated by her *cidadán*. In relation to this, Moure confirms that '[a] citizen is not defined by a territory per se, but by how he or she acts in a territory': another characteristic of her *cidadán*.[41]

Any discussion of conventions in Moure's work must also take place on the structural level of her books. Despite its idiosyncratic structure, *O Cidadán* retains structural conventions such as a preface and acknowledgements, which Moure insists on making as significant as the poems themselves. At the very end of *O Cidadán*, as Moure lists her acknowledgements, she writes: 'This book is a reading practice in a community of others' (*O Cidadán* p. 141). This last statement is key to understanding *O Cidadán* in the context of *écriture au féminin*. If *écriture au féminin* is about a gender-marked writing practised by women (who in this framework, are 'other') then Moure here is simply making her own politics of writing known. Significantly, she only tells the readers once they have reached the end of the book, perhaps in order to alert them to the discursive and reading practices they have perhaps unknowingly been engaging in. As I have already noted, in the preface to *O Cidadán* Moure notes that the word 'citizen' seems to be inflected with the masculine with, according to her, a feminine supplement. Although writing in reaction to this, it is clear that she is not attempting to 'only' represent the citizen in its feminine inflection or articulation. This would be counter-productive and simply reproduce a masculine/feminine binary. For Moure, the word *cidadán* 'inflects the generic' but from a very specific location – her location: 'I, a woman, o cidadán' (p. v). This is an excellent example of the potential of *écriture au féminin* and Moure's writing in particular to 'dislodge' concepts from their traditional positions in the dominant framework. According to Eugenia Sojka, 'the social function of language marks our civic place as women. Marks civic memory', since 'leaving language as it is would mean agreeing with the civic order'.[42]

Skibsrud shrewdly notes that '[r]ather than "obeying the rules we don't have," Moure *disobeys* the rules that *we didn't know we had*'.[43] In so doing, Moure offers her critique of the system that she calls the Law. Moure's treatment of the *cidadán* sees her (the *cidadán*) as 'an enactment across prosthetic boundaries' and given that *O Cidadán* is a communal reading practice, this understanding of enactment or enacting makes sense.[44] 'Yet when the body's boundaries are questioned, a view of the citizen as belonging perhaps becomes untenable, too passive a relation. My searches point, rather, toward the citizen as enactment' (*My Beloved Wager* p. 160).

According to Moure in 'documentı' (*O Cidadán* p. 7) there is no use in theorising the *cidadán* if she is a *solitary* enactment across boundaries; she must be thought up and conceived of in order to cross them. Previous to Moure's tentative definition of the *cidadán* (as 'just an enactment across prosthetic boundaries') she asks the following: 'Is the Cidadán a prosthetic gesture (across "languages")?' and further along, 'Is the Cidadán a prosthetic gesture, across languages?' The slightly modified configuration of these two questions is very subtle but belies a plethora of meanings. Read aloud it is difficult to distinguish between the two, but on the page the differences, seemingly minor at first, are jarring.

The first, 'Is the Cidadán a prosthetic gesture (across "languages")?' asks whether the *Cidadán* itself (herself, himself) is a prosthetic gesture.[45] Before answering this question it is perhaps worth considering the unspoken question: What is a prosthetic gesture? Throughout *O Cidadán* Moure makes repeated reference to gestures, both in terms of a gesture that expresses something (as in language) and a physical movement. According to Moure, one of the things that 'make up the citizen' is the 'capacity to "be affected by"' something (p. 7). As 'a bundle of affect, affectability', the *cidadán* is certainly a product of Moure's deep engagement with the work of Jacques Derrida, Jean-Luc Nancy, and Gilles Deleuze and Felix Guattari. This is perhaps why she wonders whether the *cidadán* is a prosthetic gesture; in this case, I suggest that prosthetic links back to her choice to write about 'O Cidadán' rather than '*unha cidada*' (p. v). In this scenario, she is also asking herself and her readers whether her treatment of the *cidadán* is useful – across languages or at all.

In the second configuration of the question, the secondary character of the phrase 'across languages', present in the first configuration within parentheses, is brought into the question fully. Now Moure asks: 'Is the Cidadán a prosthetic gesture, across languages?' If as Moure believes, all things and experiences are constituted by language, then one implication of her question is whether her *cidadán* has any power, potential, or validity across language and across human experience. She is therefore asking whether the linguistic incarnation of the feminine supplement is valid across languages. In a sense, 'documentı' and in fact all of the 'document' poems in *O*

Cidadán, resemble poetic brainstorming. Moure deliberately leaves this stage of the writing process visible and available to the reader. As Moure leaves her thinking and writing processes exposed, the reader sees the various strands of her argument in their most vulnerable, unrefined, and raw form as in the note to herself in 'document 29 (French thinking)' where she reminds herself to '(add pp. 120–1 Nancy here)' (p. 75).

This is clear as she discusses the capacity of the *cidadán* for affect, emotion, and sensibility: 'Yet sensibility, affect is always local. (J-L Nancy) Without locality there is no sensibility.' But then she wonders: 'But what is the local, the notion of the local is forever altered.' This leads her to rethink her *cidadán*, resulting in: 'The citizen is a mobile complex of: (Nancy again) rights, obligations, dignities, and virtues' (p. 75). If the citizen's sensibilities are now not limited to the local, then it is no longer restricted by either its prosthetic character or by the constraints of the local; it has the capacity to cross borders and boundaries. At this point, then: 'The citizen is just an enactment across prosthetic boundaries?' And then, with uncertainty: 'Or within them?' By the end of 'document1' Moure seems unable (or perhaps unwilling) to settle on one definition of the citizen – so she leaves it to the reader: 'You be the judge. Pandemonium', referencing the semantic pandemonium the term *cidadán* represents (p. 7). By 'document2 (inaugural)' (p. 9), however, Moure seems more certain:

> O cidadán a seal or bond with this world, nothing to do with country or origin. The cidadán stands in time as the person stands in space, liquid edge before or beyond the other she craves, the she she craves also a she, and this is space that opens time, it is a space where time tumbles backwards, *brings* a future *into* presence.

Several things stand out as significant in this last excerpt. First, Moure has clarified the *cidadán*'s 'location' or position, affirming that it has nothing to do with 'country or origin'. Indeed, she confirms this later, writing that the *cidadán* is 'sited but not rooted in soil or soil's versions, and its terms remain open to the possibility of movement beyond the "already constituted" remain open to *constitution* itself as an open act, an act of *co-situating*' (*My Beloved Wager* p. 164). This idea of co-situating recalls Moure's definition of the *cidadán* in 'document1' as an enactment – something that must be done together, as part of a community, in this case, a community of readers who constitute the *cidadán* by reading her, considering her, and struggling to understand her. Directly related to this community that co-situates the citizen is the idea of the other, since such a co-situation once again calls for acts with and for the other: 'Is the body itself just a tangle of prosthetic gestures / toward and against *another?*' (*O Cidadán* p. 47).

Here again we see the importance of community and communal thinking giving form to a concept. Once again, this connects back to *O Cidadán* as a 'reading practice in a community of others' (p. 141). Since the citizen (as a practice or enactment) is given form by a practice of communal consideration and thinking, it does not have an originary myth – and it is not, as Moure emphasises, rooted in a country or a soil. She elaborates further on this in 'document6 (originary)': 'Is there an originary marking? If there were, would we be able to "read" it / at all? Or does such a "trait" receive its function as mark not only from our / reading, our imposition of acculturated being that takes place in reading's / gesture. And is thereby not "originary"' (p. 20). And of course, these questions about community assume an aporetic character: how can there be a community of others?

Moure sees community as the basis for identity: 'To me the notion of identity contains a preceding notion of *community* [...] The structuring of community, I believe, has its seed not in likeness but in the non-identity or non-congruence that the child begins to realize – not experiences itself as identity but experiencing some "other" as being non-congruent' (*My Beloved Wager* p. 62). Such a community of 'others' can be understood as 'perhaps the community of those without community' (what Derrida understands as a different kind of fraternity). To return once again to Moure's 'not-yet': 'It defeats or refuses that "Anglo-American" notion as not always useful, as possibly troublesome, as keeping us trapped. It calls for the "not yet," which, if it is "between-ness," is not "betweenness" as a site, but is, rather, a "movingbetweenness" that obviates the primacy of its poles.'[46]

If Moure's *cidadán* stands in a 'space that opens time, / it is a space / where time tumbles backwards, brings a future into presence', then this *cidadán* represents the 'not-yet' Moure also speaks of, and represents the ' "to-come" of a certain democracy' Derrida hopes for but cannot find when he asks: 'Is it possible to open up to the "to come" of a certain democracy which is no longer an insult to the friendship we have striven to think beyond the homo-fraternal and phallogocentric schema?'[47] An integral part of this process is recognising that poetry 'contains the unspeakable. It enacts. It is an enactment of what can't be said in words or forms. It consumes its form in order to enact, but can do so only through the sign, through the Law, by disturbing the sign in its own soil' (*My Beloved Wager* p. 25). If Moure's *cidadán* crosses boundaries prosthetically – that is, in and through language if not with its physical body – then we must recognise that '[l]anguage is definitely a false border. For it keeps you caught badly in one set of structures, without the mechanisms to think yourself elsewhere. And the body is, or can be, simply a reification of accepted notions of where bodies begin and end'.[48] Closely related to this is 'the language divide' in *O Cidadán*, which Skibsrud argues 'is not between French or English, Spanish or Galician, but between the language of the "subject" and the language of the "citizen"' which we later come to find are one and the same.[49] Thus the language divide is only so because we choose it to be so, and because we need to have 'other' languages from which to differentiate 'our' language and ourselves. Moure's agenda is to make her readers aware that all language is exclusionary, and uses writing in the feminine as a strategy to move beyond this, both in terms of language and community building practices. Indeed, the community of others that she calls for is conceived of and written in the feminine, and as such, the 'generic blending insists further on the crossing of disciplines with one another – of theory and creativity, of philosophy, linguistics, psychoanalysis, and literature – inscribing a theory of writing and of subjectivity within the poetic or prose work itself'.[50] As a result, what is expected of Moure's readers is an openness to read for the traces of the 'not-yet' in which the common language is continuously dislodged from itself in a persisting process of transformation. The act of reading thus becomes an *enactment* of reading in which reading practices take place in a community of others. This community of others constitutes the very language of writing and reading; like the term *cidadán*, the new generic term comprises the self and the other without excluding either or unbalancing the terms of identification.

Such acts of reading become civic in their constitution of civic subjects in a new narrative of community and this chapter has sought to clarify the reading and writing practices embedded within Moure's *O Cidadán* in order to identify their impact on the civic reader and her relationship with the status and practice of citizenship, challenging as this may seem.

Notes

1 Erín Moure, *Empire: York Street* (Toronto: House of Anansi Press, 1979).
2 The previous books in the trilogy are *Search Procedures* (Toronto: House of Anansi Press, 1996) and *The Frame of a Book* or *A Frame of The Book* (Toronto: House of Anansi Press, 1999).
3 Johanna Skibsrud, 'If We Dare To:' Border Crossings in Erín Moure's *O Cidadán*', *The Brock Review* 11:1 (2010): pp. 15–27, at p. 20.
4 Erín Moure, *O Cidadán* (Toronto: House of Anansi Press, 2002), p. 1. All subsequent references to this collection will be included in parentheses in the main body of the text.
5 Titus Livy, *The History of Rome*, trans. Rev. Canon Roberts (London: J. M. Dent and Sons, 1905). http://mcadams.posc.mu.edu/txt/ah/Livy/Livy01.html (accessed 19 November 2010).
6 Ibid., n.p.
7 Erín Moure, *My Beloved Wager: Essays from a Writing Practice* (Edmonton: NeWest Press, 2009), p. 59. All subsequent references to this text will be included in parentheses in the main body of the text.
8 Gloria Anzaldúa, *Borderlands/La Frontera: The New Mestiza* (San Francisco: Aunt Lute Books, 1997 [1987]), p. 100.
9 Eugenia Sojka, 'Canadian Feminist Writing and American Poetry', *CLCWeb: Comparative Literature and Culture* 3.2 (2001). http://docs.lib.purdue.edu/clcweb/vol3/iss2/12 (accessed 28 April 2011).
10 Ibid.
11 Ibid.
12 Karen Gould, *Writing in the Feminine: Feminism and Experimental Writing in Québec* (Carbondale: Southern Illinois University Press, 1990), p. xvi (emphasis in original).
13 Erín Moure, quoted in Dawne McCance, 'Crossings: An Interview with Erín Moure', *Mosaic: A Journal for the Interdisciplinary Study of Literature* 36:4 (2003): pp. 1–9, at p. 2.
14 Morag Shiach, *Hélène Cixous: A Politics of Writing* (London and New York: Routledge, 1991), p. 16.
15 Gould, *Writing in the Feminine*, p. 49.
16 Erín Moure, quoted in ibid., p. 37.
17 Ibid.
18 Ibid., p. xv.
19 Marie Carrière, *Writing in the Feminine in French and English Canada* (Toronto: University of Toronto Press, 2002), p. 20.

20 Ibid., p. 54.
21 France Théoret, *Entre raison et deraison: Essais* (Montreal: Les Herbes Rouges, 1987), p. 152.
22 Teresa de Lauretis, quoted in Stephen Scobie, *Signature Event Cantext* (Edmonton: NeWest Press, 1989), p. 26.
23 Susan Rudy, '"what can atmosphere with / vocabularies delight?" Excessively Reading Erín Moure', in *Writing in Our Time: Canada's Radical Poetries in English 1957–2003*, ed. Pauline Butling and Susan Rudy (Waterloo, ON: Wilfrid Laurier University Press, 2005), pp. 205–16, at p. 205.
24 Ibid.
25 William Large, *Emmanuel Levinas and Maurice Blanchot: Ethics and the Ambiguity of Writing* (Manchester: Clinamen Press, 2005), p. 161.
26 Rudy, '"what can atmosphere with / vocabularies delight?"', p. 205.
27 Skibsrud, 'If We Dare To', p. 16.
28 Ibid., p. 23.
29 Moira Gatens, quoted in Carrière, *Writing in the Feminine in French and English Canada*, p. 36.
30 Gilles Deleuze and Felix Guattari, *Kafka: Towards a Minor Literature*, trans. Dana Polan (Minneapolis: University of Minnesota Press, 1986).
31 Erín Moure, *Little Theatres* (Toronto: House of Anansi, 2005).
32 Caroline Bergvall, 'UNMOORED: On and with Erín Moure'. www.asu.edu/pipercwcenter/how2journal/vol_3_no_3/bergvall/pdfs/bergvall-unmoored.pdf (accessed 15 September 2010).
33 Stephen Scobie, *Signature Event Cantext* (Edmonton: NeWest Press, 1989), p. 118.
34 Ibid., p. 158.
35 Louis Althusser, 'Ideology and Ideological State Apparatuses', in *Lenin and Philosophy and other Essays*, trans. Ben Brewster (New York and London: Monthly Review Press, 1971), pp. 121–76, at p. 158.
36 Ibid., p. 174. Classically, Althusser uses the example of a policeman calling a person on the street to illustrate his point. 'Hey you!' shouts the policeman. The individual on the street will inevitably assume that 'you' refers to him/her. In so assuming, s/he is inducted into ideology.
37 Scobie, *Signature Event Cantext*, p. 113.
38 Althusser, 'Ideology and Ideological State Apparatuses', p. 177.
39 Ibid., p. 163.
40 Erín Moure, quoted in Bergvall, 'UNMOORED', n.p.
41 Erín Moure, quoted in McCance, 'Crossings', p. 2.
42 Sojka, 'Canadian Feminist Writing and American Poetry', n.p.
43 Skibsrud, 'If We Dare To', p. 20.
44 Moure, *O Cidadán*, p. 7.
45 It could very well be that Moure's choice of words here (prosthetic) is connected to her reading of Deleuze and Guattari's 'body without organs'.

For more on this, see Gilles Deleuze and Felix Guattari's *Capitalism and Schizophrenia*, trans. Robert Hurley, Mark Seem, and Helen R. Lane (London and New York: Continuum, 2004 [1972]). Alternatively, or perhaps, simultaneously, 'prosthetic' may well refer to Moure's reading of Donna Haraway's 'A Cyborg Manifesto', itself not unrelated to Deleuze and Guattari's projects.

46 Erín Moure, quoted in McCance, 'Crossings', p. 3.
47 Jacques Derrida, *The Politics of Friendship*, trans. George Collins (London and New York: Verso, 1997), p. 87.
48 Erín Moure, quoted in McCance, 'Crossings', p. 3.
49 Skibsrud, 'If We Dare To', p. 23.
50 Carrière, *Writing in the Feminine in French and English Canada*, p. 26.

6

Reading for hemispheric citizenship in Junot Díaz's *The Brief Wondrous Life of Oscar Wao*

In his 1992 Nobel Speech, Saint Lucian poet and Nobel Laureate Derek Walcott theorised Caribbean art as working to achieve the recovery and reconstruction what he called the region's 'shattered histories'. As he put it: 'Antillean art is this restoration of our shattered histories, our shards of vocabulary, our archipelago becoming a synonym for pieces broken off from the original continent.'[1] Walcott's comments on the connections between art and history encapsulate the redemptive relationship between literature and historical memory in Junot Díaz's 2007 novel *The Brief Wondrous Life of Oscar Wao* and emphasises Caribbean writing's ability to 'conjugate both tenses simultaneously: the past and the present'[2] even as it envisions and synthesises the region's future. It is fitting, then, that Díaz partially frames his first novel with lines from 'The Schooner Flight', one of Walcott's most celebrated poems, and one that reflects on the colonial legacies that precipitated the formation of a Caribbean diaspora. By invoking questions of Caribbean diasporic identity even while he contributes to a canon of American literature, Díaz offers readers a way of understanding a citizenship that is tied to 'fragmented memory' and lost or stolen national and personal histories, as well as presenting readers with a diasporic, hemispherically focalised novel that demands a readerly engagement through its experimentation with literary hybridity, narrative voice, and linguistic register.

The Brief Wondrous Life of Oscar Wao, which won Díaz the Pulitzer Prize for Fiction in 2008, follows the lives of titular character Oscar de León and his family, sister Lola, mother Belicia, and grandfather Abelard as they negotiate the curse, or fukú, on their family. Narrated by Yunior, a family friend and a character who appears elsewhere in Díaz's literary universe, the novel is framed as a bildungsroman of sorts. However, the novel displaces readerly expectations of a biographical bildungsroman. Instead of offering a linear account of the titular character's life and times, Díaz's novel weaves multiple intergenerational narratives, moving back and forth in time in service of the narrator's memorialisation of the titular Oscar himself.

This chapter explores Díaz's novel as a Caribbean text that offers a revisionist history of the Dominican Republic, with specific focus on Rafael Trujillo's thirty-year dictatorship, and theorises how Díaz crafts what I call a dictator-narrator in Yunior, whose presence allows readers to reflect not only on the dangers of dictatorship but also on the transformative possibilities of multilingual, hemispheric citizenship. Regularly featuring in showcases of twenty-first-century fiction, the novel has been described by Alison Flood as 'the best novel of the 21st century to date'.[3] Critics credit Díaz with having crafted a novel that fuses 'science fiction, fantasy, and testosterone'.[4] Similarly, in his review of the novel, Christopher Taylor notes Díaz's success in 'coupling the book's interest in genre to the creolisation he values in Caribbean culture'.[5] Taylor is perhaps simplistic in his appeal to creolisation, but he is right in identifying the hybrid character of the novel, which is foregrounded by Díaz from the outset.

Indeed, as the novel opens, readers encounter two epigraphs which they must likely mine to understand how they frame the novel. The first is a question posed in a 1966 issue of Stan Lee and Jack Kirby's comic series *The Fantastic Four*: 'Of what import are brief, nameless lives ... to **Galactus**?' (emphasis in original).[6] The novel's readers will not all be familiar with the Marvel Comic Universe in which Galactus is a villain and the only remaining cosmic entity in existence to have survived the Big Bang. In the original comic, Galactus is speaking to a Watcher, a member of another ancient and powerful species in the Marvel Comic Universe, and his question is followed by an attempt to justify what he distinguishes as the unintended but nonetheless anticipated consequences of his plan to drain planets for his survival: 'It is not my intention to injure any living being! I must replenish my energy!' In a novel that meditates on the nature of dictators as super-villains, this epigraph is fitting because it problematises the simple distinction between good and evil in the face of cosmic curses that are rooted in legacies of colonisation.

The second epigraph is an excerpted stanza from Derek Walcott's celebrated persona poem 'The Schooner Flight' (1990). Here, as in the other literary works I discuss in this book, Díaz begins his novel with a poem that is preoccupied with the effects of colonisation, borders, and hybridity: 'I had a sound colonial education', readers are reminded by the poem's speaker, Shabine, who goes on to describe the 'Dutch, nigger, and English in me', suggesting neither identification nor disidentification, but fact. Unlike Gloria Anzaldúa, Walcott's speaker does not directly connect hybridity to empowered identity or citizen. Instead, by beginning the next line with 'and', Walcott's speaker is made active agent not through a causal relationship, but through an additional declaration: 'and either I'm nobody, or I'm a nation'. The speaker's 'colonial education' and hybrid identity does not automatically confer 'insider' status; insider status is *chosen* through the opposition of 'nobody' paired with 'nation' (*Brief* p. xi).

Díaz's novel, likewise, seems to be about a 'nobody': its titular character, Oscar, is described as ordinary, and by some standards, as the novel's first chapter explains, a failure, but is rendered extraordinary – or in Walcott's terms, a nation – by the narrator we later find to be Yunior, whose act of writing works, as he notes, as countercurse or 'zafa of sorts' (p. 7) against the fukú or curse of a nation as it manifests through Oscar and his family. The opening passage of the novel explains the nature of the *fukú americanus* or fukú: 'generally a curse or a doom of some kind; specifically the Curse and the Doom of the New World' (p. 1). The original culprit of this curse is named by Yunior as 'the Admiral', Christopher Columbus, whose arrival in Hispaniola 'unleashed the fuku on the world, and we've all been in the shit ever since' (p. 1). This language, akin to biblical 'original sin', sets in motion Oscar's origin story while also functioning as a humorous expletive that signals the narrative's resistance to the legacies of colonialism.

As an immigrant who moved to the United States from the Dominican Republic as a young child, Díaz draws on his own personal experiences of displacement and diasporic identity in this novel. Accordingly, Díaz's own peripheral position informs his writing and his own perceptions of diasporic Caribbean identity structure the work. As he puts it, 'In my mind the book was supposed to take the shape of an archipelago; it was supposed to be a textual Caribbean. Shattered and yet somehow holding together, somehow incredibly vibrant and compelling'.[7] This textual Caribbean in *The Brief Wondrous Life of Oscar Wao* is rendered evident to the reader in a range of ways, which I explore over the course of this chapter. As Silvio Torres-Saillant observes, 'Perhaps recognizing the centrality of the Caribbean to the core structure of the Dominican experience, Díaz owns his regional descent in a manner that makes him into a kind of American to whom the Antillean world matters at the level of existential immediacy'.[8] At its core, *The Brief Wondrous Life of Oscar Wao* allows readers to reflect on the hybridity of contemporary American literature, offering them routes to conceiving of citizenship as an archipelago of rights and responsibilities, or status and habitus, and fusing the key components of citizenship that this book theorises: readerly, participatory, and queered in its emphasis of looking beyond the borders of national identity.

Hybrid and hemispheric textual identities

In *The Brief Wondrous Life of Oscar Wao*, Díaz evokes a clear Caribbean aesthetic, particularly in the way that his writing 'embraces', as Joshua Jelly-Schapiro puts it, Walcott's 'dictum' on Caribbean art.[9] By situating Díaz's writing as part of a tradition of Caribbean writing as well as being part of and drawing on the contemporary US literary, science fiction, and popular culture scene, I argue that he is able to stage his first novel as one that is 'writing back', to borrow Bill Ashcroft, Gareth Griffiths, and Helen Tiffin's term, to the fukú brought about by colonial power and its dictatorial legacy in the Dominican Republic. In narrator Yunior's terms, then, writing back operates as his 'very own zafa' to ward off Columbus' curse (*Brief* p. 7). Reading the novel hemispherically and as intersecting and engaging with both Caribbean and American literary traditions opens up an identifiable site where his writing can be read as a hybrid text that impels readers to reconceive of citizenship as hemispheric and hybrid while simultaneously nationally inflected. As Rigoberto González notes, the novel 'reaffirmed the strong connections Latinos maintain with their ancestral homeland's culture, language and history. It also re-energised these questions: Who is American? What is the American experience?'[10] González's comments here, while broad and rhetorical, resonate with the key questions of this book: how do contemporary authors engage with the multivalent character of American identity and citizenship?

Díaz sets *The Brief Wondrous Life of Oscar Wao* in the same fictive universe as his two collections of short stories *Drown* (1996) and *This is How You Lose Her* (2012). This universe is one in which readers familiar with Díaz's work will recognise the narrator as Yunior, despite Yunior identifying himself explicitly only late in the novel, when Oscar's sister Lola is said to have used his name to ask him to drive her home (*Brief* p. 169). His continued presence in Díaz's work can be read as part of a trope in Caribbean writing in which characters 'escape fixity both within and between texts' (p. 153). Describing Díaz's work, Jelly-Schapiro suggests that *The Brief Wondrous Life of Oscar Wao* 'evince[es] an avowedly regional, and Caribbean, approach to history and to writing', one that is 'centrally engaged with the impossibilities of nation for small islands and, as such, concerned with more encompassing conceptions of Caribbean identity'.[11] Monica Hanna also sees Díaz as 'creating a pastiche that attempts to capture the Caribbean diasporic experience', which, for readers possibly encountering such a text for the first time, has the effect of both including them and alienating them from the text because of the sheer number of allusive references.[12]

As well as being read for its explicitly Caribbean tropes, Díaz's work is often read as contributing to an existing tradition of US ethnic and immigrant writing. As a Latino writer whose work contributes to the rich tapestry of US literature, his work has been read as 'a harrowing meditation on public and private history and the burdens of familial history'[13] and 'a self-reflexive work that catalogues and meditates upon its variety of narrative modes'.[14] Here, I explore how his novel enacts a hybrid literary citizenship that reaches back to the colonisation of the Americas, the *fukú americanus*. I read Díaz's novel as one that is concerned with hemispheric citizenship and belonging, as theorised by Jose Martí, for example, the Cuban revolutionary and poet, who in 1891 exhorted us to consider the continent from what Caroline Levander and Robert S. Levine describe as 'a comparative, hemispheric perspective—to think of the hypothetical villager's relation to the larger "American" cosmos'.[15] Only through the development of what Levander and Levine call 'a multilayered positionality in relation to local, national, and hemispheric cultures' can 'full civic representation in a hybrid American world' be achieved.[16] Likewise, in his *Contrapunteo cubano del tabaco y del azúcar* (1947), Fernando Ortiz theorises *transculturación*, the process by which hybrid cultures emerge, defined by Bronislaw Malinowski as 'a process in which a new reality emerges, compounded and complex; a reality that is not a mechanical agglomeration of characters, not even a mosaic, but a new phenomenon, original and independent'.[17] These appeals to broadening definitions of culture and identity find resonance in notions of hemispheric citizenship, where conceptions of 'nation' are opened up to consider how continental, hemispheric, colonial, and postcolonial flows have impacted cultural and civic belonging.

In his depiction of hemispheric identity and citizenship, Díaz allows readers access to a range of characters, experiences, and languages. As Sam Anderson puts it, Díaz's work 'is defined by this kind of radical inclusiveness — the language of drug dealers and Tolkien dorks; the problems of destitute Dominican women and their more privileged American sons'.[18] The 'radical inclusiveness' Anderson describes is democratising while also meditating on the historical circumstances that impact Díaz's characters. As he puts it: 'I am interested in what I witnessed as a diasporic subject, in what happens to families when they're shattered and scattered, what is possible when one attempts to reinvent themselves in a new land and what is impossible.'[19] Díaz's comments here resonate with Michiko Kakutuni's comments on 'the two worlds [Díaz's] characters inhabit: the Dominican Republic, the ghost-haunted motherland that shapes their nightmares and their dreams; and America (a k a New Jersey), the land of freedom and hope and not-so-shiny possibilities that they've fled to as part of the great Dominican diaspora'.[20] Likewise, Lev Grossman recognises that 'Having escaped to New Jersey, [Díaz's characters] still suffer the manifold curses of the old country, still shiver in the chilly shadow of the departed Dominican dictator Rafael Trujillo'.[21] The violence of the Dominican Republic is replaced with a different variety once characters arrive in the United States.

Díaz's hybrid novel continues to invoke the violent histories of the Caribbean and the Americas in its titular engagement with Bartoleme de las Casas' *A Brief Account of the Devastation of the Indies* (1542) even while overlaying the play in his title with the imagery of the magical and miraculous – *The Brief Wondrous Life*. Significantly, Yunior shares his surname with de las Casas, and perhaps his first name too, if we choose to read him as a descendent, further suggesting that Yunior's writing serves as more than a mere biography of Oscar de León. Like the sixteenth-century de las Casas' *Account*, Yunior's records his view of history of the Dominican Republic with a view to exposing atrocities perpetrated by those in power: Indigenous and enslaved people in the case of Bartoleme de las Casas, and the victims of Trujillo's rule in the case of Oscar and his family. Bartoleme's rather grandiose title, 'Protector of the Indians', finds its parallel in Díaz's novel in repeated references to The Watchers – both a reference to the Marvel comic book characters and to Yunior himself, the god-like, seemingly omniscient narrator able to step outside time to relate the stories of the de Leóns. The novel's title is also evocative of Ernest Hemingway's 1936 short story 'The Brief Happy Life of Francis Macomber', which, in Hemingway's recognisable style, succinctly depicts the life of Francis Macomber, who is a on hunting safari in Africa before he is shot, perhaps unintentionally, by his wife, Margot, who has cheated on him with their guide, Wilson.

By titling the novel in such a way that it simultaneously calls to at least two national and regional literary traditions, Caribbean writing and canonical US literature and historiography, Díaz primes readers for contingent, parallel, and simultaneous narratives and frames the novel as a hybrid yet originary text. Similarly, excavating the etymology of the name Oscar opens up multiple strands of interpretation, both of which imbue the name with elements of the supernatural and are consistent with Díaz's allusive writing style. Given Díaz's own preoccupation with the science fiction genre and the mythical or marvellous, it does not seem unreasonable that the name evokes the Old Norse *Ásgeirr*, which is composed of the words 'god' and 'spear'. Asgard is also the realm of the Norse gods, and in the Marvel Comic Universe, the fictional realm of the Asgardians, including the comic superhero Thor. Given this, it is also not strange that this god-like name be juxtaposed with the Irish etymology of the name Oscar, which finds its roots in, *os*, or 'deer', and *cara*, which means 'friend'. The story of 'Oscar' that precedes Yunior's story of Oscar is especially relevant given that Oscar Wao is a nickname he is given by Yunior and other boys who are making fun of his Doctor Who Halloween costume, humorously missing the sci-fi reference and instead mistaking it for a different literary reference that allows them to taunt him about his perceived homosexuality: 'I couldn't believe how much he looked like that fat homo Oscar Wilde, and I told him so' (p. 180) so that Oscar Wilde is changed to Oscar Wao by the Spanish inflection of English and its engagement with Irish literature and history: 'Oscar Wao, quién es Oscar Wao, and that was it, all of us started calling him that' (p. 180). That Oscar's mere name is to be read as a palimpsest is consistent with his own character development as well as Díaz and Yunior's own palimpsestic novel, in which various narratives as well as other formal elements come together in service of the broader de León story being told in the novel.

The novel's settings also reflect the multivalent nature of citizenship conveyed by Díaz. As Silvio Torres-Saillant puts it, 'the crossnational setting of the novel may be said to expand the physical territory that the country's literary imagination can cover to encompass genealogies, places, histories, and people in sites located elsewhere'.[22] This expansion of readers' 'literary imagination' allows readers to explore what Elisabeth Maria Mermann-Jozwiak calls 'narratives of multiculturalism'.[23] Accordingly, 'by portraying the cultural flows that reach beyond the borders of the nation', Díaz exposes readers to alternative narratives of citizenship and belonging beyond national frames.[24] By framing discourses of citizenship as extending outside national borders of readers' literary imaginations, Díaz offers a queering of citizenship that is concerned with hemispheric literary and civic identity.

Rewriting Dominican history

The hemispheric citizenship developed by Díaz can best be identified in Yunior's writing (and rewriting) of the history of the Dominican Republic. However, Díaz complicates Yunior's historiography by casting him into a writerly role that I call the dictator-narrator. As with any narrator, Yunior is read as omniscient; however, by calling Yunior's omniscience into question, Díaz encourages readers to overthrow Yunior's dictatorial narrative. In this way, Díaz posits the possibility of a post-dictatorial future. In this section, I theorise how Díaz, through Yunior, writes a readerly history of the Dominican Republic with a particular focus on the brutal dictatorship years of Trujillo. As Hanna puts it, 'Yunior becomes a writer-historian in the process of researching Oscar's family, but the history that he tells is not one of linear progression like conventional representations of history'.[25] Yunior relegates the history of Trujillo, cast as a villainous character in the Great Man theory of history, to the extensive footnotes of his novel, so that Yunior is able to focus on a character-driven narrative. Instead of individual narratives being read as footnotes to a broader history, in this novel, Díaz foregrounds the stories of members of one family, showing the devastation wrought by Trujillo's rule, itself only rendered in footnotes in his text. In figuring the history of the de León family as extending back to the 'discovery' and subsequent exploitation of the new world, Díaz casts the de Leóns as existing outside time, even though the family 'line' dies with Oscar. As Elisabeth Maria Mermann-Jozwiak notes, 'History does not function as the backdrop for the plot; instead, the story of the family is deeply interwoven with the history of the nation'.[26] Indeed, regardless of the family being fictional, the de Leóns have real-life ancestors, as Felipe Fernández-Armesto uncovers in his own revised, Hispanic history of the United States: 'Juan Ponce de León, a Castillian gentleman of obscure origins, had made a favorable impression as governor of the town and province of Higüey in Hispaniola.'[27] While there is no evidence that either Díaz or Yunior has access to (or interest in) this information, Yunior's rewriting of Dominican history is made more relevant and credible by the existence of real life ancestors for the de Leóns.[28]

However, it is wise to read Yunior, as both a narrator and a character, with suspicion. He goes to great pains to cast himself as a Watcher, another allusion to the Marvel Comic Universe species, described as 'the oldest species in the universe, committed to observing and compiling knowledge on all aspects of the universe without any interference'.[29] The Watchers, then, possess limitless knowledge and powers, and in the Marvel Comic Universe are intended to act as neutral observers – something Yunior, who we discover at the end of the novel is now a writer and teacher of composition and creative writing, recognises as a useful trait in a narrator. However, one Watcher, Uatu, reveals himself to the Fantastic Four and is later put on trial for contravening his species' policy of non-interference. Yunior has no such policy of non-interference and much of the narrative is based on memories of his own interactions with Oscar and Lola.

Like the Watchers, Yunior is god-like, as well as being a narrator whose proper name we are never told, though Díaz admits 'Yunior' is a nickname of his, and the name is at least in part intended to be a joke about the mispronounciation of Díaz's own first name by non-Spanish speakers and readers. The book Yunior writes is not simply the life story of Oscar de León and the contingent life stories of his sister, mother, and other family members, but also the story of the process through which Yunior writes a book based on his own reading and interpretation of the writing Oscar has left behind, which comprises letters, unfinished book manuscripts, writing notebooks, and space operas. Yunior's act of writing is, therefore, predicated on the act of reading Oscar's work, which is referenced over the course of the novel and most explicitly in its closing pages, when Yunior discloses that he has 'four refrigerators' in his basement containing Oscar's 'books, his games, his manuscript, his comic books, his papers' (p. 331). In this way, Díaz's novel is narrated by a writer with his own agenda (to ward off the fukú), and whose material is drawn from his own readerly interpretations, so that by the time the novel is read, it is utter hearsay.

In a section towards the end of the novel, entitled 'A Note from Your Author', Yunior addresses the question of his own unreliability, offering the reader more 'believable' scenarios at this juncture of the plot and asking: 'Would this be better? Yes? But then I'd be lying. I know I've thrown a lot of fantasy and sci-fi in the mix but this is supposed to be a *true* account of the Brief Wondrous Life of Oscar Wao' (p. 285). Yunior's appeal to his readers in the final pages of the novel serves as a reminder of his own lack of credibility. He undermines his own authority in his admission that his narrative draws on fantasy or sci-fi, not because these are 'lesser' genres but because of his insistence that his account of Oscar Wao's life is true. The juxtaposition here of Oscar de León with his interpellated Oscar Wao personal adds a further layer of fantasy, pushing readers to remain sceptical of Yunior's narrative.

Formally and stylistically, Díaz's novel confounds readerly expectations, not least because of its relentless allusions to comic books, science-fiction, and fantasy literature. As well as his use of intertextual allusions to a range of material from *The Fantastic Four* to *The Lord of the Rings* to Stephen King, Díaz employs footnotes – usually focused on exposing the 'true' – or at least revised – history of the Dominican Republic to provide a supplementary narrative line for the reader to follow. In providing readers with an alternative narrative of the history of the Dominican Republic, Díaz's novel has the effect of, as Anne Garland Mahler puts it, 'collapsing the difference between historiographical and fictional registers by inextricably blending the two'.[30] Indeed, over the course of the novel, Díaz's thirty-three extensive footnotes offer the reader additional commentary to the main plot of the novel, predominantly in relation to Trujillo and the modern history of the Dominican Republic. However, following the Derridean interpretation of supplementarity, I argue that Yunior's footnotes are used as devices to supplement the gaps in written history that Trujillo's rule rendered unrecorded. These footnotes work as testimony in the accounting of Trujillo while also continuing to textually evoke a Caribbean aesthetic. In the first footnote, which runs across two pages of the novel proper, Trujillo is described as 'a personaje so outlandish, so perverse, so dreadful that not even a sci-fi writer could have made his ass up. Famous for changing ALL THE NAMES OF ALL THE LANDMARKS in the Dominican Republic to honor himself [...] for expecting, no *insisting* on absolute veneration from his pueblo [...] and for his almost *supernatural* abilities' (pp. 2–3). In a novel that casts an ordinary young man, Oscar, as a superhero, these footnoted comments about Trujillo's 'supernatural abilities' allow Díaz to 'centralize the marginalized character of Oscar and marginalizes the dictator as a minor character'.[31] This contrapuntal writing of history not only 'plays out power relations structurally within the text' but also foregrounds the orality of the novel, since the footnotes' spatiality 'reproduces the asides and interruptions that constitute oral narrative'.[32]

Reading the footnotes as a parallel narrative or supplement not only has the effect of making present the gaps in the officially recorded history of the Dominican Republic by metafictionally representing the narratives of those who suffered under Trujillo, but also resists official accounts. Writing on the concept of the supplement, Derrida suggests that it 'has not only the power of procuring an absent presence through its image; procuring it for us through the proxy of the sign, it [also] holds it at a distance and masters it'.[33] As well as the mastery they symbolise, the footnotes also serve to protect Yunior's narrative, which must be written down, for 'when speech fails to protect presence, writing becomes necessary. It must *be added* to the word urgently'.[34] Once again, however, Yunior's own unreliability must be reckoned with, because as Hanna observes, 'Yunior consumes and embodies the stories of Oscar, Lola, Belicia, and Abelard as a way to write Dominican Americans into history'.[35] In his consumption and embodiment of the de Leóns, Yunior's history is exposed as constructed, like any other. This allows Díaz to emphasise to readers 'the constructed nature of all histories and narratives in general', while also compelling them 'to examine the power structures behind the act of telling'.[36] Accordingly, Díaz uses Yunior as a dictator-narrator but only as a foil in a broader agenda of questioning history. As Hanna reminds us, the novel 'implicitly implores readers to question [Yunior's] authority in taking over the narration of the lives of Oscar and his family'.[37] In this way, Anne Garland Mahler is right when she suggests that 'Díaz promotes a writing that does not repress its own inherent violence but rather exposes it in order to disarm tyrannical power of perhaps its most effective weapon: the written word'.[38]

In one of his many interviews, Díaz himself reflects on his use of footnotes. As he puts it:

> The footnotes are there for a number of reasons; primarily, to create a double narrative. The footnotes, which are in the lower frequencies, challenge the main text, which is the higher narrative. The footnotes are like the voice of the jester, contesting the proclamations of the king. In a book that's all about the dangers of dictatorship, the dangers of the single voice—this felt like a smart move to me ... This novel (I cannot say it enough) is all about the dangers of dictatorship—Trujillo is just the face I use to push these issues—but the real dictatorship is in the book itself, in its telling; and that's what I think is most disturbing: how deeply attached we all are to the institution of dictatorship.[39]

Multilingual futures

If Díaz's crafting of Yunior as what I call a dictator-narrator is intended to alert readers not only to the novel's complex historical and historiographic narrative but also to our own 'disturbing' attachment to dictatorship, his use of language looks instead to the future, and the potential of a new, multilingual generation of characters becoming capable of escaping the fukú. As Monica Hanna, Jennifer Harford Vargas, and José David Saldívar suggest, Díaz's writing works 'to envision and articulate alternatives to the logics of coloniality' and here, I map how *The Brief Wondrous Life of Oscar Wao*, while focusing on the history of a family as it reflects that of a nation, also offers a view of the future through its experimentation with languages.[40] Yunior's reconstruction and restoration of the Dominican Republic's 'shattered history' is rendered not only in English, but also often unitalicised and generally untranslated Spanish, as well as what Díaz calls 'a mash-up of codes'.[41] Here, I explore how theories of multilingualism, and specifically the practice of translanguaging, can be used to offer a reading of the novel that interpellates readers as empowered, multilingual citizens, even as the same readers follow Oscar to his eventual demise.

Díaz himself has a complex relationship with the English language. As a first-generation immigrant who grew up in Santo

Domingo and who learned English slowly, only upon moving to New Jersey as a young child, the process of adopting the language 'was a miserable experience' that Díaz describes as 'torturous' and 'a brutal slog'.[42] While he still suffers from 'the trauma of English acquisition' – the humorous phrasing here evokes a relationship of colonisation – he does describe his sense of language as 'a life where both English and Spanish are in italics in [his] brain'.[43] Díaz's simultaneous identification and disidentification with languages is perhaps not especially unusual for a first-generation immigrant, but it does allow for a reading of his work as reflecting Wilson Harris' description of Caribbean writing as the 'limbo gateway',[44] which Ashcroft, Griffiths, and Tiffin suggest allows for 'the de-imperialisation of apparently monolithic European forms, ontologies, and epistemologies'.[45] The limbo gateway is an especially useful metaphor for reading Díaz's diasporic work as the novel's narrative settings are in constant motion, often looking away from the 'place' of the narrative at one particular moment towards either the Dominican Republic or the United States, as when Yunior describes Oscar's life and job after he has graduated from university in relation to his plans for the summer, which are to visit the Dominican Republic: 'Every summer Santo Domingo slaps the Diaspora engine into reverse, yanks back as many of its expelled children as it can' (*Brief* p. 271). The reading experience is therefore also one of constant displacement, both in terms of setting and in terms of linguistic register, and reflects the experiences of Díaz's immigrant characters.

Díaz's fusion of languages, a further articulation of the literary hybridity discussed at the beginning of this chapter, is made evident from the outset of the novel. As Yunior opens by speculating on the many origin stories of fukú, he offers evidence that even Columbus, as fukú's 'midwife' (p. 1), suffered from the curse: 'despite "discovering" the New World the Admiral died miserable and syphilitic, hearing divine (dique) voices' (p. 1). Only three sentences into the novel, Díaz gestures towards a different language, giving readers none of the standard readerly cues to translate the word 'dique'. Even a more diligent reader who researches the word 'dique' will find multiple, unrelated (and probably incorrect in this context) translations of the word: Google Translate suggests that dique can variously mean dam, dike, dock, levee, and dyke. However, Díaz's clue lies at the start of the very next sentence, which begins: 'In Santo Domingo'. Indeed, in the Dominican Republic, dique can mean 'supposedly' or 'it is said'.

This in itself echoes the first words of the novel: 'They say' (p. 1). In the space of four sentences, then, Díaz draws on three languages: English (the bulk), Dominican Republic Spanish (dique), and Latinised Spanish and English (the term or concept of *fukú americanus*, designed of course to simulate scientific naming practices of living things).

The linguistic simultaneity that frames the start of the novel can be found throughout, and although, as I have discussed, Yunior writes with the authority of an omniscient narrator, each of the characters he 'inhabits' speaks, writes, and thinks in the same seamless multilingual register. Díaz himself finds multilingualism thrilling, if mystifying: 'The older I get and the more time I spend in language work, the more aware I am of how little I understand the powerful forces that have allowed both English and Spanish to spread across the world, to thrive, to create entirely new edifices for themselves, which permits the kind of linguistic simultaneity that I so thrill in'.[46] Where Díaz revels in the seemingly cosmic power of language and coloniality, Ashcroft, Griffiths, and Tiffin remind us that 'Language becomes the medium through which a structure of power is perpetuated, and the medium through which conceptions of "truth", "order", and "reality" become established'.[47] By not privileging one language over another in *The Brief Wondrous Life of Oscar Wao*, Díaz destabilises the primacy of English in order to reflect on not only the multilingualism of his characters, but also his readers, and the nature of language in the United States. As Fernández-Armesto notes, 'The status of English could and probably will change. The English of the United States has already borrowed many peculiarities of its grammar and lexicon from other languages, especially Spanish and Yiddish'.[48]

Reading the novel through the lens of translanguaging, a process that theorises 'the linguistic practices of speakers labeled as bilingual or multilingual, and to describe as well the many ways that those practices are leveraged for a variety of purposes',[49] is useful as it offers a framework through which to understand how 'multilingual individuals ... integrate social spaces (and thus "language codes") that have been formerly practiced separately in different places'.[50] In the context of the novel, translanguaging allows for a hemispheric analysis of linguistic citizenship, shedding light on the sites at which US citizenship and citizenship of the Dominican Republic intersect and merge to form a hybrid linguistic space in which characters and their readers are able to envisage multiple modes of linguistic belonging. However, translanguaging is not simply the theorisation of a 'hybrid' space of multilingualism. As Ofelia Garcia and Li Wei put it, 'Translanguaging goes beyond hybridity theory that recognizes the complexity of people's everyday spaces and multiple resources to make sense of the world'.[51] By reading citizenship as it plays out through the interplay of language choice, readers are offered a way of 'capturing the expanded complex practices of speakers who could not avoid having had languages inscribed in their body, and yet live between different societal and semiotic contexts as they interact with a complex array of speakers'.[52] Not only do these characters interact with a range of speakers, but also an equally 'complex' array of readers, since, as Fernández-Armesto puts it, 'There was never a time when most Americans, or most people in what is now the United States, were white English Protestants'.[53]

In recognising the already existing complexity of US identity and making explicit the multilingualism of many US readers, Díaz's work can be read as helping 'to disrupt the socially constructed language hierarchies that are responsible for the suppression of the languages of many minoritized peoples'.[54] As he puts it, 'By keeping the Spanish as normative in a predominantly English text, I wanted to remind readers of the fluidity of languages, the mutability of languages. And to mark how steadily English is transforming Spanish and Spanish is transforming English'.[55] This is modelled for readers in a humorous encounter between Yunior and Oscar when they move in together at university. Yunior remembers:

> Hail, Dog of God, was how he welcomed me my first day in Demarest.
> Took a week before I figured out what the hell he meant.
> God. Domini. Dog. Canis.
> Hail, Dominicanis. (p. 171)

This is the clearest model that Yunior provides to readers so that they can understand the complex multilingual processes at work in the lives of characters (and people) who 'hail' from more than one place or language of citizenship. Yunior's account of this exchange serves as a cipher for all other multilingual moments in the novel. Presented with this cipher, readers must then 'do extra work' of translating and positioning themselves within a multilingual translanguaging framework in order to fully comprehend the novel, in the same way that Yunior, as Oscar's first reader, does.[56] Evelyn Ch'ien describes

'Spanish as an assumed American language' in this novel, where untranslated Spanish appears normatively in reported and recounted conversations and accounts.[57]

As well as English and Spanish, Díaz also identifies the genre of science fiction as having a language of its own, and one that he mobilises because he sees it as 'a third language for our cultural moment'.[58] This perhaps helps to explain the abundance of science-fiction references in the novel, which can make reading it a challenge for those readers who are not well-versed in the genre. In this way, translanguaging is best understood as 'refer[ing] to using one's idiolect, that is, one's linguistic repertoire, without regard for socially and politically defined language labels or boundaries'[59] and the prevalence of science fiction in the novel pushes readers to 'manage the dislocations and confusions and fantasies of "progress"', as well as, Díaz suggests, 'help[ing] us read the present in ways that are indispensable'.[60]

Yet Díaz sees his relationship with readers as one of hospitality and generosity, terms associated less with the politics of reading and more often with the politics of identity: 'what I've discovered is that I'm sort of of the generation that belonged to the time when writers were more securely embedded in readers and hadn't been isolated into a professional cadre with each other [...] Because when you're writing for other readers, readers bring to the experience of reading, when they like your book, a tremendous generosity'.[61] By working together with readers, then, this novel is a model for collaborative reading that reflects the parallel and contingent narratives that are unravelled in the text itself.

Díaz demonstrates the potential for such a practice of collaborative reading when Yunior, writing from the novel's fictive present and as himself, imagines a future meeting between him, the guardian of Oscar's writing and memory, and Lola's daughter, Isis, who he describes as 'happy' and 'speaks Spanish and English' (p. 329). In Yunior's reverie, Isis 'will come looking for answers' about the fukú on her family (and nation), and Yunior will have 'prepared it all' (p. 330) and show her where he stores Oscar's 'books, his games, his manuscript, his comic books, his papers --- refrigerators the best proof against fire, against earthquake, against almost anything' (p. 330). Yunior sees his act of preserving, reading, and recording Oscar's life as only one in a process of ending the fukú. This process must be completed by Isis, who Yunior believes will 'take all we've done and all we've learned and add her own insights and she'll put an end to it' (pp. 330–1). By collaboratively reading Oscar's writing, the insipiration for Yunior's writing of *The Brief Wondrous Life of Oscar Wao*, Isis will live up to her mythical namesake, who restored her brother, Osiris, to life after he was murdered and his body parts scattered across the world. In turn, in collaboratively reading, the novel's Isis looks to the future and ends the *fukú americanus* that has shattered the histories of the Antilles. Isis is protected by 'powerful elder magic' (p. 229) and is the embodiment of the hemispheric, hybrid citizenship this chapter has explored.

Notes

1. Derek Walcott, 'The Antilles: Fragments of Epic Memory' (7 December 1992). www.nobelprize.org/nobel_prizes/literature/laureates/1992/walcott-lecture.html (accessed 15 July 2016).
2. Ibid.
3. Alison Flood, '*The Brief Wondrous Life of Oscar Wao* Declared 21st Century's Best Novel so Far' (20 January 2015). www.theguardian.com/books/2015/jan/20/brief-wondrous-life-of-oscar-wao-novel-21st-century-best-junot-Díaz (accessed 11 October 2015).
4. Jane Ciabattari, 'The 21st Century's 12 Greatest Novels' (19 January 2015). www.bbc.com/culture/story/20150119-the-21st-centurys-12-best-novels (accessed 11 October 2015).
5. Christopher Taylor, 'Performance Art' (23 February 2008). www.theguardian.com/books/2008/feb/23/featuresreviews.guardianreview20 (accessed 11 October 2015).
6. Junot Díaz, *The Brief Wondrous Life of Oscar Wao* (London: Faber & Faber, 2008 [2007]), p. ix. All subsequent references will be included in parentheses in the main body of the text.
7. Megan O'Rourke, '*The Brief Wondrous Life of Oscar Wao*: Questions for Junot Díaz' (8 November 2007). www.slate.com/articles/news_and_politics/the_highbrow/2007/11/the_brief_wondrous_life_of_oscar_wao.html (accessed 11 October 2008).
8. Silvio Torres-Saillant, 'Artistry, Ancestry, and Americanness in the Works of Junot Díaz in *The Brief Wondrous Life of Oscar Wao*', in *Junot Díaz and the Decolonial Imagination*, ed. Monica Hanna, Jennifer Harford Vargas, and José David Saldívar (Durham, NC and London: Duke University Press, 2016), pp. 115–146, at p. 120.
9. Joshua Jelly-Schapiro, 'Ground Zero(es) of the New World: Geographies of Violence in Junot Díaz and Edwidge Danticat', *Transforming Anthropology: Journal of the Association of Black Anthropologists* 21 (2013): pp. 169–86, at p. 172.

10   Rigoberto González, qtd in Ciabattari, 'The 21st Century's 12 Greatest Novels'.
11   Jelly-Schapiro, 'Ground Zero(es) of the New World', p. 170.
12   Monica Hanna, 'Reassembling the Fragments: Battling Historiographies, Caribbean Discourse, and Nerd Genres in Junot Díaz's *The Brief Wondrous Life of Oscar Wao*', *Callaloo* 33:2 (2010): pp. 498–520, at p. 500.
13   Michiko Kakutani, 'Travails of an Outcast' (4 September 2007). www.nytimes.com/2007/09/04/books/04Diaz.html (accessed 11 October 2015).
14   Maria del Pilar Blanco, 'Reading the Novum World: The Literary Geography of Science Fiction in Junot Díaz's *The Brief Wondrous Life of Oscar Wao*', in *Surveying the American Tropics: A Literary Geography from New York to Rio*, ed. Maria Cristina Fumigalli, Peter Hulme, Owen Robinson, and Leslie Wylie (Liverpool: Liverpool University Press, 2013), pp. 49–74, at p. 50.
15   Caroline F. Levander and Robert S. Levine, eds, *Hemispheric American Studies* (New Brunswick and London: Rutgers University Press, 2008), p. 8.
16   Ibid.
17   Bronislaw Malinowski, quoted in Ofelia García and Li Wei, *Translanguaging: Language, Bilingualism and Education* (Basingstoke: Palgrave Macmillan, 2014), p. 21.
18   Sam Anderson, 'Junot Díaz Hates Writing Short Stories' (27 September 2012). www.nytimes.com/2012/09/30/magazine/junot-diaz-hates-writing-short-stories.html (accessed 11 October 2015).
19   Henry Ace Knight, 'An Interview with Junot Díaz' (n.d). www.asymptotejournal.com/interview/an-interview-junot-diaz/ (accessed 10 January 2017).
20   Kakutani, 'Travails of an Outcast'.
21   Lev Grossman, 'Top 10 Fiction Books. #1. *The Brief Wondrous Life of Oscar Wao*' (9 December 2007). http://content.time.com/time/specials/2007/article/0,28804,1686204_1686244_1691840,00.html (accessed 11 October 2015).
22   Torres-Saillant, 'Artistry, Ancestry, and Americanness', p. 121.
23   Elisabeth Maria Mermann-Jozwiak, 'Beyond Multiculturalism: Ethnic Studies, Transnationalism, and Junot Díaz's *Oscar Wao*', *Ariel: A Review of International English Literature* 43:2 (2013), pp. 1–24, at p. 7.
24   Ibid.
25   Hanna, 'Reassembling the Fragments', p. 500.
26   Mermann-Jozwiak, 'Beyond Multiculturalism', p. 9.
27   Felipe Fernàndez-Armesto, *Our America: A Hispanic History of the United States* (New York and London: Norton, 2014), p. 7.
28   As well as this, the novel is dedicated to Elizabeth de León, Díaz's fiancée.

29 'Watchers' (n.d.). http://marvel.wikia.com/wiki/Watchers (accessed 12 July 2017).
30 Anne Garland Mahler, 'The Writer as Superhero: Fighting the Colonial Curse in Junot Díaz's *The Brief Wondrous Life of Oscar Wao*', *Journal of Latin American Cultural Studies* 19:2 (2010), pp. 119–40, at p. 120.
31 Jennifer Harford Vargas, 'Dictating a Zafa: The Power of Narrative Form as Ruin-Reading in *The Brief Wondrous Life of Oscar Wao*', in *Junot Díaz and the Decolonial Imagination*, ed. Monica Hanna, Jennifer Harford Vargas, and José David Saldívar (Durham, NC and London: Duke University Press, 2016), pp. 201–27, at p. 213.
32 Ibid., p. 216.
33 Jacques Derrida, *Of Grammatology*, trans Gayatri Chakravorty Spivak (Baltimore and London: Johns Hopkins University Press, 1997 [1967]), p. 155.
34 Ibid., p. 144.
35 Monica Hanna, 'A Portrait of the Artist as a Young Cannibalist: Reading Yunior (Writing) in *The Brief Wondrous Life of Oscar Wao*', in *Junot Díaz and the Decolonial Imagination*, ed. Monica Hanna, Jennifer Harford Vargas, and José David Saldívar (Durham, NC and London: Duke University Press, 2016), pp. 89–111, at p. 91.
36 Hanna, 'Reassembling the Fragments', p. 501.
37 Hanna, 'A Portrait of the Artist as a Young Cannibalist', p. 95.
38 Mahler, 'The Writer as Superhero', p. 120.
39 O'Rourke, '*The Brief Wondrous Life of Oscar Wao*: Questions for Junot Díaz'.
40 Monica Hanna, Jennifer Harford Vargas, and José David Saldívar, 'Junot Díaz and the Decolonial Imagination: From Island to Empire', in *Junot Díaz and the Decolonial Imagination* (Durham, NC and New York: Duke University Press, 2016), pp. 1–29, at p. 8.
41 Junot Díaz, quoted in Evelyn Nien-Ming Ch'ien, *Weird English* (Cambridge, MA and London: Harvard University Press, 2004), p. 204.
42 Knight, 'An Interview with Junot Díaz', n.p.
43 Ibid.
44 Wilson Harris, 'History, Fable and Myth in the Caribbean and Guianas', *Caribbean Quarterly* 54:1/2 (2008): pp. 5–38, at p. 11.
45 Bill Ashcroft, Gareth Griffiths, and Helen Tiffin, eds, *The Empire Writes Back* (London: Taylor & Francis, 2003 (2nd edn)), p. 151.
46 Karen Cresci, 'Junot Díaz, "We exist in a constant state of translation. We just don't like it"' (n.d.). www.buenosairesreview.org/2013/05/diaz-constant-state-of-translation/ (accessed 16 October 2018).
47 Bill Ashcroft, Gareth Griffiths, and Helen Tiffin, 'Introduction', in *The Empire Writes Back* (London: Taylor & Francis, 1989), pp. 1–13, at p. 7.
48 Fernàndez-Armesto, *Our America*, p. xxvii.

49 Ricardo Otheguy, Ofelia García, and Wallis Reid, 'Clarifying Translanguaging and Deconstructing Named Languages: A Perspective from Linguistics', *Applied Linguistic Review* 6:3 (2015), pp. 281–307, at p. 282.
50 García and Wei, *Translanguaging*, p. 24.
51 Ibid.
52 Ibid., p. 18.
53 Fernàndez-Armesto, *Our America*, p. 5.
54 Otheguy *et al.*, 'Clarifying Translanguaging', p. 282.
55 Junot Díaz, quoted in Ch'ien, *Weird English*, p. 204.
56 Madeleine Brand and A. Martinez, 'Junot Díaz Reflects on Love in His Latest Book' (13 September 2012). www.scpr.org/programs/brand-martinez/2012/09/13/28399/junot-Díaz-love-immigrant-this-is-how-you-lose-her/ (accessed 12 October 2015).
57 Ch'ien, *Weird English*, p. 205.
58 Knight, 'An Interview with Junot Díaz'.
59 Otheguy *et al.*, 'Clarifying Translanguaging', p. 297.
60 Knight, 'An Interview with Junot Díaz'.
61 Tracy O'Neill, 'Podcast #95: Junot Díaz on the Game of Fiction and Intimacy' (19 January 2016). www.nypl.org/blog/2016/01/19/podcast-junot-Díaz (accessed 21 October 2016).

Conclusion: Yann Martel's lonely book club

Soon after Donald Trump's presidential inauguration in January 2017, and in response to a range of articles citing evidence that the president 'does not read books',[1] anti-Trump protesters began to make plans to 'bury the White House'[2] in literary texts that engage with some of the 45th US president's more divisive and exclusionary policy issues. Frequently appearing on these reading lists is writing by nineteenth-century abolitionist Frederick Douglass, who Trump famously described as 'an example of someone who's done an amazing job and is getting recognized more and more',[3] and Canadian author Margaret Atwood's *The Handmaid's Tale* (1985), a novel set in a dystopian near-future New England where women are socially, civically, and sexually subjugated under a new theonomy premised on Old Testament-inspired religious fanaticism. Of course, this was not the first or only time literary texts have been used in (or as) individual and collective citizen action, and, as I show over the course of these concluding comments, simply sending books to an ill-informed and expert-averse world leader is a strategy not without its problems. In fact, the act of merely prescribing literature as an absolute antidote to bigotry and ignorance is one that has failed in countless civil and social movements. Instead, these final notes are concerned with recognising and exploring the communities of protest that can result in and emerge from such campaigns. Here, I explore one such campaign as it is related over the course of Canadian author Yann Martel's *101 Letters to a Prime Minister: The Complete Letters to Stephen Harper* (2012), a collection of letters drawn from the author's 'What is Stephen Harper Reading?' project.

If the authors and works discussed in previous chapters may have at times seemed to deal with the civic act of reading more figuratively, this chapter offers an exploration of a concrete way that reading can function as a civic act in what I have called the queering of citizenship. Where the writing of Gloria Anzaldúa and Dorothy Allison theorises abstract or fictional spaces of queer belonging, Gregory Scofield's and Guillermo Gómez-Peña's poetry and performance pieces focus on hybrid identities and the importance of their authorial and cultural roles as mediators in finding and navigating new spaces for survival, and in their experiments with literary form, Erín Moure and Junot Díaz enact new kinds of citizens whose existence across the borders of languages is dependent on what Moure would call 'a reading practice in a community of others', and a hemispheric articulation of citizenship and history in Díaz's case. In an important way, Martel's work in *101 Letters to a Prime Minister* can and should be read as working beyond the book. In a sense, then, each of the chapters in *Crossing borders and queering citizenship* can be read as being part of a trajectory of radical civic action based on the singular act of reading. In this way, the reader of this book has been offered multiple entry points to consider how reading can be translated into civic work.

It is important to note that Martel is different from the other authors discussed in this book, primarily because he is a white, male, Canadian citizen. In this sense, he is not peripheral in the same way that I have categorised Anzaldúa, Allison, Scofield, Gómez-Peña, Moure, and Díaz, each of whom occupy identities that are rendered marginal by the exclusionary activities of state-sanctioned citizenship. In this way, then, Martel is the exception that proves the rule; in another sense, his civic action is problematic precisely because he occupies the privileged position of white, male Canadian citizen. Nonetheless, his work can be productively read in its concrete engagement with the queering of citizenship as it has been theorised here.

Martel's *101 Letters to a Prime Minister* marked the end of a three-year project in which the Canadian writer, perhaps most famous for his *Life of Pi* (2001), began writing a series of letters to then-Prime Minister Stephen Harper, enclosing a novel, a collection of short stories, a children's book, a play, or a collection of poetry with every dispatch. Martel never received a personal response from Harper, who in 2004 famously (but perhaps apocryphally) noted that his favourite book was the *Guinness Book of World Records*.[4] Martel has

Conclusion

since described the experience as like being in 'the loneliest book club in the world'.[5]

While Anzaldúa, Allison, Scofield, Gómez-Peña, Moure, and Díaz frequently address their readers directly, such addresses are often to implied, imagined, or postulated readers.[6] This book understands readers as *real*, in opposition to Wolfgang Iser's classical definition of the implied reader, who, for Iser, is 'a construct and in no way to be identified with any real reader'.[7] In Martel's *101 Letters to a Prime Minister*, the idea of the reader is explicit and specific: his letters are addressed to Stephen Harper. Following on from this, it makes sense, then, that each of Martel's letters began with a standard inscription or address: 'To Stephen Harper, / Prime Minister of Canada, / From a Canadian writer, / With best wishes, / Yann Martel.'[8] However, Stephen Harper's lack of engagement with Martel, and Martel's subsequent publication of the letters complicate the seemingly straightforward naming of Martel's intended reader. The fact of Harper's non-responsiveness to Martel's 101 letters and dispatches and Martel's public sharing of these letters opens up and broadens the intended readership, enacting a community of co-readers, both of the letters and books recommended therein. As Martel puts it, 'Communities are made and then gain by sharing books' (p. 15), and in the case of his letter writing and book recommendation project, the sharing of books works to directly address the Canadian prime minister responsible, during his tenure, for CAD 45 million worth of cuts in Canadian arts, culture, and heritage funding, dubbed by pundits as Canada's Culture Wars (or more accurately, a war on culture).

In *101 Letters*, Martel traces his project back to March 2007, when he was invited to Ottawa to take part in the celebrations commemorating the 50th anniversary of the Canada Council for the Arts, as he was a recipient of a Council Grant in 1991 and again in 1997. He recalls how he felt while contemplating the House of Commons, where the celebrations were taking place, and, as he puts it: 'I got to thinking about stillness' (*101 Letters*, p. 7). At these celebrations, the Minister for Canadian Heritage at the time, Bev Oda, delivered a short speech. Martel remembers that Harper 'didn't look up', leading Martel to wonder, 'Who is this man? What makes him tick?' (p. 8). In particular, as Martel reflects, Harper had never declared his 'imaginative assets', those facets of his mind that with the power of elected office can become his dreams but Martel's 'nightmares' (p. 14). For Martel, effective leadership must be informed by art 'in all its incarnations, from the frivolous to the essential' (p. 16), and he saw no evidence that Harper is 'informed by literary culture or, indeed, by culture in general' (p. 12) except in Harper's elimination of arts funding and initiatives over the course of his leadership. As he puts it, 'If Stephen Harper were shaped and informed by literary culture, if he read novels, short stories, plays and poetry, he would love them, he would defend them, he would celebrate them. He would not try to scuttle the public means of sustaining our nation's artistic culture, retreating from doing so only when it's politically expedient' (p. 12). Reading for Martel, then, is a powerful civic act, whether it is undertaken by a political leader or by the citizens 'represented' by that leader. In exercising his civic right to publicly advocate for reading, Martel opens up his tiny, two-person book club to the public, who he implores: 'if you have a book you think Stephen Harper should read, by all means send it to him' (p. 15), providing the address of the Office of the Prime Minister and Privy Council in Ottawa. Invoking the very address of the prime minister serves as a reminder to readers (Harper included) that his is a public office, subject to public scrutiny and accountability.

Martel's view that a political leader should be in possession of 'a deeply thinking, fully-feeling mind', capable of appreciating 'the greatness of literature, and its paradox', encapsulates what Martel sees as the power of literature: that which can '[leap] from the bounds of the local to achieve universal resonance' (p. 19), and instigate change in a reader. Martel uses his own literary celebrity to theorise the power of the citizen, empowering his broader readership with civic agency: 'It is citizens who must move first, and art is an ideal way to help them do that. Art wrestles with its subject matter on a level that the individual, the man, woman, teenager and child on the street, can engage with and react to' (p. 222). Harper's cuts to arts and culture funding serves only, according to Martel, to disempower citizens; in the letter accompanying dispatch 51, William Shakespeare's *Julius Caesar*, Martel asks Harper directly, 'Is it really your aim to transform Canada into a post-literate society?' (pp. 217–18).

In using literature and the act of reading as an act of resistance, then, Martel works to galvanise his readers to enact their own resistance to Harper's policies (and politics). Ultimately, Martel never receives a direct response from Harper – though there are seven form replies from aides and deputies – but he does receive an unsolicited letter from US President Barack Obama in 2010, which he relates

Conclusion

to Harper in dispatch 76 (Alexander Solzhenitsyn's *One Day in the Life of Ivan Denisovich*). Martel uses Obama's letter, which thanks Martel and simply notes of *Life of Pi*, 'It is a lovely book—an elegant proof of God, and the power of storytelling' (p. 318), to offer Harper a reproachful jab as he sends him Solzhenitsyn's famous novel about a day in the life of a gulag prisoner: 'Not all heads of government are as good' (p. 318).

In terms of an engagement with the arts, there is little use in comparing Harper to Obama, who famously noted 'when I think about how I understand my role as citizen, setting aside being president, and the most important set of understandings that I bring to that position of citizen, the most important stuff I've learned I think I've learned from novels'.[9] It is worth noting, however, that Harper's successor, Justin Trudeau, is vocal in his appreciation and support of the arts (temporarily leaving aside his other, more problematic policies). This is not to suggest that Harper lost the 2015 federal election because he does not read, but it does suggest a recognition that working to actively remove arts and literature from the lives of citizens is an unpopular policy, and that public resistance to such policies can make a difference in raising awareness of alternative electoral choices.

Such alternative choices are rendered differently in the writing examined in this book. For Gloria Anzaldúa, individual citizens and readers are called to join a community of new *mestizas* whose multiple and hybrid identifications can work to resist the exclusionary workings of the state – crafting a new architecture for citizenship. Dorothy Allison's writing reminds readers that when left alone, 'trash rises', but this isolation must lead to inclusive, intersectional identities to be successful. For Gregory Scofield questions of citizenship are inextricably linked to the revision of history – both personal and political – and maintaining the connection to Indigenous languages. In his case, his identification as a two-spirited Métis man is reflected in his use of Métis two-spirit vernaculars, and he shares these vernaculars with his readers, who, in reading his work, will learn more of the experiences of the Métis in Canada and elsewhere. Guillermo Gómez-Peña builds alternative civic communities and his performances work to create a more concrete, 'real' text, in collaboration with his readers and audiences. For Gómez-Peña, performance art holds within it a distinct and special potential to sow the seeds of social and political change, because of its immediacy. Erín Moure's writing, while complex and often intimidating, seeks to build a community of readers through the very act of deciphering her work. Moure's community hinges on a readiness on the part of the reader to actively take part in her work. Junot Díaz's articulation of hemispheric citizenship, across languages, exposes and revises the history of tyranny in the Dominican Republic and reminds readers that we have an unhealthy attachment to dictatorship, whether it comes in the form of a political figure or in the form of a dictatorial narrator. Yann Martel publicly resists regressive and conservative cultural policies by encouraging public political figures to read more widely (or at all). Each advances a model for resistance against the exclusionary and marginalising work of contemporary citizenship in North America.

Over the course of this book, I have argued that the civic act of reading works on and blurs the relationship between the status and performance of citizenship and can transform what I have called the 'real conditions' that spurred Gloria Anzaldúa, Dorothy Allison, Gregory Scofield, Guillermo Gómez-Peña, Erín Moure, Junot Díaz, and Yann Martel's work. In focusing on these varied and various lived experiences, this book has sought to engage a critique of state-sanctioned citizenship (and marginalisation), not by merely theorising alternative spaces of belonging for marginalised groups, but by theorising how readers can be mobilised to enact shifts in national understandings of belonging in the United States and Canada.

The act of reading, according to Martel, 'is no longer an elite pastime' (*101 Letters* p. 27). This optimistic, if reductive, statement reveals Martel's own position of privilege, and also suggests that literacy and reading is accessible to everyone, and that the civic empowerment brought on by reading work by peripheral people – as I have shown in this book – can be accessed simply by walking into a public library because, as Martel puts it, 'public libraries are just that, public' (p. 27). While reading should not be an activity only for the privileged, it does mark privilege, and so it becomes all the more important for those occupying the positions of civic, racial, class, and other privileges to read and access work by those who occupy positions of civic exclusion on the basis of race, class, and other 'minority' identifications.

Crossing borders and queering citizenship shows that through the civic act of reading, citizenship – both as a discourse and as a practice – can be changed, queered, and may be able evolve into an iteration of one the models articulated by Allison, Anzaldúa, Scofield, Gómez-Peña, Moure, Díaz, and Martel. State-sanctioned citizenship cannot (yet) exist without a sense of territoriality, and an attachment to territory calls for the sovereignty of the nation state. What is at stake, then, is the legitimacy of the nation state to confer and maintain citizenship in its current exclusionary forms. In different ways, each of the writers in this book calls for the blurring of the distinction not only between the status and habitus of citizenship, but also an interrogation of the validity of the nation state as an entity, if its insistence is to continue to erode the civic rights of a range of minority peoples. Along these lines, I would agree with Kwame Anthony Appiah's assessment that 'the primary mechanism' for the rights of citizenship 'remains the nation-state'.[10] As Appiah puts it, 'Accepting the nation-state means accepting that we have a special responsibility for the life and justice of our own; but we still have to play our part in ensuring that all states respect the rights and meet the needs of their citizens'.[11] The queering of citizenship entails a radically different and intersectional understanding of how recognition, rights, and representation should operate in the contemporary US and Canadian political spheres. Such an understanding must engage with reading because, the act of reading, as Kjell Ivar Skjerdingstad and Paulette Rothbauer remind us, 'precisely makes us see what we did not remember, know, or even imagine'.[12]

Crossing borders and queering citizenship has travelled across the borders of the United States and Canada to explore the writerly strategies deployed by a range of writers – novelists, poets, performance artists, cultural theorists – who position their readers as active agents in the critique and queering of state-sanctioned citizenship. In my use of the term 'peripheral peoples', I have examined work originating from the US–Mexico border, the queer white trash community in the US South, the Indigenous yet precarious position occupied by the Métis, the borders of languages, and from an immigrant Latino writer concerned with hybrid linguistic and historical identities. All the authors and texts under examination seek to craft new *habita* of civic belonging through an engagement with active readers. In these concluding notes, I have sought to theorise, however briefly, articulations of a new *status* of civic belonging, bearing in mind, of course, that these authors are not *representative* of all the possibilities of civic status. Aside from the political and civic connotations of representation, I mean of course that these peripheral identities do not encompass *all marginal identities* in the United States or Canada. I have not, for example, explored writing by African American or

African Canadian authors, or considered writing by those who, for example, identify as Pacific Islanders, as coming from Nunavut communities, or as Puerto Rican, all communities that maintain an equally problematic relationship with either the United States or Canada (and sometimes, both), and whose writing both merits and demands sustained and sensitive attention. In focusing on writing by Anzaldúa, Allison, Scofield, Gómez-Peña, Moure, Díaz, and Martel, I have explored only a few ways in which citizenship can be encountered, acknowledged, critiqued, troubled, and queered by readers, who, more than ever before, are in a position to collaborate and work in solidarity with the continuing struggle for recognition, rights, and representation experienced by minority communities in North America and around the world.

Notes

1. Maggie Haberman, 'A Homebody Finds the Ultimate Home Office' (25 January 2017). www.nytimes.com/2017/01/25/us/politics/president-trump-white-house.html (accessed 31 January 2017).
2. Claire Fallon, 'Trump Doesn't Read, So Protesters Are Flooding His Office With Books' (6 February 2017). www.huffingtonpost.com/entry/send-trump-books-valentines-day_us_5898b09be4b0406131382138 (accessed 15 March 2017).
3. David A. Graham, 'Donald Trump's Narrative of the Life of Frederick Douglass' (1 February 2017). www.theatlantic.com/politics/archive/2017/02/frederick-douglass-trump/515292/ (accessed 20 February 2017).
4. Sonya Bell, 'Fact Check: Stephen Harper and the Guinness Book of World Records' (28 November 2012). www.ipolitics.ca/2012/11/28/dnp-fact-check-stephen-harper-and-the-guinness-book-of-world-records/ (accessed 14 December 2014).
5. Sonya Bell, '101 Letters to a Prime Minister: Yann Martel Opens up His Book Club' (28 November 2012). www.ipolitics.ca/2012/11/28/101-letters-to-a-prime-minister-yann- martel-opens-up-his-book-club/ (accessed 14 December 2014).
6. For more on implied and imagined readers, see Wolfgang Iser, *The Implied Reader: Patterns in Communication from Bunyan to Beckett* (Baltimore and London: Johns Hopkins University Press, 1974). For more on postulated readers, see Wayne C. Booth, *The Rhetoric of Fiction* (Chicago: University of Chicago Press, 1961).
7. Wolfgang Iser, *The Act of Reading: A Theory of Aesthetic Response* (Baltimore: Johns Hopkins University Press, 1978), p. 34.

8 Yann Martel, *101 Letters to a Prime Minister: The Complete Letters to Stephen Harper* (Toronto: Vintage Canada, 2012), p. 17. All subsequent references will appear parenthetically in the text.
9 Barack Obama and Marilynne Robinson, 'President Obama & Marilynne Robinson: A Conversation — II', *The New York Review of Books* (19 November 2015). www.nybooks.com/articles/2015/11/19/president-obama-marilynne-robinson-conversation-2/ (accessed 28 November 2015).
10 Kwame Anthony Appiah, *Cosmopolitanism: Ethics in a World of Strangers* (London: Penguin Books, 2006), p. 163.
11 Ibid.
12 Kjell Ivar Skjedingstad and Paulette M. Rothbauer, 'Introduction: Plotting the Reading Experience', in *Plotting the Reading Experience: Theory/Practice/Politics*, ed. Paulette M. Rothbauer, Kjell Ivar Skjedingstad, Lynne (E. F.) McKechnie, and Knut Oterholm (Waterloo, ON: Wilfrid Laurier University Press, 2016), pp. 1–15, at p. 5.

Bibliography

Acoose, Janice. 'Post *Halfbreed*: Indigenous Writers as Authors of Their Own Realities'. In *Looking at the Words of Our People: First Nations Analysis of Literature*, ed. Jeannette C. Armstrong (Penticton: Theytus, 1993), pp. 27–44.

Adams, Howard. *Prison of Grass: Canada from the Native Point of View* (Toronto: New Press, 1975).

Adams, Howard. *A Tortured People: The Politics of Colonization* (Penticton: Theytus, 1995).

Adams, Rachel. *Continental Divides: Remapping the Cultures of North America* (Chicago: University of Chicago Press, 2009).

Agarwal, Nisha. 'This Bridge Called My Back: A Retro Look at Women of Color and Power' (25 May 2011). www.huffingtonpost.com/nisha-agarwal/this-bridge-called-my-bac_b_418196.html (accessed 30 June 2011).

Alexander, M. Jacqui and Mohanty, Chandra Talpade, eds. 'Introduction: Genealogies, Legacies, Movements'. In *Feminist Genealogies, Colonial Legacies, Democratic Futures* (New York and London: Routledge, 1997), pp. xiii–xlii.

Allison, Dorothy. *Bastard Out of Carolina* (New York: Plume, 1993).

Allison, Dorothy. Interview by Kelly Anderson, transcript of video recording, 18–19 November 2007, Voices of Feminism Oral History Project, Sophia Smith Collection, p. 6. www.smith.edu/libraries/libs/ssc/vof/transcripts/Allison.pdf (accessed 12 February 2017).

Allison, Dorothy. *Skin: Talking about Sex, Class, and Literature* (Ithaca, NY: Firebrand Books, 1994).

Allison, Dorothy. *Trash: Short Stories* (New York: Plume, 2002 [1988]).

Allison, Dorothy. *Two or Three Things I Know for Sure* (New York: Penguin Books, 1995).

Althusser, Louis. 'Ideology and Ideological State Apparatuses'. In *Lenin and Philosophy and other Essays*. Trans. Ben Brewster (New York and London: Monthly Review Press, 1971), pp. 121–76.

Bibliography

Alurista. 'Cultural Nationalism and Xicano Literature during the Decade of 1965–1975'. *MELUS* 8:2 *Ethnic Literature and Cultural Nationalism* (1981): pp. 22–34.
'An Act making Emergency Supplemental Appropriations for Defense, the Global War on Terror, and Tsunami Relief, for the fiscal year ending September 30, 2005, and for other purposes' (11 May 2005). www.gpo.gov/fdsys/pkg/PLAW-109publ13/content-detail.html (accessed 17 October 2010).
Anderson, Benedict. *Imagined Communities: Reflections on the Origin and Spread of Nationalism* (London and New York: Verso, 1991).
Anderson, Chris. *'Métis': Race, Recognition, and the Struggle for Indigenous Peoplehood* (Vancouver and Toronto: University of British Columbia Press, 2014).
Anderson, Sam. 'Junot Díaz Hates Writing Short Stories' (27 September 2012). www.nytimes.com/2012/09/30/magazine/junot-diaz-hates-writing-short-stories.html (accessed 11 October 2015).
Andrews, Jennifer. 'Irony, Métis Style: Reading the Poetry of Marilyn Dumont and Gregory Scofield'. *Canadian Poetry: Studies, Documents, Reviews* 50 (2002): pp. 6–31.
Angus, Ian. *A Border Within: National Identity, Cultural Plurality, and Wilderness* (Montreal and Kingston: McGill-Queen's University Press, 1997).
Anzaldúa, Gloria. *Borderlands/La Frontera: The New Mestiza* (San Francisco: Aunt Lute Books, 1997 [1987]).
Anzaldúa, Gloria. Gloria Evangelina Anzaldúa Papers, Benson Latin American Collection, University of Texas Libraries, the University of Texas at Austin, Box 183, Folder 2.
Anzaldúa, Gloria. 'To(o) Queer the Writer – Loca, escritoria y chicana'. In *Inversions: Writings by Dykes, Queers & Lesbians*, ed. Betsy Warland (London: Open Letters, 1992), pp. 249–63.
Appiah, Kwame Anthony. *Cosmopolitanism: Ethics in a World of Strangers* (London: Penguin Books, 2006).
Armstrong, Jeanette. 'Four Decades: An Anthology of Canadian Native Poetry from 1960 to 2000'. In *Native Poetry in Canada: A Contemporary Anthology*, ed. Jeannette C. Armstrong and Lally Grauer (Peterborough, ON: Broadview Press, 2001), pp. xv–xx.
Armstrong, Jeanette. 'History Lesson'. In *Native Poetry in Canada: A Contemporary Anthology*, ed. Jeannette C. Armstrong and Lally Grauer (Peterborough: Broadview, 2001), pp. 110–11.
Arredondo, Gabriela F., Aida Hurtado, Norma Klahn, Olga Nájera-Ramírez, and Patricia Zavella, eds. 'Introduction'. In *Chicana Feminisms: A Critical Reader* (Durham, NC and London: Duke University Press, 2003), pp. 1–18.
Ashcroft, Bill, Gareth Griffiths, and Helen Tiffin, eds. *The Empire Writes Back* (London: Taylor & Francis, 1989).

Ashcroft, Bill, Gareth Griffiths, and Helen Tiffin, eds. *The Empire Writes Back* (London: Taylor & Francis, 2003 (2nd edn)).

Baker, Moira P. '"The Politics of They": Dorothy Allison's *Bastard Out of Carolina* as Critique of Class, Gender and Sexual Ideologies'. In *The World is Our Culture: Society and Culture in Contemporary Southern Writing*, ed. Jeffrey J. Folks and Nancy Summers Folks (Lexington: University Press of Kentucky, 2000), pp. 117–41.

Bakhtin, Mikhail M. *The Dialogic Imagination: Four Essays*. Trans. Caryl Emerson and Michael Holquist (Austin: University of Texas Press, 1981).

Bartra, Roger. 'Introduction'. Trans. Coco Fusco. In Guillermo Gómez-Peña, *Warrior for Gringostroika* (St. Paul: Graywolf Press, 1993), pp. 11–14.

Barzilai, Gad. *Communities and Law: Politics and Cultures of Legal Identities* (Ann Arbor: University of Michigan Press, 2003).

Bell, Daniel. *Communitarianism and Its Critics* (Oxford: Clarendon Press, 1993).

Bell, David and John Binnie. *The Sexual Citizen: Queer Politics and Beyond* (Cambridge: Polity Press, 2000).

Bell, Sonya. '101 Letters to a Prime Minister: Yann Martel Opens up His Book Club' (28 November 2012). www.ipolitics.ca/2012/11/28/101-letters-to-a-prime-minister-yann- martel-opens-up-his-book-club/ (accessed 14 December 2014).

Bell, Sonya. 'Fact Check: Stephen Harper and the Guinness Book of World Records' (28 November 2012). www.ipolitics.ca/2012/11/28/dnp-fact-check-stephen-harper-and-the-guinness-book-of-world-records/ (accessed 14 December 2014).

Benhabib, Seyla. *The Claims of Culture: Equality and Diversity in the Global Era* (Princeton: Princeton University Press, 2002).

Bergvall, Caroline. 'UNMOORED: On and with Erín Moure' (April 2009). www.asu.edu/pipercwcenter/how2journal/vol_3_no_3/bergvall/pdfs/bergvall-unmoored.pdf (accessed 15 September 2010).

Berlant, Lauren G. *The Female Complaint: The Unfinished Business of Sentimentality in American Culture* (Durham, NC: Duke University Press, 2008).

Berlant, Lauren G. *The Queen of America Goes to Washington City: Essays on Sex and Citizenship* (Raleigh: Duke University Press, 1997).

Bleich, David. *Readings and Feelings: An Introduction to Subjective Criticism* (Urbana: NCTE, 1975).

Bleich, David. *Subjective Criticism* (London: Johns Hopkins University Press, 1978).

Bloomfield, George (dir). *Riel* (CBC, 1979).

Booth, Wayne C. *The Rhetoric of Fiction* (Chicago: University of Chicago Press, 1961).

Bibliography

Bost, Suzanne. *Mulattas and Mestizas: Representing Mixed Identities in the Americas, 1850–2000* (Athens and London: University of Georgia Press, 2003).

Brand, Madeleine and A. Martinez. 'Junot Díaz Reflects on Love in His Latest Book' (13 September 2012). www.scpr.org/programs/brand-martinez/2012/09/13/28399/junot-Díaz-love-immigrant-this-is-how-you-lose-her/ (accessed 12 October 2015).

Braz, Albert. *The False Traitor: Louis Riel in Canadian Culture* (Toronto: University of Toronto Press, 2003).

Brown, Chester. *Louis Riel: A Comic-Strip Biography* (Montreal: Drawn and Quarterly Publications, 2003).

Brown, Jennifer. 'Metis, Halfbreeds, and Other Real People: Challenging Cultures and Categories'. *The History Teacher* 27:1 (1993): pp. 19–26.

Butler, Judith. *Bodies that Matter: On the Discursive Limits of Sex* (New York: Routledge, 1993).

Butler, Judith. 'Critically Queer'. *GLQ* 1 (1993): pp. 17–32.

Butler, Judith. *Gender Trouble: Feminism and the Subversion of Identity* (New York: Routledge, 1999 [1990]).

Byrd, William. *Histories of the Dividing Line Betwixt Virginia and North Carolina* (New York: Dover, 1967 [1929]).

Calderón, Héctor and José David Saldívar. *Criticism in the Borderlands: Studies in Chicano Literature, Culture, and Ideology* (Durham, NC: Duke University Press, 1991).

Califia, Pat. *Sex Changes: The Politics of Transgenderism* (San Francisco: Cleis Press, 1997).

Campbell, Maria. *Halfbreed* (Lincoln: University of Nebraska Press, 1982 [1977]).

Carrière, Marie. *Writing in the Feminine in French and English Canada* (Toronto: University of Toronto Press, 2002).

Cash, W. J. *The Mind of the South* (New York: Knopf, 1941).

Castro, Rafaela G. *Chicano Folklore: A Guide to the Folktales, Traditions, Rituals and Religious Practices of Mexican-Americans* (New York: Oxford University Press, 2001).

Ch'ien, Evelyn Nien-Ming. *Weird English* (Cambridge, MA and London: Harvard University Press, 2004).

Ciabattari, Jane. 'The 21st Century's 12 Greatest Novels' (19 January 2015). www.bbc.com/culture/story/20150119-the-21st-centurys-12-best-novels (accessed 11 October 2015).

Cixous, Hélène. 'The Laugh of the Medusa'. Trans. Keith Cohen and Paula Cohen. *Signs* 1:4 (1976): pp. 875–93.

Constantin-Weyer, Maurice. *The Half-Breed* (New York: The Macaulay Company, 1954).

Constantin-Weyer, Maurice. *A Martyr's Folly* (Toronto: The Macmillan Company, 1934).

Coulthard, Glen Sean. *Red Skin, White Masks: Rejecting the Colonial Politics of Recognition* (Minneapolis and London: Minnesota University Press, 2014).

Coulthard, Glen Sean. 'Subjects of Empire: Indigenous Peoples and the "Politics of Recognition" in Canada'. *Contemporary Political Theory* 6:4 (2007): pp. 437–60.

Crenshaw, Kimberlé. 'Mapping the Margins: Intersectionality, Identity Politics, and Violence Against Women of Color'. *Stanford Law Review* 43 (1991): pp. 1241–99.

Damm, Kateri. 'Dispelling and Telling: Speaking Native Realities in Maria Campbell's *Halfbreed* and Beatrice Culleton's *In Search of April Raintree*'. In *Looking at the Words of Our People: First Nations Analysis of Literature*, ed. Jeannette Armstrong (Penticton: Theytus, 1993), pp. 93–114.

Damm, Kateri. 'Says Who: Colonialism, Identity, and Defining Indigenous Literature'. In *Looking at the Words of Our People: First Nations Analysis of Literature*, ed. Jeannette Armstrong (Penticton: Theytus, 1993), pp. 10–25.

Daniels, Harry W. 'Bill C-31: The Abocide Bill'. Congress of Aboriginal Peoples 1998. www.abopeoples.org/programs/C-31/Abocide/Abocide-3.htm#Membership (accessed 13 November 2009).

Daniels v. Canada (Minister of Indian Affairs and Northern Development) (T.D.), 2002 FCT 295, [2002] 4 F.C. 550. http://reports.fja.gc.ca/eng/2002/2002fct295.html (accessed 20 February 2013).

Davidson, Arnold E., Priscilla L. Walton, and Jennifer Andrews. *Border Crossings: Thomas King's Comic Inversions* (Toronto: University of Toronto Press, 2003).

De Lauretis, Teresa. 'Displacing Hegemonic Discourses: Reflections on Feminist Theory in the 1980s'. *Inscriptions* 3/4 (1988): pp. 127–44.

Dean, Jonathan. 'The Lady Doth Protest Too Much: Theorising Disidentification in Contemporary Gender Politics'. Working Paper in Ideology in Discourse Analysis No. 24 (2008). www.essex.ac.uk/idaworld/paper240708.pdf (accessed 15 November 2008).

del Pilar Blanco, Maria. 'Reading the Novum World: The Literary Geography of Science Fiction in Junot Díaz's *The Brief Wondrous Life of Oscar Wao*'. In *Surveying the American Tropics: A Literary Geography from New York to Rio*, ed. Maria Cristina Fumigalli, Peter Hulme, Owen Robinson, and Leslie Wylie (Liverpool: Liverpool University Press, 2013), pp. 49–74.

Deleuze, Gilles. *Negotiations 1972–1990* (New York: Columbia University Press, 1997).

Deleuze, Gilles and Felix Guattari. *Capitalism and Schizophrenia*. Trans. Robert Hurley, Mark Seem and Helen R. Lane (London and New York: Continuum, 2004 [1972]).

Bibliography

Deleuze, Gilles and Felix Guattari. *Kafka: Toward a Minor Literature*. Trans. Dana Polan (Minneapolis: University of Minnesota Press, 1986).
Derrida, Jacques. *Of Grammatology*. Trans. Gayatri Chakravorty Spivak (Baltimore and London: Johns Hopkins University Press, 1976 [1967]).
Derrida, Jacques. *The Politics of Friendship*. Trans. George Collins (London and New York: Verso, 1997).
Derrida, Jacques. *Writing and Difference*. Trans. Alan Bass (London and New York: Routledge, 1978).
Díaz, Junot. *The Brief Wondrous Life of Oscar Wao* (London: Faber & Faber, 2008 [2007]).
Dworkin, Ronald. *Is Democracy Possible Here? Principles for a New Political Debate* (Princeton: Princeton University Press, 2006).
Eco, Umberto. *Travels in Hyperreality*. Trans. William Weaver (London: Pan, 1987).
Eng, David L., Judith Halberstam, and José Esteban Muñoz. 'What's Queer about Queer Studies Now?' *Social Text* 23:3–4 (2005): pp. 1–17.
Fallon, Claire. 'Trump Doesn't Read, So Protesters Are Flooding His Office With Books' (6 February 2017). www.huffingtonpost.com/entry/send-trump-books-valentines-day_us_5898b09be4b0406131382138 (accessed 15 March 2017).
Fernàndez-Armesto, Felipe. *Our America: A Hispanic History of the United States* (New York and London: Norton, 2014).
Fish, Stanley. *Is There a Text in the Class? The Authority of Interpretive Communities* (London: Harvard University Press, 1980).
Fisher Fishkin, Shelley. 'Crossroads of Cultures: The Transnational Turn in American Studies'. *American Quarterly* 57:1 (2005): pp. 17–57.
Flood, Alison. '*The Brief Wondrous Life of Oscar Wao* Declared 21st Century's Best Novel so Far' (20 January 2015). www.theguardian.com/books/2015/jan/20/brief-wondrous-life-of-oscar-wao-novel-21st-century-best-junot-Díaz (accessed 11 October 2015).
Forment, Carlos A. 'Peripheral Peoples and Narrative Identities: Arendtian Reflections on Late Modernity'. In *Contesting the Boundaries of the Political*, ed. Seyla Benhabib (Princeton: Princeton University Press, 1996), pp. 314–30.
Foster, John E. 'Some Questions and Perspectives on the Problem of Métis Roots'. In *The New Peoples: Being and Becoming Métis in North America*, ed. Jacqueline Peterson and Jennifer Andrews (Winnipeg: University of Manitoba Press, 1985), pp. 73–93.
Fraser, Nancy. 'Rethinking the Public Sphere: A Contribution to the Critique of Actually Existing Democracy'. In *Habermas and the Public Sphere*, ed. Craig Calhoun (Cambridge, MA and London: MIT Press, 1992), pp. 109–42.

Fraser, Nancy and Lina Gordon. 'Contract versus Charity: Why is there no Social Citizenship in the United States?' *Socialist Review* 22:3 (1992): pp. 45–65.
Freud, Sigmund. *Group Psychology and the Analysis of the Ego*. Trans. James Strachey (London: Hogarth Press, 1922).
Fuller, Danielle. 'Citizen Reader: Canadian Literature, Mass Reading Events and the Promise of Belonging'. The Fifth Eccles Centre for American Studies Plenary Lecture pamphlet series (London: Eccles Centre & The British Library, 2011).
Fuller, Danielle and DeNel Rehberg Sedo. *Reading Beyond the Book: The Social Practices of Contemporary Literary Culture* (London: Routledge, 2013).
Fuss, Diana. *Identification Papers* (New York and London: Routledge, 1995).
Fuss, Diana. 'Interior Colonies: Frantz Fanon and the Politics of Identification'. *Diacritics* 24:2/3 (1994): pp. 20–42.
Garber, Marjorie. *Vested Interests: Cross-Dressing and Cultural Anxiety* (New York: Harper Perennial, 1993).
García, Alma M. 'Introduction'. In *Chicana Feminist Thought: The Basic Historical Writings*, ed. Alma M. García (New York and London: Routledge, 1997), pp. 1–16.
García, Ofelia and Li Wei. *Translanguaging: Language, Bilingualism and Education* (Basingstoke: Palgrave Macmillan, 2014).
García, Ramon. 'Against Rasquache: Chicano Identity and the Politics of Popular Culture in Los Angeles'. *Critica: A Journal of Critical Essays* (1998): pp. 1–26.
García, Ramon. 'Session Three: Staking the Claim: Introducing Chicana/o Cultural Studies'. In *The Chicana/o Cultural Studies Forum: Critical and Ethnographic Practices*, ed. Angie Chabram-Dernersesian (New York: New York University Press, 2007), pp. 54–132.
Gatens, Moira. *Imaginary Bodies: Ethics, Power, and Corporality* (New York: Routledge, 1996).
George, Courtney. '"It Wasn't God Who Made Honky-Tonk Angels": Musical Salvation in Dorothy Allison's Bastard Out of Carolina'. *The Southern Literary Journal* 41:2 (2009): pp. 126–47.
Gikandi, Simon. 'Globalization and the Claims of Postcoloniality'. *South Atlantic Quarterly* 100:3 (2001): pp. 627–58.
Giraud, Marcel. *The Métis in the Canadian West*. Trans. George Woodcock. 2 volumes (Lincoln: University of Nebraska Press, 1986 [1945]).
Gómez, Laura E. *Manifest Destinies: The Making of the Mexican American Race* (New York: New York University Press, 2007).
Gómez-Peña, Guillermo. 'Border Brujo: A Performance Poem (from the series "Documented/Undocumented")'. *The Drama Review* 35:3 (1991): pp. 48–66.

Gómez-Peña, Guillermo. *Dangerous Border Crossers: The Artist Talks Back* (London and New York: Routledge, 2000).
Gómez-Peña, Guillermo. 'In Defense of Performance Art'. www.pochanostra.com/antes/jazz_pocha2/mainpages/in_defense.htm (accessed 5 April 2010).
Gómez-Peña, Guillermo. 'El Mexorcist (A Performance)'. *Journal of Visual Culture* 5:1 (2006): pp. 5–15.
Gómez-Peña, Guillermo. *Ethno-Techno: Writings on Performance, Activism, and Pedagogy* (London and New York: Routledge, 2005).
Gómez-Peña, Guillermo. 'Excerpt from *Philosophical Tantrum*, 2005'. http://hemisphericinstitute.org/hemi/en/e-misferica-81/gomez-pena (accessed 20 February 2013).
Gómez-Peña, Guillermo. *Guillermo Gomez-Pena: Conversations Across Borders*. Ed. Laura Levin (London: Seagull Books, 2011).
Gómez-Peña, Guillermo. *The New World Border: Prophecies, Poems, and Loqueras for the End of Century* (San Francisco: City Lights Books, 1996).
Gómez-Peña, Guillermo. *Warrior for Gringostroika* (St. Paul: Graywolf Press, 1993).
Gómez-Peña, Guillermo and Roberto Sifuentes. *Temple of Confessions: Mexican Beasts and Living Santos* (New York: Powerhouse Books, 1997).
Gómez-Peña, Guillermo and Lisa Wolford. 'Navigating the Minefields of Utopia: A Conversation'. *The Drama Review* 26:2 (2002): pp. 66–96.
Gonzalez, Rudolfo. 'Yo Soy Joaquín'. www.latinamericanstudies.org/latinos/joaquin.htm (accessed 12 September 2015).
Gould, Karen. *Writing in the Feminine: Feminism and Experimental Writing in Québec* (Carbondale: Southern Illinois University Press, 1990).
Graham, David A. 'Donald Trump's Narrative of the Life of Frederick Douglass'. *The Atlantic* (1 February 2017). www.theatlantic.com/politics/archive/2017/02/frederick-douglass-trump/515292/ (accessed 20 February 2017).
Gray, R. W. '"... in my writing I see myself as a community worker": An Interview with Gregory Scofield'. *Arc* 43 (1999): pp. 21–9.
Grossman, Lev. 'Top 10 Fiction Books. #1: The Brief Wondrous Life of Oscar Wao'. *Time* (9 December 2007). http://content.time.com/time/specials/2007/article/0,28804,1686204_1686244_1691840,00.html (accessed 11 October 2015).
Haberman, Maggie. 'A Homebody Finds the Ultimate Home Office'. *New York Times* (25 January 2017). www.nytimes.com/2017/01/25/us/politics/president-trump-white-house.html (accessed 31 January 2017).
Habermas, Jurgen. *The Structural Transformation of the Public Sphere: An Inquiry into a Category of Bourgeois Society*. Trans. Thomas Burger with Frederick Lawrence (Cambridge, MA: MIT Press, 1989).

Halperin, David. *Saint Foucault: Towards a Gay Hagiography* (New York: New York University Press, 1995).
Hanna, Monica. 'A Portrait of the Artist as a Young Cannibalist: Reading Yunior (Writing) in *The Brief Wondrous Life of Oscar Wao*'. In *Junot Díaz and the Decolonial Imagination*, ed. Monica Hanna, Jennifer Harford Vargas, and José David Saldívar (Durham, NC and London: Duke University Press, 2016), pp. 89–111.
Hanna, Monica. 'Reassembling the Fragments: Battling Historiographies, Caribbean Discourse, and Nerd Genres in Junot Díaz's *The Brief Wondrous Life of Oscar Wao*'. *Callaloo* 33:2 (2010): pp. 498–520.
Hanna, Monica, Jennifer Harford Vargas, and José David Saldívar. 'Junot Díaz and the Decolonial Imagination: From Island to Empire'. In *Junot Díaz and the Decolonial Imagination* (Durham, NC and New York: Duke University Press, 2016), pp. 1–29.
Haraway, Donna. 'A Cyborg Manifesto: Science, Technology and Socialist-Feminism in the Late Twentieth Century'. In *Simians, Cyborgs and Women: The Reinvention of Nature* (London: Free Association Books, 1991), pp. 149–82.
Harris, Wilson. 'History, Fable and Myth in the Caribbean and Guianas'. *Caribbean Quarterly* 54:1/2 (2008): pp. 5–38.
Hartigan, John. 'Who Are These White People? "Rednecks," "Hillbilly," and "White Trash" as Marked Racial Subjects'. In *White Out: The Continuing Significance of Racism*, ed. Ashley W. Doane and Eduardo Bonilla-Silva (New York: Routledge, 2003), pp. 95–111.
Hartsock, Nancy. 'Rethinking Modernism: Minority vs. Majority Theories'. *Cultural Critique* 7 (1987): pp. 187–206.
Hele, Karl S., ed. *Lines Drawn upon the Water: First Nations and the Great Lakes Borders and Borderlands* (Waterloo, ON: Wilfrid Laurier Press, 2008).
Henninger, Katherine. 'Claiming Access: Controlling Images in Dorothy Allison'. *Arizona Quarterly: A Journal of American Literature, Culture, and Theory* 60:3 (2004): pp. 83–108.
Hicks, Emily. *Border Writing: The Multidimensional Text* (Minneapolis: University of Minnesota Press, 1991).
Hobbes, Thomas. *Leviathan* (Cambridge: Cambridge University Press, 1991 [1651]).
Holland, Norman. *Five Readers Reading* (London: Yale University Press, 1975).
Holland, Norman. *Poems in Persons: A Psychology of the Literary Process* (New York: Norton, 1973).
Horsman, Reginald. *Race and Manifest Destiny: The Origins of American Racial Anglo-Saxonism* (Cambridge, MA: Harvard University Press, 1981).
Howard, Joseph Kinsey. *Strange Empire: A Narrative of the Northwest* (New York: William Morrow and Co, 1952).
Hurtado, Aida. '*Sitios y lenguas:* Chicanas Theorize Feminism'. *Hypatia* 13:2 (1998): pp. 135–59.

The Immigration Reform and Control Act, 1986 – Public Law 99-603. www.uscis.gov/ilink/docView/PUBLAW/HTML/PUBLAW/0-0-0-15.html (accessed 9 April 2013).
Iser, Wolfgang. *The Act of Reading: A Theory of Aesthetic Response* (London: Johns Hopkins University Press, 1978).
Iser, Wolfgang. *The Implied Reader: Patterns of Communication in Prose Fiction from Bunyan to Beckett* (Munich: Wilhelm Fink, 1972).
Isin, Engin F. 'Theorizing Acts of Citizenship'. In *Acts of Citizenship*, ed. Engin F. Isin and Greg M. Neilsen (London and New York: Zed Books, 2008), pp. 15–43.
Isin, Engin F. and Greg Neilsen, eds. 'Introduction'. In *Acts of Citizenship* (London and New York: Zed Books, 2008), pp. 1–12.
Isin, Engin F. and Patricia Wood. *Citizenship and Identity* (London: Sage, 1999).
Jacobs, Sue-Ellen, Wesley Thomas, and Sabine Lang, eds. 'Introduction'. In *Two-Spirit People: Native American Gender Identity, Sexuality, and Spirituality* (Chicago: University of Illinois Press, 1997), pp. 1–18.
Jamieson, Sara. 'Âyahkwêw Songs: AIDS and Mourning in Gregory Scofield's "Urban Rez" Poems'. *Canadian Poetry* 57 (2005): pp. 52–64.
Jay Treaty. Treaty of Amity, Commerce, and Navigation, signed at London November 19, 1794, with additional article Original in English. Submitted to the Senate June 8, Resolution of advice and consent, on condition, June 24, 1795. Ratified by the United States August 14, 1795. Ratified by Great Britain October 28, 1795. Ratifications exchanged at London October 28, 1795. Proclaimed February 29, 1796. http://avalon.law.yale.edu/18th_century/jay.asp (accessed 15 June 2013).
Jelly-Schapiro, Joshua. 'Ground Zero(es) of the New World: Geographies of Violence in Junot Díaz and Edwidge Danticat'. *Transforming Anthropology: Journal of the Association of Black Anthropologists* 21 (2013): pp. 169–86.
Jones, Kathleen B. and Sue Dunlap. 'Queer Citizenship/Queer Representation: Politics Out of Bounds?' In *The Political Interests of Gender Revisited: Redoing Theory and Research with a Feminist Face*, ed. Anna G. Jónasdóttir and Kathleen B. Jones (Manchester: Manchester University Press, 2009), pp. 189–207.
Joseph, Suad. 'Women between Nation and the State in Lebanon'. In *Between Woman and Nation: Nationalism, Transnational Feminism, and the State*, ed. Cora Kaplan, Norma Alarcon, and Minoo Moallem (Durham, NC: Duke University Press, 1999), pp. 162–81.
Kakutani, Michiko. 'Travails of an Outcast'. *New York Times* (4 September 2007). www.nytimes.com/2007/09/04/books/04Diaz.html (accessed 11 October 2015).
Kaup, Monika. 'Constituting Hybridity as Hybrid'. In *Mixing Race, Mixing Culture: Inter-American Literary Dialogues*, ed. Monika Kaup and Debra J. Rosenthal (Austin: University of Texas Press, 2002), pp. 185–210.

Kidd, David and Emanuele Castano. 'Reading Literary Fiction Improves Theory of Mind'. *Science* 342 :6156 (2013): pp. 377–80.
King, Thomas. 'Borders'. In *One Good Story, That One: Stories* (Minneapolis: Minnesota University Press, 2013 [1993]), pp. 131–47.
King, Vincent. 'Hopeful Grief: The Prospect of a Postmodern Feminism in Allison's Bastard Out of Carolina'. *The Southern Literary Journal* 33:1 (2000): pp. 122–40.
Kinsman, Gary. *The Regulation of Desire* (Montreal: Black Rose Books, 1996).
Kinsman, Gary and Patrizia Gentile. *The Canadian War on Queers: National Security as Sexual Regulation* (Vancouver: University of British Columbia Press, 2010).
Knight, Henry Ace. 'An Interview with Junot Díaz' (n.d). www.asymptotejournal.com/interview/an-interview-junot-diaz/ (accessed 10 January 2017).
Konrad, Victor and Heather N. Nicol. *Beyond Walls: Re-inventing the Canada-United States Borderlands* (Aldershot and Burlington: Ashgate, 2008).
Kristeva, Julia. *Tales of Love* (New York: Columbia University Press, 1987).
Kuhnheim, Jill S. 'The Economy of Performance: Gómez-Peña's New World Border'. *Modern Fiction Studies* 44 (1998): pp. 24–35.
Kymlicka, William. *Liberalism, Community and Culture* (Oxford: Clarendon Press, 1991).
Kymlicka, William. *Multicultural Citizenship: A Liberal Theory of Minority Rights* (Oxford: Oxford University Press, 1995).
Lang, Anouk, ed. *From Codex to Hypertext: Reading at the Turn of the Twenty-First Century* (Amherst: University of Massachusetts Press, 2012).
Lang, Sabine. 'Various Kinds of Two-Spirit People: Gender Variance and Homosexuality in Native American Communities'. In *Two-Spirit People: Native American Gender Identity, Sexuality, and Spirituality*, ed. Sue-Ellen Jacobs, Wesley Thomas, and Sabine Lang (Urbana and Chicago: University of Illinois Press, 1997), pp. 100–18.
Large, William. *Emmanuel Levinas and Maurice Blanchot: Ethics and the Ambiguity of Writing* (Manchester: Clinamen Press, 2005).
Leclaire, Jennifer. 'Because They (Islam) Hate'. *The Voice*. www.thevoicemagazine.com/culture/society/brigitte-gabriel-because-they-hate.html (accessed 12 October 2010).
Levander, Caroline F. and Robert S. Levine, eds. *Hemispheric American Studies* (New Brunswick and London: Rutgers University Press, 2008).
Lionnet, Françoise. *Autobiographical Voices* (Ithaca, NY and London: Cornell University Press, 1989).
Lionnet, Françoise. *Postcolonial Representations: Women, Literature, Identity* (Ithaca and London: Cornell University Press, 1995).
Lionnet, Françoise and Shu-Mei Shi, eds. *Minor Transnationalism* (Durham, NC and London: Duke University Press, 2005).

Bibliography

Lippard, Lucy. *Mixed Blessings: New Art in a Multicultural America* (New York: Pantheon Books, 1990).
Lipsitz, George. 'Not Just Another Poster Movement: Poster Art and the Movimiento Chicano'. In *Just Another Poster? Chicano Graphic Arts in California*, exh. cat., ed. Chon A. Noriega (Santa Barbara: University Art Museum, University of California, Santa Barbara, 2001), pp. 71–87.
Littau, Karen. *Theories of Reading: Books, Bodies, and Bibliomania* (Cambridge: Polity, 2006).
Livy, Titus. *The History of Rome*. Trans. Rev. Canon Roberts (London: J. M. Dent and Sons, 1905). http://mcadams.posc.mu.edu/txt/ah/Livy/Livy01.html (accessed 19 November 2010).
Long, Elizabeth. *Book Clubs: Women and the Uses of Reading in Everyday Life* (Chicago: University Press of Chicago, 2003).
Lovell Banks, Taunya. 'Mestizaje and the Mexican Mestizo Self: no hay sangre negra, so there is no blackness'. *Southern California Interdisciplinary Law Journal* 15 (2006): pp. 199–234.
Mahler, Anne Garland. 'The Writer as Superhero: Fighting the Colonial Curse in Junot Díaz's *The Brief Wondrous Life of Oscar Wao*'. *Journal of Latin American Cultural Studies* 19:2 (2010): pp. 119–40.
Marshall, T. H. *Class, Citizenship, and Social Development* (Chicago: University of Chicago Press, 1964).
Martel, Yann. *101 Letters to a Prime Minister: The Complete Letters to Stephen Harper* (Toronto: Vintage Canada, 2012).
Martel, Yann. *What is Stephen Harper Reading?* (Toronto: Vintage Canada, 2009).
McCance, Dawne. 'Crossings: An Interview with Erín Moure'. *Mosaic: A Journal for the Interdisciplinary Study of Literature* 36:4 (2003): pp. 1–9.
McKechnie, Lynne E. F., Knut Oterholm, Paulette M. Rothbauer, and Kjell Ivar Skjerdingstad, eds. *Plotting the Reading Experience: Theory/Practice/Politics* (Waterloo, ON: Wilfrid Laurier University Press, 2016).
McLeod, Alan Lindsey. *The Canon of Commonwealth Literature: Essays in Criticism* (India: Sterling Publishers Pvt. Ltd, 2003).
Megan, Carolyn E. 'Moving Toward Truth: An Interview with Dorothy Allison'. *The Kenyon Review* 16:4 (1994): pp. 71–83.
Menchaca, Martha. 'Chicano Indianism: A Historical Account of Racial Repression in the United States'. *American Ethnologist* 20:3 (1993): pp. 583–603.
Mermann-Jozwiak, Elisabeth Maria. 'Beyond Multiculturalism: Ethnic Studies, Transnationalism, and Junot Díaz's Oscar Wao'. *Ariel: A Review of International English Literature* 43:2 (2013): pp. 1–24.
Mesa-Bains, Amalia. 'Domesticana: The Sensibility of Chicana Rasquache'. In *Distant Relations: A Dialogue among Chicano, Irish, and Mexican Artists*, ed. Trisha Ziff (New York: Smart Art Press, 1996), pp. 156–63.

Métis Nation of Ontario. 'Métis Rights in the Courts Again'. www.metisnation. org/news--media/news/metis-rights-in-the-courts-again (accessed 2 February 2013).

Mignolo, Walter D. 'Citizenship, Knowledge, and the Limits of Humanity'. *American Literary History* 18:2 (2006): pp. 312–31.

Monteith, Sharon. *Advancing Sisterhood? Interracial Friendships in Contemporary Southern Fiction* (Athens and London: The University of Georgia Press, 2000).

Morejón, Nancy. 'Race and Nation'. In *AfroCuba: An Anthology of Cuban Writing on Race, Politics and Culture*, ed. Pedro Perez Sarduy and Jean Stubbs (Melbourne: Ocean Press, 1993), pp. 227–37.

Morrison, Amanda. 'Performance Review: Guillermo Gomez-Peña Brings Borderland Aesthetics to the Avant-Garde'. *Text, Practice, Performance IV* (2003): pp. 133–8.

Moure, Erín. *Empire: York Street* (Toronto: House of Anansi Press, 1979).

Moure, Erín. *The Frame of a Book or, A Frame of The Book* (Toronto: House of Anansi Press, 1999).

Moure, Erín. *Little Theatres* (Toronto: House of Anansi Press, 2005).

Moure, Erín. *My Beloved Wager: Essays from a Writing Practice* (Edmonton: NeWest Press, 2009).

Moure, Erín. *O Cidadán* (Toronto: House of Anansi Press, 2002).

Moure, Erín. *Search Procedures* (Toronto: House of Anansi Press, 1996).

Muñoz, José Esteban. 'Choteo/Camp Style Politics: Carmelita Tropicana's Performance of Self Enactment'. *Women and Performance: A Journal of Feminist Theory. New Hybrid Identities: Performing Race/Gender/Nation/Sexuality* 7:2–8:1 (1995): pp. 39–51.

Muñoz, José Esteban. *Disidentifications: Queers of Color and the Performance of Politics* (Minneapolis and London: University of Minnesota Press, 1999).

Navarro, Moisés González. 'Mestizaje in Mexico During the National Period'. In *Race and Class in Latin America*, ed. Magnus Mörner (New York: Columbia University Press, 1965), pp. 145–69.

Neustadt, Robert. *(Con)Fusing Signs and Postmodern Positions: Spanish American Performance, Experimental Writing, and the Critique of Political Confusion* (New York: Garland Publishing Inc., 1999).

Neustadt, Robert. 'Guillermo Gómez-Peña: Dragging Representation'. http://fuentes.csh.udg.mx/CUCSH/Sincronia/neustadt.html (accessed 12 June 2012).

New, W. H. *Borderlands: How We Think about Canada* (Vancouver: University of British Columbia Press, 1998).

Nozick, Robert. *Anarchy, State, and Utopia* (Oxford: Blackwell, 1974).

O'Neill, Tracy. 'Podcast #95: Junot Díaz on the Game of Fiction and Intimacy' (19 January 2016). www.nypl.org/blog/2016/01/19/podcast-junot-Díaz (accessed 21 October 2016).

O'Rourke, Megan. 'The Brief Wondrous Life of Oscar Wao: Questions for Junot Díaz' (8 November 2007). www.slate.com/articles/news_and_politics/the_highbrow/2007/11/the_brief_wondrous_life_of_oscar_wao.html (accessed 11 October 2016).

Obama, Barack and Marilynne Robinson. 'President Obama & Marilynne Robinson: A Conversation — II'. The New York Review of Books (19 November 2015). www.nybooks.com/articles/2015/11/19/president-obama-marilynne-robinson-conversation-2/ (accessed 28 November 2015).

Otheguy, Ricardo, Ofelia García, and Wallis Reid. 'Clarifying Translanguaging and Deconstructing Named Languages: A Perspective from Linguistics'. Applied Linguistic Review 6:3 (2015): pp. 281–307.

Patton, Cindy. Inventing AIDS (New York: Routledge, 1990).

Perry, Michael J. The Political Morality of Liberal Democracy (Cambridge: Cambridge University Press, 2010).

Peterson, Jacqueline. 'Many Roads to Red River: Métis Genesis in the Red River Region, 1680–1815'. In The New Peoples: Being and Becoming Métis in North America, ed. Jacqueline Peterson and Jennifer S. H. Brown (Winnipeg: University of Manitoba Press, 1985), pp. 37–72.

Peterson, Jacqueline and Jennifer S. H. Brown, eds. 'Introduction'. In The New Peoples: Being and Becoming Métis in North America (Winnipeg: University of Manitoba Press, 1985), pp. 3–18.

Phelan, Peggy. Unmarked: The Politics of Performance (New York: Routledge, 1992).

'Presenters 1979–2011' (n.d). https://womenwriters.as.uky.edu/presenters-1979-2011 (accessed 15 June 2017).

Proops, Leanne, Faith Burden, and Britta Osthaus. 'Mule Cognition: A Case of Hybrid Vigour?' Animal Cognition 12:75 (2009): pp. 75–84.

Pryor, Hilary (dir). Singing Home the Bones: A Poet Becomes Himself (Victoria, BC: May Street Group Film, 2006).

Radway, Janice. A Feeling for Books: The Book-of-the-Month Club, Literary Taste, and Middle Class Desire (Chapel Hill: University of North Carolina Press, 1999).

Rajan, Gita and Rahdhika Mohanram, eds. 'Introduction: Locating Postcoloniality'. In Postcolonial Discourse and Changing Cultural Contexts: Theory and Criticism (Westport and London: Greenwood Press, 1995), pp. 1–16.

Rasmussen, David, ed. Universalism vs. Communitarianism (Cambridge, MA: MIT Press, 1990).

Rawls, John. A Theory of Justice (Delhi: Universal Law Publishing Co., 2008 [1971]).

Rehberg Sedo, DeNel, ed. Reading Communities: From Salon to Cyberspace (Basingstoke: Palgrave Macmillan, 2011).

Reynolds, David. 'White Trash in Your Face: The Literary Descent of Dorothy Allison'. Appalachian Journal 20:4 (1993): pp. 356–66.

Roberts, Gillian. *Discrepant Parallels: Cultural Implications of the Canada-US Border* (Montreal: McGill-Queens University Press, 2015).
Roberts, Gillian. *Prizing Literature: The Celebration and Circulation of National Culture* (Toronto: University of Toronto Press, 2011).
Roberts, Gillian and David Stirrup, eds. *Parallel Encounters: Culture at the Canada-US Border* (Waterloo, ON: Wilfrid Laurier University Press, 2013).
Romine, Scott. *The Narrative Forms of Southern Community* (Baton Rouge: Louisiana State University Press, 1999).
Rosaldo, Renato. *Culture and Truth: The Remaking of Social Analysis* (London: Routledge, 1993).
Rosenblatt, Louise. *Literature as Exploration* (London: Heinemann, 1968 [1938]).
Rosenblatt, Louise. *The Reader, The Text, The Poem: The Transactional Theory of the Literary Work* (Carbondale: Southern Illinois University Press, 1978).
Rosenblatt, Louise. 'The Transactional Theory of the Literary Work: Implications for Research'. In *Researching Response to Literature and the Teaching of Literature: Points of Departure*, ed. C. R. Cooper (Norwood: Ablex, 1985), pp. 33–53.
Rowe, John Carlos. *Post-Nationalist American Studies* (Oakland: University of California Press, 2000).
Rudy, Susan. '"what can atmosphere with / vocabularies delight?" Excessively Reading Erín Moure'. In *Writing in Our Time: Canada's Radical Poetries in English 1957–2003*, ed. Pauline Butling and Susan Rudy (Waterloo, ON: Wilfrid Laurier University Press, 2005), pp. 205–16.
Russel y Rodríguez, Mónica. 'Mexicanas and Mongrels: Policies of Hybridity, Gender and Nation in the US-Mexican War'. *Latino Studies Journal* 11:3 (2000): pp. 49–73.
Sadowski-Smith, Claudia. *Border Fictions: Globalization, Empire, and Writing at the Boundaries of the United States* (Charlottesville and London: University of Virginia Press, 2008).
Sadowski-Smith, Claudia, ed. 'Introduction'. In *Globalization on the Line: Culture, Capital, and Citizenship at U.S. Borders* (New York: Palgrave, 2002), pp. 1–30.
Saldívar, José David. *Border Matters: Remapping American Cultural Studies* (Oakland: University of California Press, 1997).
Salih, Sarah. *Judith Butler* (London and New York: Routledge, 2002).
Schinko, Carsten. 'Why Trash? Thirteen Ways of Looking at Poor (White) Folks'. *Amerikastudien / American Studies* 55:1 (2010): pp. 143–64.
Schweikart, Patricinio. 'Toward a Feminist Theory of Reading'. In *Gender and Reading: Essays on Readers, Texts, and Contexts*, ed. Elizabeth A. Flynn and Patricinio Schweikart (Baltimore: Johns Hopkins University Press, 1986), pp. 31–62.
Scobie, Stephen. *Signature Event Cantext* (Edmonton: NeWest Press, 1989).

Bibliography

Scofield, Gregory. *The Gathering: Stones for the Medicine Wheel* (Vancouver: Polestar, 1993).
Scofield, Gregory. *I Knew Two Métis Women: The Lives of Dorothy Scofield and Georgina Houle Young* (Vancouver: Polestar, 1999).
Scofield, Gregory. 'Interview with January Magazine'. *January Magazine* (September 1999). http://januarymagazine.com/profiles/scofield.html (accessed 15 October 2009).
Scofield, Gregory. *Kipocihkân: Poems New and Selected* (Vancouver: Nightwood Editions, 2009).
Scofield, Gregory. *Louis: The Heretic Poems* (Vancouver: Nightwood Editions, 2011).
Scofield, Gregory. *Love Medicine and One Song: Sâkihtown-Maskihkiy Êkwa Pêyak-Nikamowin* (Vancouver: Polestar, 1997).
Scofield, Gregory. *Native Canadiana / Songs from the Urban Rez* (Vancouver: Polestar, 1996).
Scofield, Gregory. *Singing Home the Bones* (Vancouver: Polestar, 2005).
Scofield, Gregory. *Thunder Through My Veins: Memories of a Métis Childhood* (Toronto: HarperCollins Canada, 1999).
Scofield, Gregory. *Witness, I Am* (Gibsons, BC: Nightwood Editions, 2016).
Sheren, Ila Nicole. *Portable Borders: Performance Art and Politics on the U.S. Frontera since 1984* (Austin: University of Texas Press, 2015).
Shiach, Morag. *Hélène Cixous: A Politics of Writing* (London and New York: Routledge, 1991).
Siemerling, Winfried. *The New North American Studies Reader: Culture, Writing, and the Politics of Re/Cognition* (New York: Routledge, 2005).
Singh, Amritjit and Peter Schmidt. *Postcolonial Theory and the United States: Race, Ethnicity, and Literature* (Jackson: University Press of Mississippi, 2000).
Skibsrud, Johanna. 'If We Dare To: Border Crossings in Erín Moure's *O Cidadán*'. *The Brock Review* 11:1 (2010): pp. 15–27.
Skjedingstad, Kjell Ivar and Paulette M. Rothbauer. 'Introduction: Plotting the Reading Experience'. In *Plotting the Reading Experience: Theory/Practice/Politics*, ed. Paulette M. Rothbauer, Kjell Ivar Skjedingstad, Lynne (E. F.) McKechnie, and Knut Oterholm (Waterloo, ON: Wilfrid Laurier University Press, 2016), pp. 1–15.
Smith, Sidonie. *A Poetics of Women's Autobiography: Marginality and the Fictions of Self-Representation* (Bloomington and Indianapolis: Indiana University Press, 1987).
Smith, Sidonie and Julia Watson, eds. 'Introduction'. In *De/Colonizing the Subject: The Politics of Gender in Women's Autobiography* (Minneapolis: University of Minnesota Press, 1992), pp. xiii–xxxi.
Smith, Sidonie and Julia Watson. 'Introduction' in *Interfaces: Women/Autobiography/Image/Performance* (Ann Arbor: University of Michigan Press, 2002), pp. 1–46.

Smith, Sidonie and Julia Watson. *Reading Autobiography: A Guide to Interpreting Life Narratives* (Minneapolis: University of Minnesota Press, 2001).
Sojka, Eugenia. 'Canadian Feminist Writing and American Poetry'. *CLCWeb: Comparative Literature and Culture* 3:2 (2001) http://docs.lib.purdue.edu/clcweb/vol3/iss2/12 (accessed 28 April 2011).
Soysal, Yasemin Nohŏglu. *Limits of Citizenship: Migrants and Postnational Membership in Europe* (Chicago: Chicago University Press, 1994).
Sparks, Holloway. 'Dissident Citizenship: Democratic Theory, Political Courage, and Activist Women'. *Hypatia* 12:4 (1997): pp. 74–110.
St John, Rachel. *Line in the Sand: A History of the Western U.S.-Mexico Border* (Princeton: Princeton University Press, 2011).
Staines, David, ed. *The Canadian Imagination: Dimensions of a Literary Culture* (Cambridge, MA: Harvard University Press, 1977).
Stewart, Susan. *On Longing: Narratives of the Miniature, the Gigantic, the Souvenir, the Collection* (Durham, NC and London: Duke University Press, 1993).
Stone, Albert E. *Autobiographical Occasions and Original Acts: Versions of American Identity from Henry Adams to Nate Shaw* (Philadelphia: University of Pennsylvania Press, 1982).
Stychin, Carl. *A Nation by Rights: National Cultures, Sexual Identity Politics, and the Discourse of Rights* (Philadelphia: Temple University Press, 1998).
Surber, J. P. *Culture and Critique: An Introduction to the Critical Discourses of Cultural Studies* (Boulder: Westview Press, 1998).
Tam, Henry. *Communitarianism: A New Agenda for Politics and Citizenship* (Basingstoke: Macmillan, 1998).
Taylor, Christopher. 'Performance Art' (23 February 2008). www.theguardian.com/books/2008/feb/23/featuresreviews.guardianreview20 (accessed 11 October 2015).
Théoret, France. *Entre raison et deraison: Essais* (Montreal: Les Herbes Rouges, 1987).
Thomas, Kelly L. 'White Trash Lesbianism: Dorothy Allison's Queer Politics'. In *Gender Reconstructions*, ed. Cindy L. Carson, Robert L. Mazzola, and Susan M. Bernardo (Burlington: Ashgate, 2002), pp. 167–88.
Thomas, Robert K. 'Afterword'. In *The New Peoples: Being and Becoming Métis in North America*, ed. Jacqueline Peterson and Jennifer S. H. Brown (Winnipeg: University of Manitoba Press, 1985), pp. 243–51.
Toensing, Gale Courey. 'Canadian Border Agent Confiscated Haudenosaunee Passport, Called It "Fantasy Document"'. *Indian Country Media Network* (17 August 2011). https://indiancountrymedianetwork.com/travel/canadian-border-agent-confiscated-haudenosaunee-passport-called-it-fantasy-document/ (accessed 20 September 2011).
'Top Ten Abuses of Power Since 9/11' (n.d.). www.aclu.org/other/top-ten-abuses-power-911 (accessed 18 July 2016).

Bibliography

Torres, Lourdes. 'The Construction of the Self in U.S. Latina Autobiographies'. In *Women, Autobiography, Theory: A Reader*, ed. Sidonie Smith and Julia Watson (Madison: University of Wisconsin Press, 1998), pp. 276–87.

Torres-Saillant, Silvio. 'Artistry, Ancestry, and Americanness in the Works of Junot Díaz in *The Brief Wondrous Life of Oscar Wao*'. In *Junot Díaz and the Decolonial Imagination*, ed. Monica Hanna, Jennifer Harford Vargas, and José David Saldívar (Durham, NC and London: Duke University Press, 2016), pp. 115–46.

Travers, Ann. 'Parallel Subaltern Feminist Counterpublics in Cyberspace'. *Sociological Perspectives* 46:2 (2003): pp. 223–37.

Treaty of Peace, Friendship, Limits, and Settlement with the Republic of Mexico, U.S.-Mex., Feb. 2, 1848, 9 Bevans 791 n.11 (giving the original text of Art. IX).

'UK Refuses to Grant Visas to Iroquois Lacrosse Team'. www.bbc.co.uk/news/world-us+canada-10634044 (accessed 15 August 2010).

United States Bill of Rights. www.ourdocuments.gov/doc.php?doc=13&page=transcript (accessed 20 February 2016).

Vargas, Jennifer Harford. 'Dictating a Zafa: The Power of Narrative Form as Ruin-Reading in *The Brief Wondrous Life of Oscar Wao*'. In *Junot Díaz and the Decolonial Imagination*, ed. Monica Hanna, Jennifer Harford Vargas, and Jose David Saldivar (Durham, NC and London: Duke University Press, 2016), pp. 201–27.

Vezzali, Loris, Sofia Stathi, Dino Giovannini, Dora Capozza, and Elena Trifiletti. 'The Greatest Magic of Harry Potter: Reducing Prejudice'. *Journal of Applied Social Psychology* 45 (2015): pp. 105–21.

Villarreal, José Antonio. *Pocho: A Novel* (New York: Doubleday, 1959).

Vizenor, Gerald, ed. 'Aesthetics of Survivance: Literary Criticism and Practice'. In *Survivance: Narratives of Native Presence* (Omaha: University of Nebraska Press, 2008), pp. 1–24.

Vowel, Chelsea. 'What a Landmark Ruling Means – and Doesn't – for Métis, Non-Status Indians' (16 April 2016). www.cbc.ca/news/indigenous/landmark-supreme-court-decision-Métis-non-status-indians-1.3537419 (accessed 20 April 2016).

Walcott, Derek. 'The Antilles: Fragments of Epic Memory' (7 December 1992). www.nobelprize.org/nobel_prizes/literature/laureates/1992/walcott-lecture.html (accessed 15 July 2016).

'Watchers' (n.d) http://marvel.wikia.com/wiki/Watchers (accessed 12 July 2017).

Watson-Franke, Maria-Barbara. 'To Teach "the Correct Procedure for Love": Matrilineal Cultures and the Nation State'. In *The Political Interests of Gender Revisited: Redoing Theory and Research with a Feminist Face*, ed. Anna G. Jónasdóttir and Kathleen B. Jones (Manchester: Manchester University Press, 2009), pp. 104–21.

Wray, Matt. *Not Quite White: White Trash and the Boundaries of Whiteness* (Durham, NC: Duke University Press, 2006).

Wray, Matt and Annalee Newitz, eds. 'Introduction'. In *White Trash: Race and Class in America* (New York: Routledge, 1997), pp. 1–12.

Ybarra-Frausto, Tomás. 'Rasquachismo: A Chicano Sensibility'. In *Chicano Art: Resistance and Affirmation, 1965–1985*, ed. Teresa McKenna, Yvonne Yarbro-Bejarano, and Richard Griswold del Castillo (Los Angeles: Wright Art Gallery, 1991), pp. 155–62.

Zacharasiewicz, Waldemar and Christoph Irmscher, eds. *Cultural Circulation: Dialogues between Canada and the American South* (Vienna: Verlag der Österreichischen Akademie der Wissenschaften, 2013).

Index

1986 Immigration Control and Reform Act 107
1993 Kentucky Women's Writers Conference 36
see also Allison, Dorothy; Anzaldúa, Gloria
49th parallel 1, 11, 57, 93
see also border

Agee, James 43
Algren, Nelson 43
Allison, Dorothy 2, 4, 11–12, 19, 31, 57, 125, 174–5, 177–8, 180
Bastard Out of Carolina 40
and citizenship 19, 31, 36, 37
and feminist activism 35, 38, 48
as peripheral 11, 12, 45
Skin: Talking about Sex, Class, and Literature 38, 48–50
and the South 2, 36, 46
Trash: Short Stories 37–8, 44
Two or Three Things I Know for Sure 41, 42
see also autobiographical acts; white trash
Althusser, Louis 25, 143–4
American studies 6, 9
Anzaldúa, Gloria 2, 4, 6–7, 9, 11–12, 19, 31, 57, 68, 86, 95, 99, 104, 106, 113, 125, 129, 155, 174–5, 177–8, 180

and American Studies 46
and border studies 37
Borderlands/La Frontera: The New Mestiza 46, 48–52
and the Chicano movement 35, 37
and citizenship 31, 36, 45
and feminist activism 35, 37–9, 53
and the new *mestiza* 47–50
as peripheral 11, 12, 45
This Bridge Called My Back 38
see also autobiographical acts; *bocacalle*; hybridity
Atwood, Margaret 173
autobiographical acts 36, 43, 44, 45, 52
autobiographical mode 36

berdache 60
see also two-spirit
Blackfoot 1, 11
bocacalle 47
book club 175–6
border
Canada–US 1, 8, 9, 61–2
studies 6–7, 9, 36, 46
US–Mexico 2, 6–8, 11, 36–7, 46, 48, 57, 93–6, 98–100, 104–7, 112, 115, 120, 179
wound 37, 99, 104–7, 112
Border Arts Workshop 94
border legislation 2, 7–9, 15n29

bricolage 29, 36
Butler, Judith 19, 21, 26, 28, 100–1
　see also queer

Canadian Anti-Terrorism Act 9
canon 35, 153, 159
Chicana feminism 47
　see also Anzaldúa, Gloria
Chicano movement 37, 39–40, 48, 95–7, 104
cidadán 121, 125–6, 131–50
　see also citizen; citizenship; Moure, Erín
citizen
　neighbours 10, 17, 50
　queer 10
　see also citizenship; reader
citizenship
　Canadian 1, 57, 174
　contemporary 2, 18, 178
　dissident 23–4, 27, 58
　exclusionary 3–5, 19, 21, 26, 177–9
　habitus 21–2, 36, 93, 156, 179
　hemispheric 154, 156–8, 160, 166, 169, 174, 178
　Mexican 6–7
　sexual 4
　state-sanctioned 4–5, 19, 174, 178–9
　status 7–8, 11, 21–2, 57, 59, 61, 63, 64, 66–7, 71–2, 75–7, 80, 94, 98, 107, 125, 137, 150, 156, 178
　studies 17, 20, 22, 31, 32n22, 36
　theory 10, 17–18
　US 98, 166
Clinton, Hillary R. 9
code-switching 48, 57, 80
Columbus, Christopher 70, 93, 155
community
　art and performance 104
　building 4, 26, 125, 149
　Métis 71
　of readers 119, 143, 147, 178

Deleuze, Gilles
　and Felix Guattari 135, 142, 146
democracy, theories of 18–19, 31nn7–8
Derrida, Jacques 134, 146, 158, 163
Díaz, Junot 2–4, 11–12, 19, 31, 36, 174–5, 178, 180
　Brief Wondrous Life of Oscar Wao, The 153, 155–7, 162, 164, 166, 169
　and dictator-narrator 154, 160, 163–4
　textual Caribbean 155
　see also citizenship, hemispheric; translanguaging
disidentification 24, 26–8, 155, 165
　see also Muñoz, José Esteban
dissident vernaculars 58–9, 75
Doctor Who 159

Fantastic Four, the 154, 161–2
fukú americanus 155, 157, 166, 169

Gómez-Peña, Guillermo 3–4, 11–12, 19, 36, 87, 125, 174–5, 177–8, 180
　'Border Brujo' 105–8
　as coyote 105
　and drag 99–101, 106
　'El Mexorcist (A Performance)' 118–20
　Museum of Fetishized Identities, The 112
　rasquache 94, 99–100, 102, 104, 112, 118, 120
　solidarity 95, 102, 113, 116–17
　Temple of Confessions 108–10
Guadalupe Hidalgo, Treaty of 6, 96

Harper, Stephen 173–7
hybridity 57, 141
　and borders 7, 9, 48, 52, 155
　citizens and 4
　as empowering 48–52, 155

Index

linguistic 167
literary 153, 156, 165
Métis, the 74
  as *métissage* or *mestizaje* 24, 28, 29–31, 47–9, 142
  and the new *mestiza* 7, 9, 36, 47–51, 113, 177
  readers and 4
  as third space 113
  see also Anzaldúa, Gloria

identification 3, 19, 25–6, 49, 50, 52, 65, 84, 102, 107, 114, 177–8
Indigenous people 1, 8, 58–65, 67–71, 76–9, 83, 85, 93, 100–1, 109, 158
  and border studies 1, 6, 8–9, 95
  citizenship 1, 8–9, 19, 95, 179
  and Indian Act 66, 71, 76–8
  and Indian status 59, 71–2, 76–8, 80
  languages 79, 177
  and Métis 58–65, 67–71, 86, 179
  sovereignty 1, 10, 21, 65, 179
intersectionality 4, 28, 35, 37–8, 45, 47–8, 53, 57, 177, 179

King, Thomas
  'Borders' 1, 2, 9, 11

La Pocha Nostra 94, 102–3, 111–13
  see also Gómez-Peña, Guillermo
Lionnet, Françoise 28–30, 36, 48, 52, 58, 141
  see also hybridity

mainstream bizarre 111–12
  see also Gómez-Peña, Guillermo
Marshall, T. H. 9–10, 18, 129–30
Martel, Yann 3–4, 11–12, 19, 31, 36, 180
  101 Letters to a Prime Minister 173–5, 178
  and civic action 174

Life of Pi 174, 177
  and reading 175–6, 178, 180
  What is Stephen Harper Reading? 173
Marvel Comic Universe 154, 159, 161
Moure, Erín 3, 4, 11–12, 19, 31, 36, 121, 174–5, 177–8, 180
  alternate signatures 143–4
  and the antianaesthetic 130, 132, 144
  and borders 126–7, 129, 132, 134, 147, 149
  and *écriture au féminin* 131–3, 145
  and *écriture feminine* 131–3
  and Galicia 126, 131, 138, 142, 149,
  and Livy 127–8
  and Québec 131, 133, 142, 144
  and the state 127–30, 132, 138–40, 143–4
  see also cidadán; reader
Muñoz, José Esteban 20, 26–7
  see also disidentification; queer

peripheral peoples 3, 11–12, 20, 24–5, 27–8, 37, 45, 49, 57, 125–6, 155, 174, 178–9

queer
  theory and studies 6, 17, 20–2, 27, 31, 128, 144,
  see also citizenship; two-spirit

reader
  active 11, 27–8, 79, 120, 127, 179
  as civic 3–6, 28, 36, 52, 94–5, 103, 110, 125–6, 136, 147, 149, 154, 56, 164, 174, 177, 179
  community of 143–4, 119, 147, 177–8
  engaged 3, 43–5, 51, 65, 74, 76, 120–1, 126, 134–5, 139–40, 147, 149, 153, 160, 163, 165, 167–8
  imagined 175
  implied 175

reader (*cont.*)
  intended 175
  postulated 175
  role of 25
  see also reader-response theory
reader-response theory 17, 24–5, 27–8, 31
recognition 2, 4, 6, 11–12, 19, 28, 40, 62, 64, 74, 140, 177, 179–80
representation
  historical and literary 36–7, 44, 74, 97, 101, 160
  ideology 143, 19
  legal-political 2, 4, 11–12, 37, 77, 84, 95, 97, 128, 130, 132, 157, 179–80
  in performance 97, 101, 103, 109
  self 44–5, 51, 81
reverse anthropology 101, 109
  see also Gómez-Peña, Guillermo
rights 1–12, 18–19, 21–2, 35, 37, 39–40, 63, 67, 71–2, 74, 77, 93, 96, 108, 116–17, 147, 156, 179–80

Scofield, Gregory 2, 4, 11–12, 19, 31, 36, 93, 125, 174–5, 177–8, 180
  ancestry 59, 62–3, 69–70, 78, 83
  autobiography 71, 81, 83
  as community activist 71
  and healing 82, 84
  as mediator 58, 72, 85, 174
  and Métis history 57–9, 63–75, 78, 81–2, 84–7, 89
  see also code-switching; two-spirit
solidarity 27, 29, 31, 42, 52–3, 61, 85, 95, 102, 113, 116–17, 136, 180
Spanish 29, 38, 40, 48, 60, 95–6, 98, 103, 105–6, 104, 126, 138, 142, 149, 159, 161, 164–8
subaltern counterpublics 10, 11, 24

terrorism 7–9, 20–1, 116
transculturation 113, 157
translanguaging 164, 166–8
Trudeau, Justin 177
Trujillo, Rafael 154, 158, 160, 162–4
Trump, Donald J. 7–8, 173
two-spirit 58–61, 84–5, 87
  see also berdache

US–Mexico War 6
  see also Guadalupe Hidalgo, Treaty of

Walcott, Derek 153–6
Warland, Betsy 43, 131
white trash 2, 36–8, 40–4, 46–8, 50–1, 53, 83, 179

zafa 155–6

EU authorised representative for GPSR:
Easy Access System Europe, Mustamäe tee 50,
10621 Tallinn, Estonia
gpsr.requests@easproject.com